Letters from Na

Richard Carter's *Letters from Nazareth* tells of a glorious spiritual paradox. ... letters are a lyrical record of how contemplative prayer leads to resolute action in confronting the problems of our world – how the energy of stillness built a community able to welcome the homeless and the outcast of London's West End. Tranquillity in Trafalgar Square may seem a contradiction in terms. But this book shows how it powers engagement with the violence and the injustices of the capital. The life of prayer underpins the life of service; Martha can do her work only if she regularly joins Mary in silent meditation. I have read *Letters from Nazareth* with growing attention, admiration and enrichment.

Neil MacGregor, former Director of the British Museum and National Gallery, and Chair of the Booker Prize 2022

Letters from Nazareth is a deeply moving invitation to be at home, with ourselves and with each other, and ultimately in the Lord who dwells with us. These letters are inhabited by a peace born of prayer and silence which speaks to us all in this time of homelessness, whether that of the people who live on our streets, to whom Richard is so close, or to all who suffer from the multiple forms of mental or inner homelessness of the heart that afflict our society. Home, we discover, is the place where you are so secure and fully accepted that you can even rejoice in being challenged.

Timothy Radcliffe OP, priest, Dominican friar and writer

This tender and inspiring sequence of letters keeps revealing new insights into the meanings of 'home', of 'homeless' in the heart of a city, and of a community based on the loving recognition that other people's needs are my concern. Adorned with skeleton leaf silhouettes, each torn and exquisite in its own way, ending with a beautiful poem about a cross made from splinters of a wrecked migrant boat, it reminded me of that moment in the morality play where Knowledge, alongside her sister Good Deeds, promises Everyman: 'I will go with thee, and be thy guide, In thy most need to go by thy side.' Everyone needs by their side both the knowledge this heartfelt and luminous book keeps providing every time you go back to it, and the goodness inherent within it.

Ruth Padel, award winning poet, novelist and writer, and Professor of Poetry at Kings College London 2013–22

This sequel to Richard Carter's remarkable book *The City is My Monastery* takes us further on the journey of his new 'monastic' quest in the heart of London – and beyond. This time the genre is that of 'spiritual letters', through which Carter unfolds all the agonies and challenges for his fledgling community as it confronts the lockdown, immigration crises, and ever-increasing poverty for so many in this country. But through the lens of contemplation we are able to see the depth of understanding, wisdom and hope that Christ bestows on his church precisely in this context. Everyone who cares about 'mission' should read this book: it will upend all your previous presumptions and set you on a different path.

Sarah Coakley, Anglican priest, systematic theologian, philosopher of religion and writer

Reading *Letters from Nazareth*, I am convinced that home is not a place but an irrevocable condition of the heart. Richard seems to know with both the knowledge of the knower and the knowledge of the lover that we need prayerful silence and fierce courage to tame wildernesses in us to find God as Home. 'This our crown', he is saying, 'has already been bought and paid for. All we have to do is wear it.' I will read this book again (and again). Like *The City is My Monastery* it will be part of my anchor deep down into God.

Bernárd Lynch, Irish Catholic priest, psychotherapist, writer and human rights worker

I like to think of *The City is My Monastery* as the Gospels and *Letters from Nazareth* as the Epistles: I suggest you read them side by side like the two halves of the New Testament. The power of these letters is that as Richard shares how he has turned experience into wisdom, we the readers are moved to do the same. *Letters from Nazareth* will be a source of blessing to many.

Sam Wells, Vicar of St Martin-in-the-Fields

Richard has helped us see Nazareth for what it is: God accepting the hospitality of a human home, God in human flesh making divinity a home in which we may all find ourselves and each other. This book is another gem.

Rowan Williams, former Archbishop of Canterbury

Richard Carter enables us to see life as a gift and the light in the cracks.

Sarah Mullally, Bishop of London

Letters from Nazareth is an invitation to enter a truly intimate space; to encounter the deep love of Christ and embody this love in our everyday. The reader is taken on a much longed-for journey; finding home, belonging and community. The tone of the letters and the guidance in this book are a true reflection of what the Nazareth Community is all about. I am so grateful for Richard's wisdom and believe this book will be an inspiration and important resource to individuals and churches longing for deepening faith and discipleship.

Mirjam Ngoy-Verhage, Discipleship Lead for London Diocese, spiritual director and member of the Nazareth Community

We do not write or receive many proper letters nowadays. The post mostly delivers information and adverts. Occasionally something special arrives, such as these letters from my friend and former colleague, Richard Carter. Wherever he lives, Richard has chosen to dwell in Nazareth, the ordinary place where God dwells with us. Richard is present too but does not seek to resolve all the problems of the world. His letters illuminate what it is to abide lovingly in a community. They are deep and prayerful insights written to encourage and feed us along life's way. This book is fabulous.

Nicholas Holtam, former Bishop of Salisbury

With characteristic honesty and sensitivity, Richard Carter writes letters to console, sometimes provoke but always to encourage and build up the people of God. At the hardest of times, at the bedside of a dying friend, or in the bewilderment of pandemic uncertainty, his personal call to surrender all to Christ is a call, as he outlines at the end of each chapter, not only to pray but to wonder. Read the letters written to the scattered community and you will feel they have been written only for you.

Lucy Winkett, Rector of St James's, London

Letters from Nazareth

A Contemplative Journey Home

Richard Carter

CANTERBURY
PRESS

Norwich

© Richard Carter 2023

First published in 2023 by the Canterbury Press Norwich
Editorial office
3rd Floor, Invicta House
108–114 Golden Lane
London EC1Y 0TG, UK

www.canterburypress.co.uk

Canterbury Press is an imprint of Hymns Ancient & Modern Ltd
(a registered charity)

Hymns Ancient & Modern® is a registered trademark of
Hymns Ancient & Modern Ltd
13A Hellesdon Park Road, Norwich,
Norfolk NR6 5DR, UK

Cover Painting © Nick Hedderly: *St Martin-in-the-Fields*,
with permission of the artist.

Lime leaves © Andrew Carter: https://andrew-carter.net,
with permission of the artist.

Scripture quotations are from New Revised Standard Version Bible:
Anglicized Edition, copyright © 1989, 1995 National Council of the
Churches of Christ in the United States of America.
Used by permission. All rights reserved worldwide.
And when indicated from:
The Authorized Version of the Bible (The King James Bible),
the rights in which are vested in the Crown, are reproduced by permission of the
Crown's Patentee, Cambridge University Press.

British Library Cataloguing in Publication data

A catalogue record for this book is available
from the British Library

ISBN 978-1-78622-491-0

Typeset by Regent Typesetting
Printed and bound in Great Britain by
CPI Group (UK) Ltd

Contents

Part Three Nazareth the Place of Presence

Part Four Nazareth the Place of Pilgrimage –
Letters from the Holy Land

Part Five Nazareth the Place of Struggle and Hope

And I said to them as they passed: 'Where are you going?' And they said only one thing: 'This is our home. This is where we are going to learn of the love of Jesus Christ ... this is where all peace lies.'
(Dick Sheppard 1914)[1]

Your love is more than enough for me
It is all that I am and all that I long for
There is nothing else
No extra
All is here
As deep as an ocean
As expansive as the sky
As miraculous as a new-born child
Or the sun rising
In loving Christ
I love the smallest creature
And a universe far beyond my knowledge or understanding
And I see your face in the face of my brother and sister and in
    your creation
Each day of my life Lord
Give me the grace to let your love grow

Foreword

Sam Wells

I'd known Richard Carter for five years by 2017, worked alongside him, prayed alongside him, enjoyed his companionship and shared in good times and sad; but he was still a mystery to me. A mystery because on the one hand he was a person of action, who loved drama and organized remarkable work with asylum seekers and managed impressive lecture series and pulled together memorable hospitality events; yet on the other hand he belonged in silence, and clearly still missed the Solomon Islands, where he had been Chaplain to the Melanesian Brotherhood and a brother himself. St Martin-in-the-Fields is a busy place, one that provided plenty of opportunities for the busy side of Richard, and access to theatre and galleries and fascinating people of all social classes; but how could it feed his contemplative side, in a noisy and relentless Trafalgar Square, in a constantly moving and changing community, in an environment more associated with attention deficit than meditation?

One of the early letters in this volume offers an indication of how the secret at the heart of that mystery came to be revealed. Richard relates how in 1986 he asked a brother of the Taizé community for direction when he felt his life was in fog, yet he was facing a crossroads. 'What is the grace that you most long for in your life?' the brother asked Richard. Richard replied, 'I would like to be able to teach, and to be a brother in a community, and to work in the developing world, and to be a priest and still to direct dramas ...' Then, Richard records, there was a long silence. After which the brother spoke, in words that sound somewhere between Jesus and Thích Nhất Hạnh: 'You long for many things. Perhaps you need to let go of some of them, in order that others may be fulfilled.'

I sense that Richard was still having that internal conversation when he spent a month on retreat contemplating his vocation in January 2017. It is well known that he returned from that retreat and said five momentous words: 'The city is my monastery.' The words that stand out in that sentence are 'city' and 'monastery'. But to me the transformative word, out of which the whole movement embraced by his subsequent book and this one has sprung, is the word 'is'. He was looking for a monastery; he loved the city. God's word to him offered him a way – one that he'd never perceived before – that the city could *be* that monastery: even if that meant reconceiving the notion of monastery.

It seems puzzling to reflect that the Taizé brother was wrong. But the secret at the heart of the mystery of Richard was precisely that he needed not to let go of the complexity of who he was, in order to be the blessing he was created to be. God was saying, 'I made you this way because I wanted one like you.' And so the Nazareth Community was born, and in the breadth of its components – silence *and* sharing, sabbath *and* service, scripture and sacrament, and staying with – we see the gathering-together of the breadth of Richard's personality, and the wide embrace of the complexities of the diverse people who are drawn in different ways into the penumbra of St Martin-in-the-Fields. The truth is, like Richard, like all the members of the community, we are all a mass of incoherent elements until the Holy Spirit calls us into roles and invites us into opportunities that reassemble all our experiences and gifts in a beautiful way: and we trust that our reassembling – a glimpse of the final reassembling of heaven – will be a blessing not just to ourselves but to all around us.

Much of this book concerns Nazareth – the place of Jesus' nurture and growth. In my book *A Nazareth Manifesto: Being with God*,[1] I speak of Nazareth as the place where Jesus simply *was with* people – in contrast to Galilee, where for three years he *worked with* people, and Jerusalem, where for a week he *worked for* people. Thus *being with* comprised 90 per cent (30 years) of Jesus' incarnate life. The question is, how are we to turn this being with into our model for human existence? Especially when our culture so prizes working-for lifestyles. This is what the members of the Nazareth Community are doing together. My thinking arose in the context of creating relationships of trust and dignity across social divisions; but I have come to realize how far-reaching are these principles for discipleship in general and theology as a whole. The heart of the transformation is to discover the miracle of grace that God meets our scarcity through the abundance we discover in those apparently more exposed to scarcity than ourselves.

Being with does not start with a problem – or, if it does, the problem lies with ourselves, rather than with the person in whom we perceive scarcity. We do not sit with a disadvantaged person because we are trying to solve their problem – we do so because we want to receive the wealth of wisdom, humanity and grace that God has to give us through them. We are not the source of their salvation: they are the source of ours. There is no goal beyond restored relationship. Being with is not a means to an end: it is an end in itself.

The Nazareth Community has taken these kinds of insights and turned them into a whole way of life – being with God, oneself, one another and the whole creation. It has been one of the most moving experiences of my life to witness principles I have gleaned from 30 years of ministry being turned into a rule of life and a dynamic and disarming community. Through the pandemic, such a confusing and disorientating time, came the gift of the Companions of Nazareth, an opportunity for those not able to come to Trafalgar Square daily, occasionally or ever, to belong, participate, contribute and enrich the movement. And so it is that now over 200 people are intentional members of this movement and a great many more are influenced and inspired by it. I like to think of *The City is My Monastery* as the Gospels and *Letters from Nazareth* as the Epistles: I suggest you read these two books side by side like the two halves of the New Testament. Neither is a book to be read at one sitting: both are fruit for regular consumption in small mouthfuls.

For me, it goes back to that 1986 conversation. What Richard was looking for then is what we're all looking for: a way to pull together the disparate and apparently divergent elements of our lives such that we discover that all elements are God's gift and that when we receive them as such, we blend into the rain of the Holy Spirit that showers down blessings and growth for myriad people and makes God's creation come alive. The power of these letters is that as Richard shares how he has turned experience into wisdom, we the readers are moved to do the same with our experience, so that through silence and sharing we may let the Holy Spirit make us part of that rain too. *Letters from Nazareth: A Contemplative Journey Home* will be a source of blessing to many.

May your reading of this book be an experience like Richard's 2017 retreat. May you find your own version of Richard's discovery of the word 'is' – a discovery of the secret inside the mystery of who you are and who God is. And may you find your monastery, wherever that may be.

Live close to all, lost in God. (Charles de Foucauld)

This book is dedicated to the Nazareth Community
and the Companions of Nazareth
who have been with me on the journey
and have helped me find my home.

And it is in memory of my dear friends
Annie (Blaber) Nairn
and Brother John Blyth MBH
'Full of grace and truth'.

Acknowledgements

When you pray alone it is frequently a lonely path. I have often said to the Nazareth Community and the Companions of Nazareth that when I pray with them in silence it is like being part of a choir where each different member adds to the harmony of the whole. I would like to thank all the members of Nazareth for being my teachers and friends on this journey home and for all they share so generously. I would also like to thank Sam Wells for writing the Foreword and for recognizing the vision for this community and inspiring me to follow it. And I would like to thank St Martin-in-the-Fields – I could not ever hope for a more diverse, creative, challenging or exciting family.

I am, as ever, grateful to my own family, who continue to show me the meaning of unconditional love: Tim, Jenny, Joe, George, Matthew, Siobhán, Molly, Jack, Andrew, Helen, Francis and Alice and Daniel. It is a blessing to me that Matthew is a member of Nazareth, and Jack has been a great companion on many of my contemplative walks, and George is an insightful member of our *lectio* group. I would especially like to thank my dear brother Andrew for the lime-tree leaf prints, which speak their own silent language of life and death – the intricacy of their ageing, pattern and beauty lead us through this book on our journey home. I would also like to thank my beloved brother Daniel, who not only does a full-time job, cares for my mother and looks after us all, but also closely read and commented on this text and encourages me always. He is the true Christian I long to be.

I would like to thank Christine Smith and all her team at Canterbury Press. No one could hope for a more encouraging or supportive editor or publisher. I would also like to thank Rowan Williams, who has generously written the last letter in this book and continues to be such a wonderful example and guide to me. I am so grateful for his inspiration and encouragement. Also, thank you to Martin Laird, in whose writing I find the expression of such wisdom.

I would like to thank my dear friend Jerry – she has heard me read many of these letters on the phone and listened and understood my journey for more than 40 years. Thank you to all my friends, some of whom graciously appear in the pages of this book, to my wonderful godmother Elizabeth, my faithful friend Juliette and her mother Elspeth, Cath who helped pray the Nazareth Community into being, and Matt and their baby daughter Jennifer Joy. Thanks for the kindness of Katherine Hedderly and Loren and her brother Nick Hedderly, who gave me permission to use his picture of St Martin's in the rain – it is the view from my window as I look towards the church.

I have dedicated this book of course to the Nazareth Community and Companions of Nazareth, but also it is in memory of two people: my friend Annie Blaber, whom I mention at various parts of this book – how much I have learnt from her life, generosity, hospitality and friendship. I edited this book from her home in Scotland, thanks to the kindness of Charlie, her daughter Amy and granddaughter Lyla (see Letters 18, 35 and 59).

It is also in memory of Brother John Blyth of the Melanesian Brotherhood. I will always remember John sitting on the polished wooden floor of the meditation chapel at Tabalia where we were Melanesian Brothers together in the Solomon Islands. The wind chimes he gave would be softly ringing in the wind, his long legs and stiff knee stretched out before him. It was the time of the martyrdom of the seven Melanesian Brothers. No words could express our sorrow but together we prayed through the troubles – united in silence, united in God.

This book is my prayer for all of you. I pray it will be a blessing. Thanks to all of you who continue to show me Christ in so many ways. Thank you to Nazareth, where we learn to listen with the ears of the heart.

Richard
Lent 2023

Cover Painting by Nick Hedderly: *St Martin-in-the-Fields*, oil on canvas, London, 2012, with permission of the artist.

Lime leaves: the original lino leaf prints included in this book are by Andrew Carter, https://andrew-carter.net. (Linden or lime leaves are a symbol of love, fertility, good health and happiness and resemble the shape of a heart. There are 32 prints as the leaves fragment.)

PART ONE

Nazareth the Place of Formation

Letter 1: Introduction

Dear Sisters and Brothers in Christ,

Can anything good come out of Nazareth?

All letters are about a relationship. And these letters are a dialogue, a to and fro, a conversation with myself, with God, with my community and the time we are living through – and a conversation with all of you who read these letters. They are the letters I have shared with the Nazareth Community and the Companions of Nazareth over the last four years as we have tried to build an open and generous community together based around a simple rule of life: Silence, Service, Scripture, Sacrament, Sharing, Sabbath and Staying With. They are letters that reflect my own life and struggles because that is the only way I know how to find God, through the flesh, blood of my own life and those who show me Christ. It is a journey of the heart. These are letters of spiritual encouragement that I pray will resonate or stir your own experiences of God, and through God's grace I hope will become a resource for those who seek to walk this path together. Some of these letters are more personal; many reflect the times we have been and are living through; some draw on the wisdom of others from whom I have learnt much about the nature of this path. But all of them, I pray, reflect something of the heart of our community, as our restless hearts seek to find their rest in God.

In all of these letters I am unashamedly a beginner. Because if I have learnt one thing about Nazareth it is that it is the beginning of our life with God. And it will take all of our lives. And I know I will be most receptive to the presence of Christ if I am able to keep this beginner's mind.

I am actually writing this introduction to you from Nazareth itself, in the Holy Land, where I have come by myself on pilgrimage and to pray.

Nazareth is a vibrant city of over 75,000 people, two-thirds Muslim and one-third Christian. It is the largest Palestinian Arab city in Israel, built alongside Old Nazareth, which has a largely Jewish population. Nazareth is dominated by the massive Basilica of the Annunciation, visible from every part of the town.[1] It is, of course, also one of the most important centres for Christian pilgrimage in the world – the hometown of Jesus, we believe, for 30 years of his life, the place where so little is known about him except what he became. Nazareth is therefore not just a specific place, it also symbolizes a spiritual home – the place of dreaming, the place of formation, the place of nurture, the place of becoming. It is the place of the incarnation that as Christians we carry with us wherever we are; the place where 'the Word is made flesh'. And Nazareth is not just the place of incarnation *then*, it is the story of God's presence with us *now*.

We call the years that Jesus spent in Nazareth 'the silent years'. That is just it – it is in silence, unannounced and on the edge that the gospel finds the soil to take root and begin to grow in real lives.

> Nazareth embodies socially, in the face-to-face and shoulder-to-shoulder embedding of God's divinity in human community ... Nazareth is important, not because it is a stage on the way to something more significant, but precisely because it is an extended window into heaven: God and humanity in peaceable interaction, perhaps with good work, perhaps with shared food, perhaps with learning and growing and nurturing and celebrating, but fundamentally just being, because there is no better place to be, and no better company to keep and no better thing to be doing ... the crown of creation; simply being with God.[2]

This morning I am in the Basilica of the Annunciation.

The scripture reading from the lectionary, as often happens, has a deep and particular resonance for me today in this place where Mary heard the message of an angel that would change her life and change ours – the message that she was to have a child.

The reading from Isaiah is:

> For thus said the Lord GOD, the Holy One of Israel:
> In returning and rest you shall be saved;
>   in quietness and in trust shall be your strength ...
> Therefore the LORD waits to be gracious to you;
>   therefore he will rise up to show mercy to you.

For the LORD is a God of justice;
> blessed are all those who wait for him ...

Though the Lord may give you the bread of adversity and the water of affliction, yet your Teacher will not hide himself any more, but your eyes shall see your Teacher. And when you turn to the right or when you turn to the left, your ears shall hear a word behind you, saying, 'This is the way; walk in it.'
(Isaiah 30.15, 18, 20–21)

The words I keep returning to are:

> In returning and rest you shall be saved;
> > in quietness and in trust shall be your strength.

These words feel like coming home.

When I first came to St Martin-in-the-Fields on the edge of Trafalgar Square, I remember one of the earliest activities I began was a discussion group after church, which we called 'Something Understood'. For one of the initial conversations I chose what I thought would be a non-controversial subject: 'Home'. I could not have been more wrong. 'I don't know what is meant by home,' said one person. 'I don't think I've ever really had a home.' 'No, my home life was pretty unhappy too,' said someone else. 'When people talk of their homes, I just think of looking through the window and imagining what it would be like,' said a person I knew to be homeless.

Well, as I write these letters from Nazareth, I am attempting to try to describe in my own way what I believe home is. Some of these stories you will recognize. And you will have your own stories and experiences to add. Nazareth is the place of Christ's home. It is God's home. Nazareth is sharing space with God. God becomes our home and we become God's home in us. Nazareth is not just a chance meeting, or a lay-by, or comfort break on the road. It is a relationship – a journey with God through the many years of our lives that continues to grow and change us. It's the place where we become what we are. It is the Word made flesh. Much of this will be unseen. It's the place of familiarity and intimacy but also the place of longing and challenge, because Nazareth is somehow always beyond us. It's also a place we cannot cling to but must be ready to share and give away again and again. At times it will seem like nothing. At other times it will seem the most precious gift of our lives. Sometimes we will feel we have nothing to offer and nothing to receive from Nazareth, and at other times we will be overwhelmed by all that is abundantly given and received from God.

God meets us at the point of our greatest need and deepest desire. For this deep-down desire – which is in fact God's desire, God's longing in and for us – is beyond our grasp. It can only be patiently shaped, purified, held and cherished. All the great spiritual teachers of the church over the ages speak of this – God's infinite longing for us and for the whole creation – and by which, through the Spirit of Jesus working in us, we are shaped into the pattern of his Son.

When we began our Nazareth Community I wondered if there was a space for yet another form of religious life. We didn't want a separate church, but to seek God where we were within the church we loved. We wanted not more but somehow less – a greater spaciousness and open-ness to listen and grow. Neither did we want a pious exclusive space but a community open to all, a community that was porous and with roots that all could share. People asked me if this was 'new monasticism'. But I did not want us to be confined. We are simply living out of the rich, deep traditions of our past, and by the example of communities of faith and prayer throughout the world. And at the heart this is a realization of how important silence and contemplative prayer are to discover our centre. What is it that we are seeking? We are seeking to make our home in God.

I have discovered this home through the trials and errors of the last 17 years here in the centre of London. I realized this when I wrote my last book, *The City is My Monastery: A Contemporary Rule of Life*.[3] I had been discerning where next the journey of my life would take me and then I realized that it was here, simply staying where I was: the place where you would perhaps least expect to find community and yet perhaps one of the places it is discovered and needed and valued most – it was here at on the edge of Trafalgar Square. This was my Nazareth. And at St Martin-in-the-Fields, this ever-changing family, it is wonderful to be part of a church where its edges are the church, where we do not reject because we too have known rejection, where in the pain of our own not belonging we have found a story that includes us all. Jesus' story in Nazareth makes room for us all to belong; belong, without mask, with-out shape-shifting or pretence. He is the one who reaches out to enfold the whole of us, and in the diversity of this community we see Christ's face – Christ, who shows us the way out of the church into the street where his life is shared with all those looking for home.

St Martin shared his cloak. He tore it in half so it could enfold the beggar. In the threads of the frayed edges we realize our thread is there too, woven into the threads of others so that it cannot be unthreaded. There is no separating these threads. We belong to Christ, we belong to each other; each thread is part of the same cloak.

In 2018 we founded the Nazareth Community at St Martin's, and in

6

2020 the Companions of Nazareth. Is this new monasticism? I would rather call it life, and the realization that all of life is our monastery where we seek the love of God and discover that God was with us all along.

'Blessed are the poor in spirit, for theirs is the kingdom of heaven' (Matthew 5.3). In Nazareth, God shows what that dwelling with God looks like. He takes the last place. Not a place of world recognition or fame but an obscure town that is not even mentioned in the Old Testament. 'Can any good come out of Nazareth?' We go down to Nazareth to meet Christ – down. We meet him when we go down, right down. At the very bottom of our lives, he is waiting for us. And here in the very last place, often where we can go no lower, we find him. At the bottom of our souls. There is room here, not for a pious holiness or anything that excludes. There is room to be formed by the gospel again and again. At the very heart of our religious life, if it's to be authentic, there is this self-emptying. We will only become who we are by our genuine simplicity and humility. A humility that makes room for the Christ who has no place to lay his head – so makes us his dwelling place.

When we take our promise to join the Nazareth Community this is our prayer: 'I want to live the gospel, O Lord, give me grace.' Nazareth is like a carpenter's workshop. It is the place where we learn to live the gospel. Nazareth, as it was for Jesus, is a hidden place. It is not the place for competition, fame, jealousy or selfish pride. And neither is it private property. It belongs to all. It's our hidden place with God – without delusion, without pretence, just as we are. As Charles de Foucauld wrote:

> Let Nazareth be your model, in all its simplicity and breadth ... like Jesus in Nazareth; have no cloister ... In a word, in all things: live like Jesus in Nazareth ... The life of Nazareth can be lived anywhere: live it where it is most useful for your neighbour.[4]

We aim to be brothers and sisters to all. It is not a soft romantic faith, for it will have to be strong and courageous if it is to survive the onslaught and suspicions of the modern world. But its strength will be its simplicity, its genuine love. By their fruits you will know them.

What I am discovering here in Nazareth is the heart of our Nazareth calling. It is not an invention of the mind. Indeed, I have seen it and experienced it in all of you. It is a warmth, a love without sides, an openness to God and one another, a care, a compassion, a call to humble service, a gift of time that is so needed in our church and in our world. It is the place we make space in our lives to be with God and to grow in body and spirit.

What an adventure to find the home where Jesus lives, to dwell in that space with him, to listen to him speak, see him sleep, witness his work, recognize his miracle and mystery every day. Be attentive, because this forgotten carpenter's son you meet is the Son of God.

These are my letters. They take many different forms: some are letters of encouragement, some share teaching, instruction or guidance for the path, many relate this spiritual path to the experiences of my own life and, by extension I pray, your own – memories, hopes, fears, but also places and experiences where the gospel became rooted. These letters, as the title reflects, are a contemplative journey – there are physical journeys to different places of discovery, but also we journey through the times we are living through. It is a journey, I pray, that leads us not just further but deeper into the heart of God. I hope they will be for you a contemplative journey home to Nazareth, inspiring your own story and your own response.

Blessings
Richard

What is the Nazareth Rule of Life?

We did not write the Nazareth rule of life. It wrote us. It emerged from a year of prayer and contemplation. It is simple and has seven roots, which we call 'The Seven Ss'. It is simple enough to be able to be incorporated into your life. It is flexible enough to be possible to live this rule even within the context of busy modern lives. Yet it is disciplined enough to help you to grow. It is a life-giving rule.

1 **Silence** – As we enter into silence as a community, we place ourselves inside the love of God. Contemplative prayer is at the heart of our community. It is this listening to God that converts our hearts and nourishes all that we are. Our prayer begins with listening: to Christ, to Christ's presence in one another, to Christ within creation, to Christ within our own hearts. Contemplative prayer is spending time with the One we love and centres our actions in him.

2 **Service** – In simple acts of giving, and face-to-face encounter with those in need, we discover the joy and reciprocity of service. We discover Christ in those we serve. Members of the community serve in different ways, according to their respective gifts and callings. There is no hierarchy in service, just the joy of giving and receiving, whatever the cost. It is an experience of God's kingdom.

3 **Scripture** – We humbly open our experiences of God to the wisdom and revelation of scripture. We allow scripture to speak to us through others and the context and experiences of our own lives. We seek the

insight of scholarship and theological insight. Through daily *lectio divina*, we reflect on who God is and who God calls us to be. We discover how the Word is being made flesh in the lives of others and in our own lives.

4 **Sacrament** – The sacrament of communion is central to our life together: how God in Christ is with us, and we are with one another. Not only do we recognize Christ in the breaking of bread, we recognize Christ in others who through God's grace become sacrament – the visible sign of Christ's indwelling presence. And we recognize our own calling to become the bearers of Christ to others. And we are recognizing that each moment, here and now, is the sacramental encounter.

5 **Sharing** – We meet one Saturday morning a month to discover new insight through sharing and listening to others. We share food and fellowship and encourage each other through prayer. We learn from the wisdom and insights of others, remembering that Christ often speaks through the humblest or quietest. Meeting with spiritual companions gives us guidance along the way. We remember that our faith depends on community and that when two or three or more are gathered in Christ's name, Christ is present with us.

6 **Sabbath** – We commit to creating a place and space in our lives each week for rest and relaxation and time to replenish our lives and spirits through beauty and creativity. We heed God's call to be refreshed by the wonder of God and to find life in all its fullness. We recognize that we were created to love and praise God. We recognize that our hearts are restless until we find our rest in God.

7 **Staying With** – In a world that often sees people and creation as disposable, the community has a commitment to stay with each other, in steadfast love. It also is committed to discovering a rhythm and a way of living that is sustainable and life-giving. It's a constant turning to Christ. We aim, like a mirror, to reflect that which is steadfast and true.

It is difficult to talk *about* Nazareth – much easier to be here. Which is why I am here now. In this book of letters I hope and pray we can go there together.

Letter 2: Learning to Meditate – Turning to Christ

Dear Sisters and Brothers,

Meditation is the very heart of Nazareth. This way of praying has a beginning that we learn but it has no end.

We often learn to meditate through the inspiration of others. I wonder who influenced or inspired you to seek God in silence. In this letter I would like to tell you about someone who helped me when I came to St Martin's and how she taught me to find God even in the midst of the unfamiliar.

> The fruit of silence is prayer. The fruit of prayer is faith. The fruit of faith is love. The fruit of love is service. The fruit of service is peace.[1]

These words are written by Mother Teresa. I wonder in whom you have seen these words realized.

They capture for me so perfectly the gifts of a spiritual guide and friend called Anne Duffin. If I needed words that could describe her, those are the words I would use: prayer ... faith ... love ... service ... peace. I was incredibly fortunate to know Anne. A spiritual guide is a gift. And often you do not realize the extent of the gift they have given you until the person is not there any longer.

When I first met Anne in 2006 I had just moved from the Solomon Islands on the other side of the world to live and work at St Martin-in-the-Fields in the centre of London. It was a massive move for me and I was all at sea in the centre of the city. It felt in those early days that the job I was being asked to do had no relationship with the faith that had brought me here to do it. It was dear Anne who centred me as she centred so many. She helped me reconnect spirit and body. You see, Anne's life was anchored in Christ.

At St Martin's she invited me to join her fortnightly meditation group, which I attended until she died and beyond. When we arrived for the group she would give each of us a slip of paper with words she had written in her own handwriting. Here, for example, is one of the phrases she gave: 'Let your will be my will, a spring of knowledge, springing up to life eternal within me.'

Then when we were sitting comfortably, she would begin, reading, with her deep, chesty, 20-a-day voice, a reflection, many of which she had written herself, peppered with quotations from Thomas Merton, Evelyn Underhill or Marion Dunlop.

Here is an extract from one of those reflections she wrote:

Let your will be my will, a spring of knowledge, springing up to life eternal within me.

A well spring. A deep unending source. We may in our lives have drawn water from various wells only to thirst again, but the water from the well spring of knowledge which he will give us satisfies our real need. For our source has put within us something of himself, which is our true substance, which longs to be united with him, and we cannot rest until we rest in his peace or know true joy until we know joy's full-ness in his presence.

Anne's words would lead us into three lengthening periods of silence. Each of the silences would begin with the repetition of the phrase on the piece of paper she had handed us. The phrase floating in the silence. I remember coming back to it as my mind wandered. At the end of the third silence, she would float the names of people we had asked her to pray for. Three names, she said, was best but sometimes it was more. The names simply held in the stillness. Often, it has to be said, at the end of a long St Martin's day, I was lulled into such peace by her soft medita-tions that I found myself fast asleep and once woke myself up with my own snore. I remember apologizing profusely but Anne only replied that God obviously was giving me the gift of rest. 'You obviously needed that sleep. It was your prayer.'

She often invited me to her home in Chiswick for lunch or tea. She opened the door to me on the edge of that busy carriageway with her chesty cough and twinkling eyes and led me into her flat, where I, like many others before and after me, have been lavished with hospitality.

Anne was such an alive and interesting person. Not only did she love books and literature and theatre, she was also like the best character that you have ever met in a novel because she drew you into her love for life and ideas and people and God, and made you feel when you were with her that you too were special. Her gift was a gift of attentiveness. She had been a literary editor all her life, in the days when editors formed close bonds with their authors and were wise guides through the creative process. She listened astutely, critically, wisely. She poured cups of tea for you in big bone-china cups, and gave you cake, and there was always more than one, including coffee cake, which I had not eaten since I was a child, with so much icing that it spilt over the edges of the layers and was impossible to eat without licking your fingers. And before you had finished the first piece of cake she was there with another plate of buttered sticky bread. And all the time she wobbled precariously down the steps into her tiny, cluttered kitchen she would be joyfully chatting, sharing insights and thoughts and memories with an intelligence as sharp as a razor, a spirit as clear as a meditation bell and a heart as deep as an ocean.

Like many others at St Martin's and beyond, I came to love Anne. She was quite simply a person of wisdom and goodness. She was no pushover either. Come wind or snow she would battle into St Martin's with her walking stick to lead the meditation and when, during the redevelopment at St Martin's, they said she could no longer use the church for her meditation, she led the group in the porch with the wind howling round the portico. 'They'll be putting us in the broom cupboard next!' she said. The group finally ended up at my flat on the twenty-second floor in Victoria until the church reopened. If she thought something or someone was not right, she would say so. She was not afraid to speak the truth, nor was she, despite her humility, prepared to be overlooked. 'Don't forget it's Anne with an "e",' she told me when I got it wrong on a list. Detail was important to her. She was steadfast as a rock. But also, she was not afraid to let go when the time was right. 'I have decided to start attending my local church,' she told me after more than 30 years of coming to St Martin's, after she had had a fall. 'It makes sense. It is much nearer and the journey into St Martin's is getting too much for me.' After that the meditation group met at her house in Chiswick and at those groups, alongside the wisdom of the mystics and Anne herself (with an 'e'), and after three periods of extended silence, there was of course coffee cake and sticky bread, and cups of tea for all.

She led us all into a deeper place – a place of peace and healing – a still, sacred place. She led us to the very heart of our Christian faith and the hospitality of God. It was a diverse group who met with her: an Irish

Catholic, a young man called Dave, who was very faithful and was suffering from bowel cancer and whom we visited later in hospital before he died with a courage and a grace he had found through these meditations. There was Ruth, originally from Jamaica, and Gloria from Sierra Leone and Nigeria, Joyce from Nigeria, gentle Duncan, Rosalind, a Sufi Christian and poet, the poet Natasha, and many others drawn into this circle. But it was Anne who held the space, and she did this by making space for Christ.

'What did you love about Anne?' I asked Alison Hardwick, one of her closest friends at St Martin's, when Anne died. 'I could always turn to her,' Alison said. Yes – you could always turn to Anne, because you knew Anne was turned to Christ. She turned to Christ and she taught us to do the same. Her life showed us how to do just that, practically, steadfastly, without artifice or self-righteousness or pretence. Simply to turn to Christ. To be filled by his presence.

That is of course our baptismal promise:

'Do you turn to Christ?'
'Yes, I turn to Christ.'

Looking back, I realize that's what she helped me to do. Disorientated after so many years in a different culture and place and by the grief I was still experiencing, in the silence she brought me back to Christ whose centre is everywhere and whose circumference is nowhere.

'Do you turn to Christ?'
'Yes, I turn to Christ.'

It was, I remember, like finding a compass and holding fast even in a storm. And each time I have turned away, Anne Duffin's meditation calls me back.

'Do you turn to Christ?'
'Yes, I turn to Christ.'

Letter 3: Learning to Meditate –
The Beyond in the Midst of Our Lives

I wonder when it was that you first sensed the awe and wonder of God. Not God of the rules and regulations and habits we learn, important though many of those lessons may be, but 'the eternity that awaits you'.[1] People are important inspirations. So is place. So are moments and events. I wonder if there are not revelations for all of us. Like Moses and the lit bush. Or like those in the East who looked up and saw a star that many others must have seen too, but who realized it was worth following.

I remember one day as a very young boy being in an old Norman church, St Mary's Chessington. Watching at the offertory as the bread and wine and collection were brought up and passed to my father who placed them on the altar, I experienced a deep sense of belonging. I remember my mother was amused by what I said, and repeated it to me later in my life. I had said, 'There is a piece of God in me which passes all understanding.' I remember running down the hill of that church to the church hall where in those days there was Sunday school and such exciting things as hobbies and handicraft exhibitions and Christmas fetes. There was in church for me always in my memory an awe, a sense of a mystery and a longing beyond the activity itself.

My Nazareth was growing up as a vicar's son in large vicarages where everyone seemed to be welcomed at our kitchen table; from school friends, to the lonely, to the drug addicted, the destitute, the elderly and the dying – and all my brothers and I were expected to take part, from preparing rock cakes, to peeling potatoes, to washing up, to helping an elderly parishioner down the corridor in the days before Zimmer frames. I was influenced by a mother who gathered family, and a father who centred it. I have been deeply influenced by my love for my brothers and their wives and families. It was a lively home where the dining-room table was used for table tennis and where there were plenty of arguments underpinned, even in struggle, by unconditional love.

When I was about nine, I had a best friend at school called Nicky Episkapou. He was from Cyprus and his parents ran a transport cafe. I remember the excitement of going to his house to play because I was allowed to drink my first Coca-Cola from a bottle and take the top off with a hiss using the bottle opener mounted on the wall. It was Nicky who had a Tottenham football kit, which made me long to have one too. I remember upstairs in his bedroom playing Subbuteo table football on the floor when a Greek Orthodox priest came in with Nicky's parents. They told us he was blessing their house. He prayed in Greek and then sprinkled us with water. I remember the drops of water on my face and the drops from his sprinkling thing on the felt Subbuteo football field. I remember it as something special. I told my parents about it. The water was water but it felt something more, like going to another country for the first time, as if it was something holy and unforgettable.

My elder brother Tim was and is my great hero. We used to go fishing together. I was the first one to catch a fish on a fishing trip with Tim and my father – three grayling in Downton. I was, however, not a good fisherman and was always getting into tangles. I remember getting a new fishing reel for Christmas and on the first trip out casting it into the River Thames under Walton Bridge and coming back cold and disappointed. But I always loved the river and the riverbank and in the summer canoeing and swimming in the Desborough Cut. My brother Tim continued with fishing and still does today. Tim wrote recently in a letter to the wife of his lifelong fishing friend Dick after he passed away:

> Fishing is about more than catching fish. It provides a reason for being out in the countryside, being with your brother or your best friend, just enjoying each other's company and the natural world and the fact that you are not at work or worrying about anything other than trying to catch a fish and usually failing, and then going home remembering the day and hoping for success next time.

He told me that people often think when you go fishing you have time to meditate on the meaning of life, but you don't, because it's now that matters: fishing is about becoming attentive to the moment itself – the weather, the river, the riverbank, the flow of water, the riverbed, your float, the bend in the tip of your rod – so attentive in fact that you forget all else, and that is precisely why it is so deeply pleasurable.

These encounters with the natural world enter deep inside us and become part of our formation – they root us. When I first had a holiday in London – a holy day – I could not decide where to go, until encouraged by my brother Tim, who had given me a guidebook to the River Thames. I bought a bicycle and spent a week following the Thames towards its source along the Thames footpath. There's something mystical about following a river; it's like the life that flows through you, within you but always onward, greater than you. From earliest times rivers have been deemed to be sacred – the Ganges, the Nile, the twin rivers of Mesopotamia, the Tigris and the Euphrates, the Amazon, and of course the Jordan flowing into the Sea of Galilee. All these rivers are so essential to our planet's eco-system, biodiversity and survival. You may have your own sacred river. Mine, of course, living in London is the Thames. So often I return to walk its footpaths. For me in all its moods it is like the lifeblood flowing through this city. A river takes us on a journey from its source to the sea, and this is a metaphor too for our lives.

Another sacred place for me as I grew up was Hilfield Friary. It is the Dorset home of the Society of St Francis. I remember Br Juniper, whose room was bare but for a small crucifix on the wall. 'That is a beautiful cross,' I said. 'You can have it,' he said, and took it from the wall and gave it to me, leaving the room bare. Later I lost it in the grass by an old swimming pool and I went back with a torch at night to search for it. I remember the joy of finding it in the grass. I sensed that this cross was precious. More than a small cross. All that Br Juniper had. All that he had given me … all.

I remember one night going to the Franciscan chapel to pray with my father and at one end of the chapel, suspended in the darkness, was a San Damiano cross, a replica of the cross that at San Damiano spoke to the young St Francis: 'Rebuild my Church.' I knelt for a long time in the darkness beside my father, the cross illuminated in front of us. I remember even as a child being filled with awe, as though I had entered with my father into the warmth of a silence that filled me but which was beyond and greater than us both. The San Damiano cross seemed to be calling us – glowing in the darkness.

Since that time at Hilfield Friary I have had the opportunity several times to go to Assisi and to pray in front of the original San Damiano cross that now hangs in the Basilica of Santa Chiara. Below the San Damiano cross there are these words that I pray with you now:

Most High, all Glorious God
Enlighten the darkness of my heart
Give me right faith
Certain hope
Perfect charity
With deep humility

Wisdom and understanding that I may know to do your most holy will Amen[2]

Above Assisi there is a long steep hill to the Carceri, the caves on mount Subasio where Francis and his brothers used to go to pray. I have climbed that hill each time I go back. Here I describe the experience.

There was no one on the road just me and the whole of God's creation. Over an hour's steep walk. There are moments in our lives when we are numbed by life. There are other moments when all our senses seem alert and present and awake to the beauty of everything around us. It was such a morning, clear, crisp light, up the zig-zagging road into the snow: the rhythm of the steps, the exhilaration of the climb, deep breathing, freshness. Francis chose the most beautiful sites in Italy for his places of prayer. At the Carceri the caves are surrounded by pine trees and a huge valley that opens up and drops right down to the plains below. I walked through the trees and the wind was blowing clouds of soft snow off the branches into the sunlight, falling in sparkling showers. In front of me unblemished snow. I was stopped in my tracks, held in a sheet of sunlight. I do not believe in visions but this was a vision for me. And what words did I hear? They were the words of the transfiguration, the light on Christ dazzling white: 'This is my son, my beloved, listen to him.' A light Christ wants to share, a Sonship in which we too are included. Even me. We are acceptable, we are pleasing to him. I am pleasing to God – how can this be …? Reeling from that … aware of nothing but my own sins and failures.

What, I the guest?
I the ungrateful …
I the unworthy … I cannot look on thee.[3]

Brother Carlo Carretto, from this hermitage, wrote these words:

How can we find within us the power of believing in the possibility of renewing the world, of finding peace once more and our lost joy?[4]
… Yes this hermitage speaks and says brotherly and sisterly love is possible.
It speaks and says that God is our Father, that creatures are our brothers and sisters, and that peace is joy.[5]

Wonderings

In this letter I have included just a few encounters with the beyond in the midst of our lives. I wonder what your own experiences and encounters have been.

Letter 4: Learning to Meditate in Silence

Lord Christ, you remain unseen at our side
present like a poor man
who washes the feet of his friends.
And we, to follow in your footsteps,
we are here, waiting for you
to make us into servants
of your gospel.
(Brother Roger of Taizé)

It was the Taizé Community in France that taught me to seek God in silence. I remember the first time going to Taizé in 1986: crossing the channel by ferry in rough sea and feeling very sick and then travelling by coach and being billeted into a bunk bed in a dormitory. I remember coming burdened with troubles and uncertainty, unsure of where my life was leading me. It was as though life was full of masks that people wore and that I needed to wear too or I would be hurt again.

The Church of Reconciliation, which can fit thousands, is empty of the chairs and pews that fill most churches, and this transforms it. There is a sense of great spaciousness. There was just carpet to sit on or simple prayer stools to kneel with. And there is candlelight and warm windows and icons that draw you in. A dove. A simple Madonna and Child. A painted icon of the cross in reds and umbers, browns and golds; a poor Christ holding out his hands to the world with Mary and the beloved disciple beneath. It is an icon I have carried with me ever since and which continues to centre my prayer. The beauty of the emptiness is that it is us, our bodies, that become the prayer. We pray of course not only with words but with the whole of ourselves, and at Taizé I learnt that when my posture was right, kneeling simply on this wooden prayer stool, with the crown of my head in line with the base of my spine, it felt that I was not only humbled and rooted but also opened up to the God beyond me, beyond formality, beyond the structures that often seem to control and confine. Simply by changing my posture it felt to me as if I was changing my relationship to God in prayer. And the posture itself was saying, 'Speak, for your servant is listening' (1 Samuel 3.10).

The other great revelation of Taizé was that the Church of Reconciliation was open all night. It was also the warmest space in the whole of Taizé, certainly more hospitable than the draughty dormitories or outside food queues for the simple meals. What is more, in the Church of Reconciliation, time seemed no object. Whatever time you went, there were people in there sitting or kneeling praying. And when the great bells chimed it was filled, the Taizé brothers themselves forming the centre, their positions of kneeling in prayer forming the cruciform shape around which we prayed too.

Then of course there is the singing, which is now known throughout the world. The secret of this singing is that it is simple, it is harmonious and profoundly beautiful, and it is repetitive: like a Gospel mantra that stills the mind and leads prayer from head to heart. Like one's breath the words and song are breathed in and out. There is something very powerful about praying so gently and harmoniously together. It is as though the prayer of each one of us becomes the prayer of the whole. Like threads being woven together. And this prayer leads us into stillness and total silence that seems to go on and on. In Taizé there can be thousands of young people led into that silence and stillness.

Coming home to the UK I knew in my heart I wanted to go back. At that time there was a group of Taizé brothers staying at St Martin-in-the-Fields, preparing for the London Pilgrimage of Trust. It was 1986. This was the first time I visited St Martin's and I met one of the brothers in 6 St Martin's Place, where I now live. I remember at that time the large room was empty apart from the brother's mattress on the floor. I asked the brother if it would be possible to go back to Taizé and stay for a longer time. He asked me to describe my experience of being there for the first time. I told him of how I had found prayer. I told him of how it felt as if my life was in fog but that somehow I had been led to this place where the masks of fear and defensiveness were removed and I had discovered my humanity again during the time of being there. But now since returning to London I felt in confusion again. I remember him saying that this feeling of a fog, or cloud within, was often part of the path of finding God again. He suggested I return to Taizé and he would arrange for me to spend a time of silent retreat and discernment there. And if I wanted to stay I could help them to prepare for the Pilgrimage of Trust that was coming to London. And so I went back.

I had never done a period of silence before. It felt strange and unnatural at first. I was no longer in the dormitory but had my own room in a house in the village with other young people who were on silent retreat. I made friends with a Korean who was similarly inexperienced in the art of silent retreats. We whispered together and during the first few days often broke the rule of silence when no one else was about. When the heavy bells rang for prayer I whispered to him that once again we were being called to the Taizé brainwashing sessions where everyone is converted to wearing the colour beige and speaking in French accents about the little miracle of Taizé. But as the silence progressed so did the depth and struggle of my prayer. The talking ceased and I realized my cynicism was really a longing to find healing and believe. We gathered around log fires as we ate in silence. I looked forward to the times of prayer that could still my mind from all my fears and distractions. And each day I met with Br Emil. At first I called him 'the ice man' to my Korean friend, because he sat in silence until I spoke and it felt I could never win him over. He remained detached but listening. At first I hid my depression and despair from him because I was ashamed of how I was feeling; it felt like weakness and I thought that he would see my search for God not as something genuine but as an excuse or cover up for my despair. Perhaps he would see my faith as a mental health problem. I bombarded Emil with questions. Sometimes he just kept silent. Sometimes he answered: 'That is not a question,' meaning, I guessed, 'That is not a question you need to ask now.' And that detachment began to give me courage. It was a sign to me that he trusted God and trusted in God's love for me. I remember him saying, 'God is love. He does not wish to break anyone.' Perhaps my questions did not need answering because God would only reveal his meaning in God's time. We are so often impatient for that which we are not ready to know. I remember thinking to myself that this man actually believes – he believes that there is really a love and a power greater than us. It gave me courage to see his faith and I began to hope that it may be true, albeit tentatively.

He gave me, I remember, a passage of scripture each day. I took it away with me and meditated on it in silence. I have written about our conversation in the book I wrote, *In Search of the Lost*:

'What is the grace that you most long for in your life?' Brother Emil asked me.

'I would like to be able to teach, and to be a Brother in a community, and to work in the developing world, and to be a priest and still to direct dramas ...'

There was a long silence and then he spoke: 'You long for many things. Perhaps you need to let go of some of them, in order that others may be fulfilled.'

I did not really want to let go of any of them, in fact I was unsure at that time of how to go forward. I had left Indonesia after four years of working there and I could not imagine any future that would fulfil me as much, because I was grieving for the place and the people I had got to know and a life I had experienced that seemed so impossible in the western world. It was hard to look forward, for I longed to go back.

'I want you to think of Mary when she receives the news that she, an unmarried woman, is to have a child. In my French translation it reads "she ran". She ran off to visit her cousin Elizabeth. That word ran has always struck me. She has received news that most women would fear, she is not even married, and yet we are told she hurries, she runs and when she meets Elizabeth she proclaims not her troubles but the greatness of the Lord and her joy. I would like you to meditate upon that response "ran".'

And that is what I did. I remember after that in my prayers I found that my grief at the loss of the person I loved, and the people and the place, was breaking open and being released, and instead of a dark bitter pain trapping inside me all that I felt I had lost, a new Word was coming to me: 'You will love again.'

When up close we often cannot see the workings of God, or the answers to our prayers, but when we step back it is different. When I step back I can see.

I remember the sermon Br Roger had preached all those years ago, when so many had gathered to hear him speak. It is a sermon I have often repeated because it is one of the few sermons of which I have never forgotten a single word. I remember him standing up before the thousands and all those ready to simultaneously translate his message into many different languages – he said simply: 'I have nothing to say. Let us keep silence because God speaks much better than me.' It is perhaps one of the most helpful pieces of wisdom I have heard. To keep silence and to listen. To believe in a God who answers our deepest needs. Contemplative prayer is a deeply revolutionary matter.

Letter 5: Learning to Live by Faith

This book of letters to you could never be complete if I do not mention the Melanesian Brotherhood and all they taught me and continue to teach me about prayer and the true way of service. They have so influenced the formation of the Nazareth Community. I do not have room to say much here but if you are interested in reading more then read the book I wrote from my diaries of living with them: *In Search of the Lost.*[1] From that book I gather here just a short description. The Melanesian Brotherhood live Nazareth – the hidden life of faith. Br Francis was one of the Melanesian brothers who was martyred in 2003, when seven brothers lost their lives while working for peace on Guadalcanal. He wrote in the prayer book he gave to me before his death the word 'courage'. He was a man of great courage. He knew his life was in danger because he had spoken out against the rebel group and opposed their methods and violence, and had confronted them when they had taken hostages. I told him when I last saw him to be careful. I had heard his name was on a blacklist the rebel group threatened to kill. I told him that God wanted living sacrifices not his death. He told me he would be scared if he was doing something wrong, but he was not scared of doing what is right. He then wrote this word, which I carry with me and return to in my fears: 'courage'. It is of course the word that Jesus uses again and again to his disciples. 'Courage, it is I.' I do not have Francis' courage but I have been strengthened by it. Though because of his courage Francis returned to God sooner than me, perhaps I have been given longer because I have more to learn in the lessons of faith. I have read that Nelson Mandela, in prison on Robben Island, underlined in a copy of Shakespeare's complete works these words: 'A coward dies a thousand times before his death, but the valiant taste of death but once.' I am most definitely the one who has imagined a thousand deaths, but that perhaps means I have learnt much from those who have the courage to live by faith. And I have learnt that such faith is a gift. Like Francis offering his courage to me.

The Melanesian Brotherhood are a lesson for me in learning to live by faith. Such faith is impossible without the rhythm of prayer holding our lives together. We need to create this rhythm of prayer in our lives wherever we live.

At 5.30 in the morning the Melanesian Brotherhood gathers in the silence and dark. Each day begins with silent prayer. It is the most beautiful time of the day. As the sun rises you can see the light streaming in rainbows of colour through the stained-glass window and on to the altar. Outside, the songbirds and parrots arrive and bounce on the flowering trees. And the chapel is filled each day with a community of more than one hundred men. First Office begins at 6.00 a.m. with a roar of voices. Melanesians sing in four-part harmony. These brothers are not pious or overly religious or fanatical or narrow, and are as human and diverse as anybody else; ordinary and yet extraordinary because one senses that they have a vocation to God. It is as if the doors and windows are all open and that somehow there is no division between the holy and the secular. There is just this sense of presence going up and coming down, inside and out. If you doubt me, as Jesus said, 'Come and see'.[2]

It is a bold humility that is at the heart of the gospel. This is what Matthew in his Gospel meant when Jesus said, 'Blessed are the poor in Spirit.' It is not what *we* do at all but what God does in *us* because we have given Christ the space and the place to be. It is the miracle of love by which the more love is given the more that love is also returned to bless the one who gives. And that love involves again and again a self-emptying in order to be filled:

by purity, knowledge, patience, kindness, holiness of spirit, genuine love,
truthful speech,
and the power of God;
with the weapons of righteousness for the right hand and for the left;
in honour and dishonour,
in ill-repute and good repute.
We are treated as impostors, and yet are true;
as unknown, and yet are well known;
as dying, and see – we are alive;
as punished, and yet not killed;
as sorrowful, yet always rejoicing;
as poor, yet making many rich;
as having nothing, and yet possessing everything.
(2 Corinthians 6.6–10)

Letter 6: Living Faith's Daring

Summer 2019

All the way through the Gospels, Jesus' constant refrain is 'Do not be afraid'.

These words seem to be directly addressed to our times. For while we live in a nation where some have great wealth and plenty, there is also so much destitution and need. And of course poverty is not just about our material possessions, it's about whether we feel we are loved and belong. Every age has its own fears and threats but let's just name some of ours: the fear that global warming is destroying our planet; the fear that the National Health Service cannot cope and is failing; the fear of knife crime and violence; the fear that housing is becoming unaffordable; the fear that there will be no one to care for us in our old age; the fear that our children will not receive a good education; the fear of immigration; the fear of poverty and homelessness; the fear of sexual offenders; the fear of obesity and eating the right foods; the fear of cancer; the fear of unemployment; the fear of debt; the fear of other nations like Russia or Iran or China; the fear of terrorism; the fear of Brexit or Remain; the fear of political division. Turn on the news any night of the week and you will hear a litany of those fears being endlessly discussed and expounded by people from both sides of the political spectrum.

Fear is often born of love – because we love, we want to protect. The important thing about fear is that it alerts us and forces us to address the danger and bring about safety. But we all have noticed that sometimes fear and anxiety can have the opposite effect. Rather than addressing the issue, fear makes us retreat from it, put up defences, hope it will go away by itself; or we begin to blame someone else for our fear or, most danger-ously, create scapegoats. This is known by those skilled at manipulation and winning influence and power. In times of hardship and austerity the politics of blame grows. On both sides of the political debate in this country at this time, we will hear politicians deliberately using these fears to advance their own case. And popularism, polarization and post-truth have taken on new and virulent forms in our twenty-first century.[1]

The theologian David Ford[2] writes about the way our lives are shaped by 'overwhelmings', the fear of the things that we imagine will defeat us. In fact we may spend a lot of time worrying about things that never happen and not enough time recognizing the things that do. There are wise ways of dealing with fears, but also defensive ways that exacerbate, like stocking up our larder with tins of peas and baked beans because we fear Brexit; similarly, ignoring the fear, continuing to party while the ship sinks. It is here that our faith teaches us. None of us can command ourselves to feel less fear, but through Christ we can locate our fears and vulnerabilities within a larger and greater story, the story that is God's story and a story that is ultimately one of hope not tragic futility. Our lives through Christ are the story of redemption.

I was talking to someone recently who was lamenting his life: his fail-ure to own a home, or have any wealth; his failure to have found any real security, or even a job that was fulfilling and could make full use of his talents; his failure in his eyes to be all-in-all self-sufficient. Yet as I listened to him, while I could acknowledge the truth in what he was say-ing, I could also see a different truth. For this man, who stood before me lamenting his life, was kind and generous, spirit-filled, brilliant in social interaction, energetic and motivated. What was more, he was full of joy in his Christian faith and gratitude for that faith. He seemed to me to be someone at the beginning of new life. There were thus two stories at work in his life: the judgement he felt from the world, but also the story of the life of Christ. And to me it was the second story that was his life force – the story of the generous, compassionate person who with God's grace he was.

Jesus taught his disciples that there was no way of following the king-dom of God without being willing to stake their lives on it. That is basic to our becoming. We have to head out into deeper water, often into the place where our feet can no longer touch the bottom. Abundance of life and, at the same time, immersion in struggle are inseparable. Ultimately, only by facing risk and death itself, our most primal fear, can we embrace the wonder of life. 'All you say may be true,' I said to my friend, 'but per-haps you do not see what I see.' 'What is that?' he asked. 'God at work in you,' I replied; 'God's possibility in all that you are.'

It is so easy to become infected by modern humanity's neurotic anxiety, but I wonder how we can have the courage to step out, confident in God's love. I wonder how we as Christians and we as a community can live not defensively or territorially but live faith's daring. Think of the holy family setting off from Bethlehem into exile in Egypt, with no money or protection, fleeing Herod's genocide and finally making their home in Nazareth.

It is a radical call, this living Christ's daring. We will often be tempted to cling on to what we can control or possess. The church itself often does not trust Christ's call. It becomes a place of fear, judgement and control, not the missionary church called to live sacrificially and provisionally. Christians themselves often become the most self-righteous and territorial: the church, a building to be preserved rather than God's love to be lived. The church has a long history of becoming prejudiced and repressive, grabbing and holding on to power and privilege rather than giving it away to feed the poor. Fear teaches us to possess, control, manipulate, but Jesus teaches a new freedom: 'What will it profit them to gain the whole world', he asks, 'and forfeit their life?' (Mark 8.36; Matthew 16.26).

The other day I was giving a very small grant from the charity Relief in Need to a person I know to be homeless and very poor. He thanked me but told me he no longer needed the money and that I should give it to someone whose need was greater than his own. I was taken aback, in fact felt quite affronted – how could he refuse our charity – until I realized that I myself was disarmed and challenged by his lack of need, his courage to face his difficulties with such dignity and hope. He challenged my own fears in the same way that we are often challenged when we see someone facing life's fears with courage and generosity. I realized he was right. He perhaps did not need our charity, but I needed his. I recognized all that he gave us, his energy and dedication, his kindness. He gave us a relationship and that relationship could never be transactional – it was pure gift.

Letter 7: Letters from the Desert

January 2020

There are certain books that you treasure all of your life and always carry with you. One of those books for me is Carlo Carretto's *Letters from the Desert*.[1] It has continued to be a guide to me and of course influenced the title of this book.

The call.[2] Carretto writes that God's call is mysterious: it comes in the darkness of faith. It is so fine, so subtle, that it is only with the deepest silence within us that we can hear it. And yet nothing is so decisive and overpowering for anyone on this earth. Nothing surer or stronger. This call is uninterrupted: God is always calling us. But there are distinctive moments. I wonder if you have ever heard God's call. I wonder how that call came. I wonder how you responded.

Until you are capable of an act of perfect love.[3] Setting out into the Saharan desert, in a jeep with two blankets, Carretto notices an old man shivering in the market town. He contemplates giving one of his blankets to him, but he does not stop. He thinks he may need both blankets to keep himself warm that night. In the middle of the night, he wakes to see a picture in his mind of the old man shivering. What is worse is that he himself has not used the second blanket. He knows, despite his two blankets, he will never be warm again. Will he ever be capable of an act of perfect love?

Attentive to God.[4] Carretto speaks of how in the desert you become attentive again to the things of God: 'I have been speaking to God all of my life but I have only just begun.'[5] Has this not also been our experience in these last months? His great joy of the Saharan novitiate is the solitude and the silence, true silence, which penetrates everywhere and invades his being, speaking to the soul with wonderful new strength unknown to many. Carlo's words and stories, like scripture, have a wisdom you carry with you through the desert or wilderness places of your life. He comes to the realization that for many years he thought that everything depended on him. He writes that we were so busy in our action to save the world that we forgot that the weight of the world was on Christ's shoulders, not our own. As prayer becomes richer in content, he discovers it begins to use fewer words. Rather than petitioning or explaining, he seeks rather to make more room for God – using a prayer word, perhaps, like the echo of a wave breaking on the shore. He craves to remain alone, silent, motionless at the feet of Christ: 'I thought in prayer everything depended on me and my efforts, on the books passing through my hands, and the beauty of the words which I was able to introduce into my conversations with God'[6], but, he writes: 'True prayer … requires more silence than words, more adoration than study, more concentration than rushing about, more faith than reason … true prayer is a gift from heaven to earth.'[7]

Purification of the Spirit.[8] Carretto talks of the struggle through which we come closer to the God who seeks us. It is in disaster, boredom, depression, experience of failure and sin, sickness, loss, that we begin to discover what we really are – poor, fragile, weak and mortal. God's impenetrable night wraps around us bringing a terrible loneliness and abandonment. In this deeply painful state prayer becomes true. The soul speaks to its God out of poverty and pain. Deep down the soul has understood that it must let itself be carried. What matters is to let God get on with it. How true this has been for me, and I believe for so many of us.

Contemplation on the streets.[9] Charles de Foucauld wrote that if the contemplative life were possible only behind convent walls or in the silence of the desert, we should in fairness give a convent away to every poor person and a strip of desert to everyone working hard in a bustling city to earn a living.[10] He decided to live the contemplative life on the streets: 'I do not want a monastery that is too secure. I want to live the contemplative life along the streets. If you cannot go to the desert you must make the desert in your life. Live the intimacy of God in the noise of the city.' Poverty is not a case of having or not having money. Poverty is a beatitude: 'Blessed are the poor in spirit.' It is a way of being, thinking, loving. Poverty can be a freedom, a detachment, a lightness of being, a truthfulness. It is also love. Our Nazareth home is living Jesus' true life on the streets with our neighbour.

Nazareth.[11] Carretto describes how Charles de Foucauld becomes moved by the way Jesus voluntarily lost himself for 30 years in an obscure Middle Eastern village, becoming an anonymous workman. He writes:

> Nazareth was the lowest place, the place of the poor and unknown, of those who didn't count ... Jesus is the Holy One of God. But the Holy One of God realized his sanctity not in an extraordinary life, but one impregnated with ordinary things ... obscure human activities, simple things shared by all people.[12]

De Foucauld actually went and for several years lived in Nazareth. But are we not called to live Nazareth where we are now, in the ordinary, everyday? What better way to live than to try each day in each activity and encounter to live goodness.

The revolt against the good.[13] One of his letters from the desert that I never forget is the one Carretto calls 'The revolt against the good'. He speaks of 'the ulcer of resentment' that can grow within us, which is hard to ignore. The experience of feeling we have carried the burden for too long, that our service has been unrecognized, that we have been overlooked, treated as nothing, sacrificed our lives, but for what? Each one of us at this point could add our own narratives of rejection. And then one terrible day the ulcer bursts and the poison that has built up inside us comes pouring out – and sometimes that outpouring can threaten years of relationship and self-giving. 'I've had enough.' We have not been heard. We have not been understood. We have been the victim. And of course, for each one of us there is truth in that. 'How can I really love my neighbour who repays me with indifference or even derision?' It is at this point Carretto says that the gospel begins. The rule of justice, he writes, is not enough.

It is good, it is true, but it is not complete. Something else is necessary. And then Christ comes. What Christ does is lead us beyond justice into the unconditional mercy of God. Unless we have met Christ on the cross and at the tomb we will never understand that. But once we have, we will begin to understand that God's love costs not less than everything.

Letter 8: A Letter Home from Ugo

February 2020

Dear Mum,

I have been in the UK for 11 years now. It's not easy since I came here because of my health. I have been in and out of hospital a lot. My sickle-cell anaemia causes a lot of pain, especially when it's cold like now. I am in hospital at the moment. I didn't want to tell you, Mum, as I know you will get worried, but I am still homeless. It's hard and lonely and makes me depressed – the cold, the wet, no place to call my own. It's worse at the moment because it's winter. There are also a lot of things I fear on the streets, like drugs and alcohol and fighting and many hardships.

But, Mum, you will be pleased – since I started coming to St Martin's I have found God. This church is so welcoming. I get support from everyone in the International Group. The Nazareth Community has become my family. I love them very much. I help steward in the church, and read the Bible lessons in public. I also act in the Christmas drama – it makes me happy because I belong.

I always think of Nigeria. I miss you, Mum, and my brothers and sisters. It is because of you that I am a Christian. I cannot forget that when I was young you taught me to pray, waking me every day at 5.30 a.m. for morning devotion. Those prayers really help me now. I miss your cooking too! I want you to keep praying for me so everything will go well. Do not forget that I am still your son.

My love and prayers
Your son
Ugo

Letter 9: Abraham – The Land that I Will Show You

Now the LORD said to Abram, 'Go from your country and your kindred and your father's house to the land that I will show you ... I will bless those who bless you, and the one who curses you I will curse; and in you all the families of the earth shall be blessed.' (Genesis 12.1, 3)

I first saw Abraham early one morning outside St Martin-in-the-Fields on the edge of Trafalgar Square. I remember he was wearing a grey track-suit, no coat at all, and in his hand was a white stick. It's hard enough being homeless in London and an asylum seeker, but to be totally blind as well, that seemed too much for anyone. He had fortunately found a place to stay at the Connection at St Martin's Emergency Night Shelter. Before that I heard he had been sleeping outside the 24-hour McDonald's. Yet what struck me about Abraham from the first was not his neediness but his gentle dignity. St Francis de Sales said: 'Nothing is so strong as gentleness and nothing so gentle as real strength.'[1] It's pretty rough living outside our place on the streets – believe me. I live next to the church and at night you can hear the shouts and the swearing and the smash of broken bottles, the wet sleeping bags, raw flesh on concrete, and the chaotic shouting of those even homeless charities can't handle. But Abraham became the cat-alyst for compassion among those who were destitute like him. Over the weeks I noticed the way Abraham had gathered around him a small com-munity of other homeless people: Ozzie, who led him to the church in the morning by the hand when the night shelter closed and came back later after a few cigarettes to lead him to the Day Centre; Biniam, who became like his protector and advocate, making sure he got and held a place in the queue on the Strand for the free food handouts. 'I've watched the way you look after him,' I said. 'Yes,' said Biniam, 'it's what the church should do – loving and caring and sharing – simple really.' Then there was H, also homeless, who never stopped fussing over him like a caring mother or elder sister and making sure he was all right. The whole group of them looked after him and he looked after them, bringing out their kindness, multiplying it: a parable of the gospel.

And the same thing started happening within our church too – those on the edge coming into the centre. Abraham and his community of fellow homeless friends sat together in church and joined our Bible studies and became members of our Nazareth Community. They earthed our faith and witness. There's no pretending when you are reflecting on the Gospels sitting next to someone who is blind and homeless. The gospel takes on a new meaning. Gone is the desire to masquerade our biblical abilities at exegesis. Abraham and the other asylum seekers who have become part of our community with their honesty strip away all defences so that heart can speak to heart: it's not what you know but who you are.

When Easter comes, we prepare a Passion play. Our Jesus, also an asylum seeker, knows what it is like to be tortured and screams out as his tormentors strip him and dress him in the gold insulating paper they use in the Mediterranean when migrants are pulled soaking from half-sunken dinghies shivering with the cold. And as he cries out from the cross our packed church is silenced. You know when this is not a pretence but the real thing. 'My God, my God, why have you forsaken me?' he shouts. And as Jesus' disciples gather to witness this death of human goodness, Ozzie leads Abraham to the foot of the cross with his white stick so that he and all his community of disciples can lift Jesus down from the cross and lay him on our altar with great tenderness. The altar, the place where the sacrament is broken open for us, the outward visible sign of grace. 'The body of Christ broken for you.' Amen. Be what you see. Become who you are.

We are learning in our church that there is not one group called the homeless and one group called the housed, one group called Christians and one group called non-Christians. We are all in fact homeless and longing for the risen Christ. In the Nazareth Community it is the gift of what we have learnt from one another that no one is sure who is the guest and who is the host. It is all too clear that everyone has goodness to share and longings to heal. The greatest of all poverty is to believe you have nothing to give and no way to receive the gifts of others. Everyone has grace to share if only it is recognized.

One day, I am celebrating the Eucharist and I move down the central aisle to share the peace. Coming to the back of the church I hear Abraham's voice: 'Father Richard, I can not only hear your voice, I can see you with my eyes.' It is a modern miracle. Abraham has had the cataracts removed from his eyes. First one eye and then the other. 'I can see you with both eyes!' The Lord is risen indeed. That week in our Nazareth group, as we share our reflections, we each speak about the greatest blessing of our week. 'My blessing', says Abraham, 'is that now I can see all of you.' 'Yes,' I say, 'but what about when you were blind, what was God's blessing then?' 'Oh then,' said Abraham, 'then I could see with my heart.' 'What could you see?' I asked. 'I could see kindness', said Abraham.

Abraham and many more of us in the Nazareth Community gather in the early morning. Three times a week we keep a silent hour before the day begins. It's silence that unites us, deeper than our individual longings. There is a solidarity in this silence holding us like the soil holds a seed in the mystery of our becoming. There is a temptation in any community to want to be the problem-solvers, to become the handout that takes away the struggle and the pain. The most difficult realization is that sometimes there is no solution, you just have to be there in the silence of the unknown, just as the beloved disciple was there at the cross in the hopelessness, running to the tomb hoping against hope. Our faith is not about control or formulaic redemption, it is about living both in blindness and in sight. The jagged edges of our own souls become the place where compassion is born. We are discovering how the fearful self is being held in an ocean of grace, unlocking that self, setting us free to become the people we long to be. Each one of us has our own wounds and power to wound others. The gospel is when our wounds become the signs of resurrection. To be with people means being with people as they are, not as you would like them to be. And our prayer for each other is not the diagnosis or the medication. It is the love of God for each person as they are. God above, God beside, God beneath, God within, the Word made flesh in us. It is this love that heals not just now but for all eternity.

Two weeks ago, Abraham was sitting on a bench minding his own business in St James's Park when he was approached by the police. He was searched. He was carrying nothing dangerous or illegal. They looked up his criminal record. He had no criminal record. Then they looked up his immigration status, which, due to his blindness, was not up to date. He was handcuffed and ended up locked in an Immigration Removal Centre. It hurt him especially to be handcuffed like a criminal. Although he has lived in this country for nine years and although he is terrified of being sent home to the place where his wife and daughter were killed in a fire, it seems he has little chance of his appeal being accepted, though we are trying all we can. We visit him frequently and try to encourage him. Beneath his gentle demeanour we can see the trauma arising and the despair threatening to overwhelm. 'Do you think, Father, I would have lived blind on the streets, lived destitute for nine years, if I had a home that was safe to go home to?' I have no words to answer him, only a prayer: 'Lord Jesus Christ, son of God, have mercy' – a prayer as simple and basic as breathing in and out, a prayer in the darkness. I take off my Nazareth cross made from the timber of a broken boat which sank off Lampedusa and place it round Abraham's neck, Abraham the one whom God called to leave his nation and become the source of blessing. He has.

Back at St Martin-in-the-Fields we sort through his suitcase and find his spectacles and medication which he has said are the only things he wants to take with him if he is deported. And I also find his own Lampedusa cross and place it around my own neck in solidarity, remembering the words of the carpenter Francesco Tuccio who made them: 'This cross is made of the boats' wood our brothers and sisters used to arrive in Lampedusa. Keep it with you like a sign of resurrection that comes from pain.'

Things are not looking good. I visit Abraham again. He's lost the joy that even life living out on the streets in winter did not take away. I can no longer see the light in him that I have always seen even when he was blind. He was a beacon. Now he looks down at his feet, he is broken. We have brought him a bag and a mobile phone and some money which he can take with him if he is deported. I can't give it to him of course but leave it with the prison officers and they carefully write down everything and give me a receipt.

They came for him very early in the morning, five Home Office officials, to remove this gentle man with no opportunity to tell anyone. It was only later that we heard that he had been deported. He texted me and I phoned him. 'I can hear cockerels crowing', I said. 'Yes, this is Africa', Abraham said. He keeps in touch. He said that he felt like someone on a ship crossing an ocean who has been thrown overboard in the middle of the sea so that he no longer knew in which direction to swim but is simply 'in the middle of nowhere'. He writes: 'This is the story of someone who has spent a decade in a place trying to build a new life only to be torn away and returned to face the violence and poverty you have fled.' But in one of his text messages he writes this:

Today is Wednesday, and the time for the St Martin's service of Bread for the World. I remember how I used to wait for Wednesdays like children wait for Christmas. The service was so helpful and encouraging to

35

me. It fed me. I just want you to know I may be thousands of miles away but my heart is still with you all. I miss you, I miss St Martin-in-the-Fields, I miss the Nazareth Community, I miss everyone. I am eternally grateful to Nazareth – you guys welcomed me with open heart. Though I was a slave, you treated me like a king … Thank you for being a family to me, thank you for listening to me and showing interest in my life. Thank you all for being there at the drop of a text … My light in the darkness. My shelter in the storm.

I quote these words because they show, I think, that even when we cannot provide the outcomes we hope for, even when we fail, the *being with* lives on. God's grace continues its work of salvation even when justice fails. We cannot take away the pain of Abraham's deportation but our Christian faith and community reach beyond time and space and allow us to be with him. Last week at Bread for the World, in the middle of a pandemic that has locked down both our nations, Abraham's voice was once again heard in our church. He was leading the intercessions for us and had recorded them on the mobile phone we had given him. His sound file was now being livestreamed – a modern epistle to the Londoners. You could hear the congregation listening for each word he spoke – as precious as the words of an apostle to us – against a background of traffic and cockerels crowing thousands of miles away. His words were Bread for the World.

Greetings! It is your brother in the Lord, Abraham. Almighty God, I thank you for giving St Martin's the Spirit of love to love you with all their hearts and minds and above all to love their neighbour as themselves. O Lord, continue to feed them with this Spirit of love. From you comes that love. Give us the heart to proclaim and offer this love to those who need it most. Amen.

PART TWO

Nazareth the Place of Refuge

Letter 10: Entering the Wilderness

1 March 2020

I wonder if you have ever thought, 'If only I could get out of here. If only I could escape.' I think all of us at times need escape routes. I wonder where yours is? The theme of fleeing, leaving the world behind and going into the wilderness occurs many times both in the Bible and in the writings of the Desert Fathers and Mothers. The saving event for the Jews was of course the escape from Egypt. But crossing the Red Sea was not the end of the story, it was the beginning of a new one of testing, struggle and temptation for 40 years. After his baptism, Jesus goes into the desert for 40 days and nights and also is tested. St Antony of Egypt and the Desert Fathers believed that if they fled the city they would be saved. Yet in the life of St Antony written by St Athanasius we read how Antony, like Christ himself, struggles with the devil. Athanasius writes:

> The devil, who hates and envies what is good, first of all tried to lead him away from his discipline, whispering to him the remembrance of his wealth, care for his sister, claims of kindred, love of money, love of glory, the various pleasures of the table and the other relaxations of life, and at last the difficulty of virtue and the labour of it; he suggested also the infirmity of the body ... In a word he raised in his mind a great dust of debate, wishing to debar him from his settled purpose.[1]

Sound familiar?

I wonder how often in our prayer life we have been beset by a similar 'great dust of debate' – worries, fears and distractions. We may not call it the devil, but how often are we too worn down by self-doubt and despair that anything good will come from this path? I was on the phone yesterday to a friend I have known for 40 years. She was telling me how her brother had been very sick in hospital and she had been visiting him each day to look after him and then she said, 'But I am so crap at caring for people.' This from a woman who cared for both her parents until they died and every neighbour too. So I said to her, 'I wonder if you recognize that tune.' 'What do you mean?' she said. 'That tune that keeps telling you you're no good and useless. I remember you playing that tune to me when we first met 40 years ago. It wasn't true then and it's certainly not true now. You are truly one of the most wonderfully caring people I have ever known in my life. Perhaps there is a different song to play.' 'If only,' she said, and laughed. Martin Laird writes that we all have these inner tunes, or what he calls our 'inner videos', like devils that plague us, which we endlessly play and which divide us against ourselves and deplete our spirit. I wonder what yours are – inner videos of anxiety, hurt, rejection, shame, loss, not being good enough, not coping, failing in love, betrayal, pride, fear ... Sometimes we even mistake this video for the condemnation of God. We need to recognize, however, that what is of God will draw us back to God. But often the spirit of condemnation, the negative spirit, drives us away from God, depleting us. We may mistake this judgement as coming from God, but a spirit that constantly drives you away from God's love, making you feel useless and unworthy, cannot be of God. Martin Laird offers this wisdom that the video may be going on but we don't have to watch it.[2]

As any of us enter more deeply into the life of prayer of Nazareth, like any true relationship or covenant we begin to discover that we bring all of ourselves, not just the initial idealized love on its best behaviour but everything, including the bits of ourselves that we hide and fear and which can fill us with regret or unhappiness. It's a bit like a marriage: after the initial infatuation we have to live love with all its moods, struggles and irritations, which may be as seemingly trivial as 'Have you put the cap on the toothpaste and cleaned the basin after shaving?'

The desert becomes the place of learning and formation, and this involves recognizing, allowing, illuminating and nurturing. Thomas Merton said that we are called to heal in ourselves the sins of the world. We need to discover an inner truthfulness, recognizing the good and acknowledging that we too have feet of clay and that we stand in need of God's redemptive love.

In the fourth century AD the deserts of Egypt, Palestine, Arabia and Persia became the refuge of Christian hermits and monks who had abandoned the cities of the pagan world to live in solitude.[3] The prototype of the hermit life was St Antony of Egypt.[4] One day, when he was 20 years old and rich, following the death of his parents, he heard in church the saying of Jesus, 'Go, sell your possessions, and give the money to the poor, and you will have treasure in heaven' (Matthew 19.21). He felt these words were addressed directly to him. In 269 he began a life that led to increasing solitude in the desert. He had many disciples and imitators, and it is from Antony and this tradition that many of the sayings of the Desert Fathers and Mothers come. 'These Fathers distilled for themselves a very practical and unassuming wisdom that is at once primitive and timeless ... Our time is in desperate need of this kind of simplicity.'[5]

The true wisdom of the desert begins with the experience of the radical consciousness that a person stands before God, in a relationship that is all-embracing because there is nothing that is outside of it. In the desert, the seeker of God comes face to face with the person he or she is. Far from an escape from the world, the desert becomes the place of struggle and transformation where individuals face themselves and their compulsions.

What the Fathers sought above all else was their true self in Christ. And in order to do this, they had to reject completely the false, formal self, fabricated under social compulsion in 'the world' ... They sought a God whom they alone could find, not one who was 'given' in a set, stereotyped form by somebody else. Not that they rejected any of the dogmatic formulas of the Christian faith: they accepted and clung to them in their simplest and most elementary shape.[6]

The desert was not an attempt to escape from other people or from community. Far from it. They came into the desert to discover their 'ordinary self' and to let go of all that divided them from themselves.

The Coptic hermits who left the world as though escaping from a wreck, did not merely intend to save themselves. They knew they were helpless to do any good for others as long as they floundered about in the wreckage. But once they got a foothold on solid ground, things were different. Then they had not only the power but even the obligation to pull the whole world to safety after them.[7]

The journey was not into isolation but into unity – into love. In the spiritual life, learning to live one's faith where you are rather than where you would like to be is one of the greatest lessons of our lives. 'Bearing your own company and the company of those immediately and unavoidably around you requires some very special graces.'[8]

Love in fact is the spiritual life, and without it all other exercises of the spirit, however lofty, are emptied of content and become mere illusions ... Love means an interior and spiritual identification with the other so that they are not regarded as an object to which one 'does good.' The fact is that good done to another as to an object is of little or no spiritual value. Love takes ones neighbour as one's other self and loves them with all the immense humility and discretion and reserve and reverence without which no one can presume to enter into the sanctuary of another's subjectivity ... We have to become, in some sense, the person we love. And this involves a kind of death.[9]

It is in the desert that we recognise these conflicts within. And it is ultimately in defencelessness that we learn to whom we truly belong.

When Jesus is led into the desert he is led by the Spirit. It is God who leads Jesus into this place of testing. The wilderness is not the place of escape. It is in fact the place of facing who we are and what God really wants us to become. Jesus faces three temptations, and perhaps we do too at various times.

The first temptation is the temptation to provide for all material wants: 'If you are the Son of God, command these stones to become loaves of bread.' How wonderful would that be to be able to change stones into bread. To find a solution to human desire and need as direct and simple as that. How often in our own lives we want to provide the quick fix that ends the problem and shortcuts the struggle: 'If only I could win the national lottery that would solve everything.' Our transactional ways of living lead us to believe that solutions come like this. 'If you give me £10, I will have a place in a hostel for tonight.' But what about tomorrow night? And the next? 'If God would only provide what I need now, then everything would be all right.' How often have I thought that at St Martin's: 'If only, if only I could just provide for every need.' But Jesus replies: 'One does not live by bread alone, but by every word that comes from the mouth of God.' I have begun to learn that every problem does not have a solution. Sometimes you learn most from hunger and living among the stones, and that, dare I say it, without ignoring or underestimating the anguish of the cry, it is in recognizing our deeper hunger that we begin to seek the bread that is eternal. How easy it is to give our leftover sandwiches to a homeless person or bag of old clothes to the charity shop and still be home in time for tea. How hard it is to recognize in others our own poverty and walk with them the longer distance. As I watched my mother's gradual slide into dementia, the temptation was to long for a fix, a solution, the tablet, the diagnosis, the answer to end or reverse the loss, but the recognition over the last eight years is to learn to live the whole journey with love and steadfastness, not just by bread alone but by every word that comes from the mouth of God.

The second temptation from the pinnacle of the Temple is the temptation of miraculous and spiritual power: 'If you are the Son of God, throw yourself down' and the angels will protect you. Have we not all somewhere within us harboured that superstition too that somehow our faith can help us live chosen, charmed lives, as though blessing and prosperity were God-given rights purchased by prayer or acts of righteousness, rather than pure undeserved gift? Notice how the devil plays upon one's spiritual pride – if you are the special one, if you are better than others, then do this thing that is reckless, dangerous, senseless, abusive: prove yourself. For how many people does religious faith *not* become the path to generous wisdom and respect for all life, but leads to a sense of self-righteousness, or still more a narrow bigotry of superiority, a justification for behaviour that may be unacceptable? God answers my prayers. God supports what I want him to support. God agrees with me. How many lives have been senselessly sacrificed in war in the delusion that God will save his own? It is this same spiritual pride that justified slavery or the exploitation or subjugation of women, or continues to tell LGBTQ+ Christians that they cannot be saved, or that their love, partnerships and same-sex marriages cannot be accepted or blessed. This is not the life that sets us free; this is where our religion becomes the means to manipulate others to become what we want. And Jesus answers: 'Do not put the Lord your God to the test.' He is not your God to manipulate for your agenda or prosperity. He is the God of all creation.

Why, God? Why do people suffer? Where is your power to save me? Last week after an hour of silent meditation a member of the Nazareth Community came to me and said: 'In my prayers I kept on asking Jesus on that cross I saw in our east window, "How do you cope? How do you cope in a world like this where there is so much suffering?" And eventually Jesus answered me.'

'What did he say?' I asked.

'He said, "I don't cope."'

We both laughed. It seemed a relief that sometimes Jesus can't cope too with the suffering of the world; indeed, that is why he was on the cross. You see, he didn't cope. No one copes on a cross. They die. *Cope* is a limited, limiting word; it's a word about self-preservation and providing temporary solutions. Jesus didn't cope, he loved. There's a world and an eternity of difference. Often we will not cope or be able to control, and that's when we depend on God's love.

And the third temptation. On the top of a high mountain the devil shows Jesus the kingdoms of the world: 'All these I will give you, if you fall down and worship me.' It is the temptation of worldly power and authority. But at the cost of his soul. We may think this temptation is so far removed from our own life experience, but is it? Listen to the leaders of our world promising to make us great again. The whole of creation stands on the precipice of this mountain at this very time. The decisions that we make now will directly influence the future of our planet, and the dilemma, though couched in different language, is in fact very similar. Do we decide to serve God and humanity or do we continue to exploit the world for our own self-interest and advantage? Jesus' answer is very clear. 'Away with you, Satan! for it is written, "Worship the Lord your God, and serve only him."'

In the wilderness Christ confronts his demons and chooses his path. I wonder what path we will choose. It is not preordained. Christ does not bribe us with our material needs, or spiritual or worldly power; instead we are given freedom to choose. The temptations of the devil will lead humanity to the crucifixion of the Son of God, but Christ himself points us to a greater freedom, the place beyond the tomb. For just as sin comes into the world bringing death, 'so all will be made alive in Christ' (1 Corinthians 15.22).

Follow the Blessing

At the beginning of this letter I told you of a phone call I had with a friend of 40 years. She still does not see the light that shines from her in the darkness. Perhaps all I can do is witness to the goodness I see within her. This is what I write to her:

Dear Jerry,
I am so sorry you are going through such a very difficult time.
I know there are times when it is impossible to see the good.
I too, you know only too well, have been through times like this
and you, with love and infinite patience,
have talked me through the stress and darkness.
If only I could help you to see all the beautiful things in your life
that may at this time seem hidden or lost.
Like your friendship which is so life-giving to me,
like our memories of joy and laughter stretching back over so
    many years,
like hours of conversation on the phone across the miles,
like your dogs who past and present have become my friends too:
Jati, and Tarra and Cinta and Jamut,

44

and most of all Murray,

who found in you the one person he could trust,

after years of trauma – the steadfast love and healing that he looked
     towards, nervously, fearing he would lose if he looked away,

until he realized you were the one who would never ever turn away.

He learnt to bask in your company

and through you in the company of every living creature you have ever
     loved and nurtured.

There are so many memories of blessing:

Our walks together by the Yarra River,

The many years we ate at the Thai restaurant together before both
     admitting that it made us feel sick and we'd both kept going because
     we thought each other liked it.

And your wonderful sense of humour:

Singing the Carpenters' hits down the road,

with your Morris Minor windows open at the traffic lights to cheer up
     the traffic,

and your wobbling plastic flowers and monkeys on the windscreen
     ledge that make everyone smile,

And those yellowing sheepskin seat covers that your elderly next-door
     neighbour Brian lent you to collect me from the airport,

And the gifts you hung for him over the fence to show him he was
     not forgotten,

And feeding your chickens in the back garden

and the raven who eats raw meat from your hand,

even though you are a vegetarian and hate 'dead animal'.

Your love and compassion for the world, especially the forgotten or
     overlooked ones:

Conversations with the lollipop lady in the middle of the street,

Or the woman in the post office who responds to your warmth.

Then swimming in the outside pool, your freestyle as smooth as an
     otter gliding through the water with barely a ripple.

And breakfast – my poached eggs on rye with avocado

and a man in the same Tasmanian-coloured socks as you,

kneeling down to take my coffee order.

And I searching the internet to buy you those same socks again in
     wonderfully exotic colours – greens, blues, purples and aquamarine.

You make this world a better place,

You may not realize it, but you do.

You make my life special not just then but always.

I know life is tough and dark,

And sometimes it feels unbearable,

But I want you to know your life is beautiful to me and those who
   love you,
You have opened my life to the smallest, gentlest, most
   overlooked things
As small, as miraculous and as tender and hidden
as the Witchetty grub you long to save in your back-garden tree stump.
You may think this is nothing but it is everything,
It is why I love you so much and Maire loves you, and your father Harold
who shared your kindness and generosity gene.
Your life I know is tough and often lonely,
But it's also beautiful and loving,
Why do birds suddenly appear every time you are near?
And follow you down the road,
Just because, just like me, they long to be
Close to you.
Please don't give up.

Letter 11: Lockdown

18 March 2020

God made us, God loves us, God sustains us.

I look out of my window and Trafalgar Square is empty. Never before has London been so strangely and eerily quiet. There is suffering, deep concern and uncertainty. The death toll from this frightening virus is mounting daily. I think of Julian of Norwich living through the fears of the Black Death and holding on to three truths revealed at that time to her: 'God made us; God loves us; God sustains us.'[1]

I wonder if in the pain and uncertainty of our time we can seek the one who is at the centre of all things, the one who made us, loves us, sustains us. I wonder if in our lockdown we can find:

A greater stillness
The song of the birds
A new attentiveness to neighbourhood
A compassion for those in need
A greater generosity of heart
A greater simplicity in the way we live and the things we depend upon
– is there life beyond searching for toilet paper?
The importance of the space and place in which we live.

When the Desert Fathers and Mothers taught the novice to 'learn to love their cell, for your cell will teach you everything',[2] they were guiding them to be at peace within the confines of their own dwelling place and especially within themselves. Perhaps the hardest thing to face is ourselves. Our contemplative prayer must seek to discover the freedom of God even in the midst of lockdown. Fear diminishes, fear is a contraction. And stuck with ourselves we recognize our uncertainties, the things we do not like. The stuff we would rather forget. And locked down with other people has its own tensions. I hear from my family how their children are finding it so difficult. Of course there are very real fears, especially for those most at risk and for those we love who are at risk. Worst of all is to be forcibly separated from those who need us. How frightening to fear infecting the ones we love most. How terrifying it must be to die alone. This is a recognition of our own vulnerability and mortality.

Our prayer is a call to look beyond the fear. Think of the image of the storm clouds that come and go. The temptation is to see our lives as those dark clouds that engulf us and to identify our own lives with them and not to see beyond the darkness. But we are not the clouds. We are the sky. The clouds come, the clouds cover us, the clouds depart. But we do not stay inside them. We need the courage to stay, allowing the storm to pass. Christ within us is our height, our breadth, our depth: the very ground of our being. Christ is much more than the struggle we face. Our love for Christ is even a love beyond death itself. Nothing can separate us from it.

It breaks my heart to see the gates of our church closed each day, this church with the ever open door. But it is we who are the church and we who must continue to remain open to God, to one another and to the suffering of our world. I had no idea when I wrote *The City is My Monastery* that this city and cities throughout the world would indeed become like monasteries. London, this complex, thriving city that never sleeps, now deserted. This week I saw a picture of the Pope praying and giving a blessing in a deserted St Peter's Square. This is the time that our contemporary rule of life is needed more than ever. In this totally unexpected way many of us have become like monks and nuns for a time, separate and set apart from one another but learning to centre our lives again in silence, service, scripture, the sacrament of the ordinary, sharing, sabbath time and staying with. Perhaps this great silence can become the place of listening and transformation, a time, as we imagined in Nazareth, to grow in intimacy with God, neighbour, self and our fragile miraculous world. Perhaps in this forced silence we will have time to rediscover the treasures beyond all price.

Contemplative prayer

We have been told, for some reason I cannot fully understand, that we cannot pray in the church even alone. The churches must be closed because of the pandemic. So we must pray at home or perhaps pray during the one hour when we are allowed to go for a walk. So my home has become my place of prayer. I kneel on my prayer stool looking out over Trafalgar Square. Praying for it. And over the next weeks within me I have the dawning realization of what I have always known: God cannot be confined to a building but is present wherever we are. God is out there on these empty streets and it's now we need his presence more than ever. We are livestreaming Morning Prayer each day but on Saturdays at 8.00 a.m. I begin livestreaming Contemplative Prayer. At first I begin with a simple example of how to still the mind and body. How our body itself is our prayer. I practise breathing deeply, letting the breath of life fill the whole diaphragm, in and out; filling the lungs, holding the breath of life within, breathing out that life breath to share with the world:

> Breathing in peace. Holding peace within. Breathing out that peace to share with the world.
> Breathing in Christ's presence. Dwelling in Christ's presence. As I breathe out, sharing Christ's presence.
> Breathing in God's love. Dwelling in God's love. As I breathe out, sharing God's love for the world.

As the breathing deepens so the stillness deepens and the spring light streams through my window. Never before or perhaps again will London be so still. I feel the warmth of the light from the crown of my head to the soles of my feet. And gently on the livestream I invite those watching, wherever they are, into this stillness of God. Into this prayer. Then taking a prayer word or phrase I float it into the stillness, calming any thoughts that may distract. 'Peace, be still, do not be afraid.' I invite each person, wherever they are, to make the place they are now become their sacred space, their place of peace. Over the next few weeks I discover that many people from around the country have started to join me, to enter into this silence and still centre with me, held together by the unseen chain of God's love.

Letter 12: Palm Sunday

4 April 2020

Today it's Palm Sunday. We begin, with our church like an empty tomb, to tell the story of a week that changed the world for ever. It is a story that goes on telling itself, making itself known in the context of our own lives. It is a story that speaks to our own time and these last few weeks of our lives, which have undoubtedly changed how we live in a way we never imagined possible and changed our world for ever.

In the Passion narrative the stage for this story is Jerusalem, but the stage is also the place where you are living in this country or whatever country in the world you are living in. At the beginning of this week Jesus knows the pain and the struggle he is facing. He has read the writing on the wall. He has predicted several times to his disciples his realization of all that is impending. It is this moment that takes the greatest courage, to face an unknown and painful future with faithfulness and truthfulness and not turn back. Instead, Jesus goes to the place where he is needed most, Jerusalem, the city which has so often rejected its prophets and stoned its prophets of peace. It is action that so often speaks so much louder than words. For Jesus this entry into Jerusalem will be for ever remembered because he chooses a donkey, the sign not of a conquering king but a beast of burden, a sign of humility and service. So where in a world in lockdown is our own Palm Sunday?

Just one example. On Thursday night my sister-in-law Siobhán and one of her best friends, Noriece, were sitting on separate benches in the Fountain Garden outside St Thomas' Hospital and beneath the statute of

the amazing Jamaican nurse Mary Seacole. They sat there decompress-
ing from all the stress, overlooking the river Thames and the Houses
of Parliament at Westminster. Both of them had just had a very long
and tough day working alongside hundreds of other nurses and health
workers at St Thomas' Hospital. It was nearly eight at night. Siobhán was
feeling exhausted. It was her birthday, but she knew in the present crisis
a birthday would have, of course, to be put on hold. Both Siobhán and
Noriece have families, Siobhán two children and Noriece three, but they
knew that St Thomas' Hospital was where they had to be. Just before
eight o'clock, outside Westminster, Siobhán noticed blue lights had
started to flash. For one awful moment she thought that there might be a
terrorist attack, and then she heard suddenly an incredible shouting and
a clapping from all around her as people opened windows and started
calling out, 'Come on, NHS!' And cars and trucks starting honking their
horns, 'Come on, NHS!' She suddenly realized that they were shouting
in encouragement for ordinary people like her and the thousands like
her who were continuing to show they cared about others and about this
nation and the world. These frontline workers really do love neighbour
as they love themselves. 'We felt this great wave of encouragement lifting
our spirits as I looked round at St Thomas' and knew of all the hundreds
of staff in there, the doctors, nurses, technicians, cleaners, cooks, admin-
istrators, caretakers, who were continuing to do their work because they
wanted more than anything to save lives.' She said it was like the best
birthday present she had ever received. 'Come on, NHS! Thank you,
NHS!' Or was it, 'Blessed are those who come in the name of the Lord.
Hosanna to the ones who bring God's blessing of peace and healing and
hope. Hosanna! Hosanna to those who bring salvation.'

I want to move now to later in this Holy Week, to the day we call
Maundy Thursday. Jesus calls his disciples together to celebrate the Pass-
over. It is going to become a meal they will always remember, the Last
Supper, a sign that God's love was not a memory of the past but real,
palpable and with them always, as real as bread and wine. This supper
would be the visible sign, until this very day, that Christ dwells in us here
and now. 'This is my body you eat. This is my blood you drink.' – I in
you and you in me. 'Do this in remembrance of me.' At present you may
feel somewhat strange and separate from the bread and wine but you are
still sacrament, you are still the body of Christ, called to become the visible signs of Christ's presence. Wherever you are in whatever part of the
city, the nation or the world, you are called to be the body of Christ held
together in him, and he in you.

On Wednesday David phoned me. He had a bad fever and he was
vomiting. On Thursday it was worse and he could not eat anything with-

out being sick and I was worried he was dehydrating. The ambulance came and decided not to admit him, but David was very anxious and weak. David, who has very recently been granted asylum in this country, has only just moved to a new bedsit and knows no one in the place where he is living. By Friday his fever was lessening, but he still had not eaten all week and felt too weak to go out and knew he couldn't anyway as he may still be infectious. Asanka from our congregation phoned him and asked him what he most liked to eat. David described a list of his favourite local foods from the country he was born. Asanka, who is a wonderful cook, made four dishes for him – spinach, pumpkin and butternut squash, rice, dal and boiled eggs – to eat later. Jonathan made leak and pumpkin soup, and then they drove to his bedsit. He was watching out of the window and waving. They left the food for him in a bag on the wall and he came down and took it, calling out in gratitude. Later he texted on WhatsApp with pictures of the dishes of food and some of himself eating for the first time in days. 'Your food', he wrote, 'was like the food my mother cooked for me when I was a child and sick.' This is Eucharist. This is Communion, the supper which Jesus celebrated, today a visible sign of God's invisible love. How can we be Eucharist for one another even when we cannot meet? How can we still be part of the same body of Christ? Perhaps now is the time when to be Communion we have to be more inventive than ever before.

But of course our story moves on. Holy Week moves into the agony of Calvary, where Christ is left alone and comes face to face with the brutality and agony of death. On Good Friday we will hear him cry from the cross. As we read in the Passion today, 'Eli, Eli, Lama Sabachthani?' that is, 'My God, my God, why have you forsaken me?' Our worst fear, to be abandoned and lost in death. Christ faces that agony and that sense of total aloneness when even God seems far away. In the last week we have heard stories of great suffering and abandonment in our hospitals and care homes. The idea of someone you love deeply, alone and dying in a place you cannot reach them, is a nightmare and we can all feel the tearing of our hearts. We realize our own vulnerability or the vulnerability of those we love most. Pictures of thousands of beds waiting for the sick, and mortuaries being prepared, fill us with dread and perhaps ignite in us that nightmare of abandonment and loss as we head into an unknown. What if that's someone you love? What if that's you in that bed in a ward the size of an aircraft hangar? And no one to visit you. Last week I spoke through a mobile phone to someone on a ventilator. She could not reply of course but the nurse offered to hold the phone close to her ear with such great thoughtfulness so I could pray for her. I said to her, 'Shirley, you are not alone, we are all praying for you.' All I could think to say over and over was 'The Lord is with you. Jesus is with you.' Today when I called, the nurse said she hoped Shirley had turned the corner: she was breathing a little easier and, she hoped, on the way to recovery.

I know too there will be many experiences of Calvary in the next few months all over the world.

But though we walk through the valley of the shadow of death we need fear no evil for he is with us. As we follow Christ into this unknown we do so with open hands. 'Blessed is the one who comes in the name of the Lord.' God is with you. God is with us. That's what Holy Week shows us, that nothing, nothing can separate us from the love of God that is ours in Christ Jesus. And is it not now, at this time of greatest need, that we are rediscovering the meaning of a faith that does not end in death but leads us through death, from death to life? For is this not the journey through Holy Week with Christ – the journey not into death but through death into life everlasting – for with Christ and in Christ death shall have no dominion?

Letter 13: Death and Resurrection

18 April 2020

I've been imagining what the disciples must feel after the days they have just been through – both crucifixion and resurrection. Resurrection does not mean back to business as usual. Everything has been unalterably changed. They have seen both hell and heaven. They have seen fear and death and then, in the pit of their loss, a hope they never believed possible and revelation of the life of eternity. I believe we are experiencing something of the same. There is no going back. What we are going through will transform the way we see the world. The suffering throughout the world is enormous. And yet when life itself is at stake and we are forced to see beyond, then a new heaven and a new earth begin to open up.

At times it can feel as though we are seeing the world through clean glasses that were so smeared before we could not see. Now, everything has been brought into focus. Mel wrote this morning on our Nazareth WhatsApp page: 'Somehow the green is greener, the blue is bluer, the sounds are more intense, the fragrance more perfumed, but maybe this is how it always is ... maybe in deprivation sensory responses are sharpened.' Or maybe at such times we are given, as Bev said, 'new windows into the soul'. We are stripped of so many of the things we thought we could not live without and here, raw, real, now, we find the gardener who speaks our name. When our name is spoken, even wounds can become signs of resurrection. The secret is to see even the difficulty and our own struggle and weakness, not as the end of our path but as something 'entrusted to us'.[1] St Augustine, who certainly went through his own struggles, 'is convinced that there is nothing, no matter how defeating, that is beyond God's ability to use for our good',[2] writes Martin Laird, and that 'All wounds flower ... The flower of the wound is the flower of awareness that is our grounding essence. The flower of awareness beholds the unity in all the joyous particularities of creation. To perceive with all the all-inclusive unity of creation is to be seen through by love.'[3]

I am continuing to livestream my Saturday Contemplative Prayer at 8.00 a.m. But now I have left my flat behind and have been drawn into London's parks. They are so alive at this time with birdsong. It's as if for this time when humanity is in lockdown we have allowed the space for nature to take over. My brother Daniel has bought me a steady-cam on the internet so with my iPhone I can walk out smoothly into nature without the camera jogging in my hand. The steady-cam means that the camera glides through the landscape. And behind the camera, not in shot myself, I can become the eyes, the ears – the eyes and ears of prayer. There is something so freeing about prayer when you are moving. Your walking finds the rhythm of your breathing so that you glide too. In this contemplation you are becoming part of something much bigger than self, the wonder of the park, the wonder of morning. As John the Baptist said, 'We must decrease. Christ must increase.' In my very soul I feel this. The diminishment caused by this pandemic is opening up a far greater sense of wonder in response to the miracle of creation all around us, which is more abundant to me than it has ever been. In these contemplative walks my sense of church is expanding out of the building into the streets and parks. Each week I expand the prayer: through St James's Park, Green Park, Hyde Park and around the Serpentine, then Kensington Gardens; then I discover the Peace Garden in Holland Park, and on my bicycle the Pagoda in Battersea Park and wonderful Chiswick Park with its lake. The place I come back to time and time again is the River Thames, the artery of London that goes on flowing, and as I walk its banks it flows through me. I whisper my prayers, reflect upon what I see, sense, touch, smell or hear, and as I walk, invite those who are watching to enter into the prayer. I notice that more and more people are joining. In their messages and comments and sharing with one another they are forming a community of prayer, taking the prayers from these walks into their own sacred spaces, homes, gardens and memories, and adding to them. Together we are sensing a wider church, not confined by individualism or organization but beyond us and including us all. It is both humbling and freeing to discover this unconfined space. There is in the physical isolation of this time, strangely, a far greater sense of unity with all that is beyond us. In this act of attentive contemplation we are gathering each other – gathering into God.

And all this is happening in the middle of a pandemic. Somehow, we have to learn. Somehow, even when this pandemic is over, we have to hold on to this radical simplicity – God, heaven, earth, goodness, love. We have to become as simple and wordless as the growing grass or the falling rain. We must just be.

Wonderings

I wonder what it is you fear.
I wonder what you have learnt.
I wonder if there can be a blessing in this tragedy.
I wonder what you are discovering about the neighbourhood in which you live.
I wonder what God is saying to us at this time.

Letter 14: Staying With

March–June 2020

From 1 March to 31 May 2020, in the death certificates of 43,763 people, Covid-19 was found to be the cause of death. This tragedy unfolding around us is overwhelming. It is attacking the most vulnerable in our nation.

I look out of my first-floor window towards Trafalgar Square. The gates of St Martin-in-the-Fields, the church with the ever-open door, are still shut because of the virus. How quickly the steps of our church have a derelict feel, littered with cups, broken bottles and discarded takeaways that even the pigeons have abandoned. The government's advice is being constantly repeated: stay safe, sanitize your hands, socially distance, work from home. But what if you've got no home, no place to sanitize or socially distance? Westminster Council, working with the homelessness agencies, had done well getting many into hotels, but now everywhere is shut – the day centres, the libraries, the bus station, the public toilets, the museums, the night shelters, even Heathrow Terminal 5 is closed at night. Those who live hidden lives of destitution, or live on zero-hour contracts with *zero* hours, are gathered in Trafalgar Square, waiting in hope for street-food handouts and hotel places that never come. But everything is closed and no one wants cash.

It's painful to see raw need. You want to turn away, not because you don't care but because you care too much. The desperateness seeps into you. You feel the guilt and frustration of powerlessness building within like a pressure cooker with no way out. Ian, the elderly man sitting out-side for the last two weeks, is still looking for cigarette ends to smoke even though he knows how dangerous it is. One contaminated butt and he too will have the virus. 'Please don't smoke dog ends,' I pleaded with him. 'I'm addicted, Father,' he says. But this virus can kill you. I buy him some tobacco and cigarette papers. What a waste. Fiona from upstairs and I feed him cups of tea and sandwiches. 'I do like food you know,' he says to me. 'I know you do, Ian.' Every day I phone up the council for him. Every day he waits for hours on my steps. I feel the intensity of it. The guilt and the pain lie in having no answer. I give him my coat. It's a good one, real fleece. But the next day he's lost it. 'I used it as a pillow last night and the next day it was gone.' I'm cross with him. 'That's the last time,' I say. Ian disappears for several days and I find myself looking for him. 'I didn't mean it,' I say. He's back and I'm pleased to be making him cups of tea and sandwiches again. I wonder who is helping whom. 'I like tuna baguettes,' he says.

What should I do? And the only answer is, 'Stay.' So often we long to be the solution, the answer, to be the saviour ourselves, instead of recognizing the saviour is on my doorstep. Remember Lazarus? Remember the story of St Martin? It's not the compassionate St Martin who is Christ, it's the beggar. 'It's not your fault,' my godmother says to me on the phone as I stand looking out of the window feeling the pain in my guts as I see all those waiting around my door. 'What do you mean?' I ask. 'Covid-19 is not your fault,' she says. There's a lesson in this. There's a lesson in the stress we're all feeling. I remember back to my time in the Solomon Islands when seven members of my community were taken hostage and murdered. I wanted to save their lives so much; carried their suffering with me; felt the pain of their deaths; felt the survivor's guilt. I feel the same now; feel I must not let people suffer on my watch. 'It's not your fault.' Somehow the 'me' must become 'us'. You can't sort other people's lives; but neither can you turn away.

Our own work with refugees facing destitution at our International Group can't continue indoors for fear of spreading the virus. But they can't just go home and self-isolate. Neither can we just turn away. They are our family here at St Martin's. So we begin meeting on our doorstep instead – 40, but then others join them, 60. Then 100. Then 160 people lining up, waiting patiently for food. We attempt to feed everyone who comes. We try to preserve two metres social distancing, round the block; and we give out masks. There's not enough food for them. It's impossible to cook for more than 60 from my small kitchen. But then the local Punjab restaurant offers help – a weekly curry for 70 or more. No payment; Amrit, the manager, simply asks that I say a prayer of blessing for his family and staff. They arrive with huge pots of steaming pilau rice, Amrit's Amritsari Chole, and village Tarka daal.

I stand there praying through my mask for Amrit and his family, who are Sikhs, and for Joaquim Menino Fernandes who works for him and is a Catholic from Goa and whose wife in Goa has just had a baby girl whom he can't get home to see, and then a group of St Martin's volunteers originating from the UK, Nigeria, Ghana, Nepal, Norway, Philippines and Botswana who join me preparing and handing out simple takeaways in a bag. Eucharist – hot chicken or vegetarian curry, daal and rice, hand sanitizer, a clean mask, a bottle of water, a cereal bar and a piece of fruit. And then, because so many are so cut off – mobile phones; £10 and a top-up.

'Do you have any tuna baguettes?' asks Ian. 'I don't like curry or rice or pasta. But I do like protein,' he adds.

Some of those who are homeless are vulnerable and are known so well to us but all the council places are full. One of the members of our congregation who is homeless is 72 years old and sleeping on our church steps. I phone and phone again to try and get a place for him. But no one is answering now. I am sure they see me as the problem rather than the problem I am trying to report. We manage to find another hotel ourselves with individual kitchens and bathrooms. A wonderful manager reduces the price and says he trusts us and does not ask for ID from those who have none if we vouch for them. We don't know how we can afford it, but St Martin's Trust offers to help. Katy Shaw the Trust director and I have long conversations on the phone. She understands and has a big heart. 'We will find the money,' she says. Miraculously donations arrive from members of our congregation and beyond. Sophie becomes the grace given by God to help me organize everything and organize the budget. With her husband Dan, twice a week, we take down supplies to the hotel near Olympia – me on a bicycle, large Sainsbury's bags full of my homemade chicken or lamb casserole swinging from the handlebars.

'Do you have an exit strategy?'

'No.'

'What will happen in three months? Where will they go then?'

'I don't know, but nor does anyone know what will happen in three months.'

All I know is that when your family has a problem you have to respond even when you don't know, do what you can. 'Don't think how you can transform the lives of the masses,' Mother Teresa used to say, 'just think how you can help today the person in front of you.' When did I see you hungry? Now. Don't ask if an act of kindness can change the world. It's the only thing that ever has. I have learnt over and over again if you treat people with genuine respect and care then that respect and care will be reciprocal. 'No good turn goes unpunished,' they say. But also no good turn goes unblessed. These days feel like blessing – such goodwill, such a sense of solidarity in adversity.

Of course we need global action to end poverty – but how often so much of our social action begins at a level that never roots itself in real lives. It becomes a strategy, a talking shop, a mission plan or a form of trying to assume control in a way that is simply not present. Our greatest strength as Nazareth is that we belong to the community, we dwell in it, we are neighbours. We can't go home – because this is our home. This is Nazareth. Global poverty is sleeping on my doorstep tonight or lining up in the rain for a food handout that doesn't arrive. Jesus suggests that the kingdom of God begins from the bottom up. When I was hungry you fed me. When I was thirsty you gave me something to drink. That means now.

I have often thought of Jesus' commandment to love our neighbour as we love ourselves as two separate actions. We love our neighbour. We love ourselves. One should not love one more than the other or there will be an imbalance. These days in a culture of far greater self-assertiveness we are often enjoined, for the sake of our own self-esteem and well-being, not to forget to love ourselves and to make sure our own deepest needs are met. But the two sides of this commandment are inseparable. It is in loving others that we do most truly love and fulfil self in the way God intended and the way we never realized possible.

Jesus does not ask us to end world poverty. He does not ask us to answer the problems of the coronavirus or to have the strategic plan to safeguard the future. Neither does he call upon us to sacrifice our only child, as Abraham learnt much to his relief. What he does call for is something much simpler, immediate and direct, something total. He calls upon us to realize, even in the midst of uncertainty and pain, even in the face of our own failure and mortality, that the Lord does not want our sacrifice, he wants our love, and when we love, God will provide. There is no mistaking the real thing. When we truly care and give attention, the world is a better place. It is at once the simplest of all messages that could help a child in a school playground but also one that presidents and prime ministers find impossible to grasp. 'Whoever welcomes you welcomes me, and whoever welcomes me welcomes the one who sent me …' The world is not your battlefield, your neighbours are not your competition or your enemies. Welcome them as you would welcome Christ. Whoever gives a glass of cold water to one of the vulnerable or rejected will be blessed.

A glass of water has been especially important to people with no credit cards in a heatwave. Some argue that food and drink handouts are just exacerbating the problem, encouraging a kind of do-gooder's dependency. But most of those whom I have heard say this are working from home. Jesus suggests that the kingdom of God begins with the water. Last night I did just that, I gave a bottle of water and some help to a homeless man on the steps of our church. Then from my window I watched how unasked he took a black plastic sack and cleared the steps and street and doorstep of all the discarded rubbish. It was a job I would not have wanted to do in this time of the virus. I rushed downstairs with sanitizing gel and plastic gloves. He smiled, surprised that someone should care about his hands, just as I was surprised that he should have cared about the rubbish on my doorstep and the church steps. As I was going back into my house a woman, about my age, who is always in the queue for the food that is handed out, said to me with no intended irony, 'Stay safe, Father.'

What are the events that have changed your life? Who are the people that turned you around and gave you hope, made you feel the future was possible? I remember a few years ago at the First Front Line Workshop of our St Martin's Charity, one of the frontline workers from a homeless people's drop-in centre began his address to the conference by saying this: 'I would not be here today if an outreach worker had not taken twenty minutes out of his day to say to me, "You look as if you need to talk ... come in, sit down and have a cup of tea." That may sound like nothing to you but on that day in my life that was the difference between life and death.'

Maybe this all sounds extreme, but perhaps we are all saved quite frequently by small acts of human kindness. We often think of the poor as some kind of project out there. You will find the greatest acts of generosity are often from those whom you would have thought would be the recipients. For example, the most elderly in our congregation are often the very heart of it and the generosity and goodness that binds us all together. All of us could name members of our own community or congregation who, though they may appear the most frail, are in fact the pillars of our common life. And there are those who think they have nothing to give who, if only they could see, are giving so much of themselves on a daily basis. Just think of a person who changed your life, who made you see that a better way was possible, who did not force you to believe but made you want to believe. Jamie phones me. 'I'm sorry to disturb you,' she says. 'Jamie, you never disturb me,' I say and mean it. 'Your phone calls and your prayers keep me going.' 'Oh, thank you,' says Jamie, and means it too.

Letter 15: Only Believe

10 May 2020

The worst thing about depression is the thought that it will never end and the darkness you are experiencing will last for ever. The worst thing about a broken heart is the realization that it will never be unbroken. The worst thing about doing something wrong is the fear within that you can never really be forgiven. The worst thing about trauma is the thought that it will go on and on repeating like a video on an endless loop. The worst thing about being rejected is the thought that you will never be worthy of acceptance. The worst thing about losing someone you love is the anguish that you will never be with them to love them again. The worst thing about grief is the realization that there can be no return because nothing can undo the death and bring them back. The worst thing about our present epidemic is the not knowing how or if it will end.

We like to count our successes and achievements as the turning points of our lives – the moment when I took control, the moment I seized the day, the moment I proved my courage. I wonder what the turning points of your life really were. All too often they are the moments of seeming fear and defeat. The time you wanted to run away, or did; the time you did not stand up for what was right but were complicit in a wounding or betrayal of another; when you lost the person you loved most and heard your heart snap; the time you lost out so badly that all your securities crumbled; the time you heard the diagnosis; the time you lost the job you thought your life depended on; the time you prayed and prayed for the miracle to happen and it did not; the time you hurt someone in a way that you could never put right; the time of sickness, the time of suffering, the time of death. It is here in the midst of these painful wounded places, these wilderness places, that Christ plants his words: 'Do not let your hearts be troubled. Believe in God, believe also in me.'

Believe. Believing begins in the storm of uncertainty. Believing begins as you reach out for the life raft in the storm, believing begins in the abject failure of your own plans to save yourself. Pain makes theologians of us all, forces us to confront who and what we ultimately are and what we long for. Again and again, we realize we are not saved by our own self-righteousness. In the wasteland of our plans, we cry out to God. As one of the text messages, last week, on our Nazareth Community WhatsApp group simply read: 'Help me! Help! I can't get through this! I need help!'

In my own life I have a very specific memory of that broken place. I am standing in the vestry of St Mark's Chapel, in the motherhouse of the Melanesian Brotherhood in the Solomon Islands. It is 2003. We have just heard from the police commissioner that seven members of my community, who were taken hostage, who we night and day have been praying for, have in fact been tortured and murdered and all seven are dead. In the vestry of this church I say to Br Caulton, the senior brother, 'I am sorry, I don't think I can go on being chaplain any more. I feel I have failed. Our prayer has failed.' To be honest, more than that, I feel God has failed. I remember to this day this feeling of total powerlessness. My inability to save those I loved, and the crushing grief and sense that I should have somehow prevented this tragedy. I cannot remember the exact words of Br Caulton's reply, but it was something like, 'It's now that God needs you.' The realization I remember was that it was not actually about me; I had vacated. It was about God. Here, in this utterly broken place, the place that *I* had vacated, faith began. Jesus answers, 'I am the way and the truth, and the life.' And here is where in my memory I say, 'I believe.' I believe. I believe in the one who is my way, my truth, my life. And, if only I have the courage, I want to stand with you. And here, in this broken place, is where Christ takes over. This is my body broken for you. *For you.* In my empty space, my derelict space, the place I had vacated, I see now that God moved in to dwell. And Christ showed me the way forward.

It is now today, May 2020, and more than ever we realize that Christ is a frontline service and a frontline worker. How do we know the way? Because it is the way of Christ.

The reason we are all clapping the NHS is because they are the ones who are embodying unconditional sacrificial service. Loving their neigh-bour as themselves – 'no one has greater love than this, to lay down one's life for one's friends.' Why do we celebrate the neighbour who goes beyond the call of duty? Or the carer who on minimum pay still turns up to care for the elderly, the Punjabi restaurant preparing 500 meals for homeless and destitute people each day, or Captain Tom Moore, aged 100, walking 100 times up and down his garden to raise money for others? What did we learn from the Second World War, six years of brutality and the ultimate sacrifice of those who died? We learn to celebrate the gift of peace. What will we learn from Covid-19? Well, we could learn to return to business as usual, or an even greater inequality, or survival of the fittest. I wonder if we will continue to spoil our planet, exploit the earth, poison the air and disregard the consequences of our food chains and trade deals. Or could this be the beginning of a new way of living and a new way of caring? How will we know the way?

Jesus answers us. 'Have I been with you all this time ... and you still do not know me?' 'I am the way, and the truth, and the life.'

Lord Jesus Christ, Son of God, help!

Letter 16: Living the Beatitudes

16 May 2020

Our contemporary rule of life is something that we did not create for its own sake. It is a practice that holds us fast even when we face the fear of all that is unknown, indeed face our own doubts. We are learning to live with an attentiveness to God both on the top of the mountain and in the valley of the shadow of death, where we need fear no evil. Our rule of life was always meant to be life-giving and that is never truer than now.

Martin Laird's writing continues to be such a helpful guide to me through this time. It has directed me back to the anonymous fourteenth-century spiritual classic *The Cloud of Unknowing*, which invites us 'to look over the shoulder of our distraction'.[1]

> In order to look over the shoulders of distractions we have to meet distraction with stillness instead of commentary ... this implies that not only do we allow distractions to be present but we also allow them to help us steady our gaze as we look over their shoulders, as it were, searching for something else. This advice from the author of *The Cloud* teaches us a new way of being present to distractions and moods.[2]

The struggle becomes the means to seeing into a greater truth. This time, even when it may feel like a disintegration, can become the place of our becoming. In the cloud of unknowing we meet the one who is both beyond and intimately present.

Martin Laird points to another image. In prayer it is often thought that we are asking God for help. If we imagine ourselves in the midst of a storm, and God as the rock that we need to hold on to, it's as if we are trying to haul this rock towards us or into our boat. But think of it the other way round. We are not hauling the rock to us, we are hauling ourselves towards the rock. We are pulling ourselves into God. What felt like drowning becomes the moment of rediscovering the rock. While the storm may rage around us, the rock is abiding, stronger and far more solid than the storm. Thus the disintegration is actually leading us to a greater and eternal strength.[3]

I spoke to a chaplain in a hospital who has been pastorally caring for the dying and their families. She told me of how when families could not visit she held up her iPad to those on the ward so they could whisper messages of love across the divide. We think of the dying as other people, not us, somehow removed from us. 'It's not true,' she said. 'It could be any one of us.'

I keep on thinking of what it must be like to be on a ventilator. A man on television describes the experience like one coming back from the dead with a whole period of his life missing. We are beginning to realize that even for those who come off ventilators, recovery will take a long time.

I dream that I am drowning, and every time I come up to the surface of the water to try and take a breath I am being pushed back under. And then under the water, in the stillness beneath the pounding of the waves above, I see Christ swimming towards me. And he breathes the breath of life into me and says, 'You can breathe underwater.' And with his breath, I realize I can. I encourage you all to keep our discipline of contemplative prayer, breathing in life, thankful for life within, breathing out and sharing life with the world.

Wonderings

I wonder where your help and strength come from at this time.
I wonder if contemplative prayer helps you to breathe under water. How?

Letter 17: In-Between Times

13 June 2020

I am more aware than ever that we are living in in-between times. The difficulty of in-between times is that everyone either wants to return to what things were like before or know what the future is going to be like. Now is the time when the strategic planners are making plans that seem to unravel as fast as they plan them. But it's hard to simply live that maxim of childhood, 'Wait and see.'

Perhaps that is what we have to do in the in-between time – to wait and see. This is the place not of solutions or outcomes but faith. Not of holding on to the past or grasping towards a future but of living with the present. Even as I write this I know the struggle. I know too that every new beginning begins with a dissolving, every new journey begins with a parting, and the new life of a tree begins with a seed falling on the ground and dying.

It is here and now that our Nazareth promise of 'staying with' becomes so important, the need to keep on turning up for God, holding the pattern we have learnt, living the rhythm of our contemporary rule of life, so that it becomes in us an internal compass that keeps on returning us to God like a magnetic north. A prayer phrase I recommend to you is this: 'Jesus has gone ahead of you.' This does not mean he has left you but that he has prepared the way for us.

I prayed those words this morning: 'Jesus has gone ahead of me.' It brought hope.

The Benedictines take a vow of stability. I wonder if we too can discover that stability, even in the storm. The importance of staying with is
not how we bring about solutions but how we live with people, events
and difficulties that won't go away. I'm always going to be faced with
that which I cannot control – how do I even then live beyond resentment,
murmuring, anxiety and pain without being defined by it? How can I be
fully alive even in the midst of trial? I wonder if we can drink the cup of
suffering and not be poisoned by it but rather let it become for us the cup
of salvation.

Empty yourself of all your preconceptions. Empty yourself of all expectations. Empty yourself of your worries, your fears. Because when you are
fully empty, God comes, and can fill you with himself in a way you never
believed possible. There are moments, in the most difficult, empty times,
when we can experience this ecstatic sense of a world alive with beauty.

The word that comes to mind is 'magnify', to enlarge, to amplify, to
exalt, to extol – to make great:

My soul magnifies the Lord. Our souls amplify,
God finding space in us, in us to be exalted.
Μεγαλύνει
Magnifying the Lord.

I think this time can work a bit like that. It is a time that magnifies. It is
like holding a magnifying glass and looking out on life and seeing some
of the detail magnified and at the same time feeling one's own inner life
magnified. It can be extraordinarily beautiful as one becomes awakened
to the life around us. It can also be at times disorientating, frightening and
exposing. Magnifying glasses can also burn and start fires. I am suddenly
aware of all that I have taken for granted and all that I have failed to
cherish. And I am more aware than ever that our creation is also mortal.
I watch *News at Ten*, a clip of the daughter visiting her elderly mother
in hospital. The daughter outside the window, pressing her hand to the
glass. The elderly mother trying to beckon her to come inside, failing to
realize they are not allowed to meet or touch or hug each other. When
we contemplate, really contemplate our world, we are in solidarity with
all those who suffer.[1]

Letter 18: Friendship – The Flower with a Thousand Petals

I have a very dear friend, Annie, who is very unwell with cancer and she is of course unable at this time to receive visitors. I remember when she told me. She knew the prognosis was not good. 'It's now in my bones too, which is why I have been experiencing this backache. The doctor said I have three years at most, probably less.' And then without evasion she went on, as is her way, with such concern to ask about me: 'How are you getting on in this awful pandemic? How are the International Group getting on? It must be so difficult if you are facing homelessness at this time.' When I came off the phone I was shaken, moved most of all by how in the face of a diagnosis we all fear, her goodness just seemed to be carrying on. There was her and there was a terminal illness, but the illness was not her, it did not define her or diminish her. She is so rooted and grounded in love and care for others. Last week one of her friends who is a composer asked her friends to put together a CD to celebrate her eightieth birthday. Her friends recorded songs or played instruments and shared messages of encouragement. I chose to read a short poem by Kabir. My friend is a great gardener and she loves nothing more than to plant and watch flowers grow and bloom. But at the moment that is something she is not able to do, so this is the poem I read:

Don't go outside your house to see flowers.
My friend, don't bother with that excursion.
Inside your body there are flowers.
One flower has a thousand petals.

That will do for a place to sit.
Sitting there you will have a glimpse of beauty
inside the body and out of it,
before gardens and after gardens.[1]

That was it you see. The thousand petals, the flowering that never ceases. This is what I wanted to tell her: 'You have such a gift of friendship, every time you met with me you made me feel that I was one of the most special people in your life. And I am sure every one of your friends would say exactly the same. You made me feel you had time for me, time to listen, not because you were a good listener, which you were of course, but because my life mattered to you. You welcomed the whole of me. That is the gift of true friendship. Not something turned on and then off, but the gift of a generous heart, before the garden, in the garden and after the garden, you helped us see the flower with a thousand petals.'

Postscript

Nine months later I called my dear friend Annie. I have been unable to see her for months because of Covid restrictions. She is too weak to speak to anyone, her carer tells me on the phone. Five minutes later the phone rings again. 'She would like you to come,' the carer says. I cycle there immediately. She is lying in bed looking so frail. She sees me but does not speak. I sit holding her hand on the edge of eternity. I think of Woven Gold, the choir from the Helen Bamber Foundation she organized, loved and gathered, the choir that took my breath away and made hearts pound, the choir to whom she was a mother, John Barber their composer and leader in whom she recognized such brilliance and goodness, the choir my dear brother Daniel and Helen spent so many months filming, the choir from countries as diverse as Myanmar, Iran, Congo and Kurdistan, asylum seekers she gathered to find a voice. I saw the power of music and friendships and Annie, to change hearts and to change lives. Their songs are the sound of hope, where those who have fled nations and home because of persecution or violence are no longer victims or even survivors but human beings set free to express their courage, their dignity, their perseverance, their creativity, their joy, even in the face of injustice. I remember how they sang at St Martin's, and the cheers and standing ovation that went on and on.

I hold Annie's hand for a long time, praying and giving thanks.

How we will all miss her, how I will miss her, this true gift of love and friendship.

The next day I hear from her daughter she has died peacefully.

Woven Gold sing these words by Rumi at her memorial at St Martin's:

Alone
You are a single feather
Blown in all directions
Together we grow wings and master the wind
Do you know what the music is saying?

And at the end they sang a traditional Zimbabwean farewell song:

Ndo Famba Naye my baba
Ndo Famba Naye kuchikira narini

(Chorus for everyone to join in)
Famba naye
Famba naye naye baba
Famba naye
famba naye my baba

It means 'Go with her, Father, take her gently.'

I am writing this from her Bothy in Castle Weary in Scotland, the place Annie often invited me to write and where in the evening I would go across to the main house to have supper with her and talk about everything in the world.

I still come here to write, blessed by Charlie and her daughter Amy, Ben and beloved granddaughter Lyla. I remember Annie showing me round the garden she planted, which in the spring will bloom with snowdrops and daffodils again, continue to flower with a thousand petals.

Real friendship is pure gift. It's the gift that surprises and goes on giving. Neither is it soft or sentimental. Indeed, it has to face death. But even in death it goes on yielding, yields a hundredfold. And you never quite realize how much it meant until you are parted.

Letter 19: Pride

June 2020

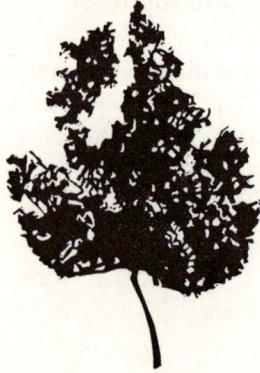

This week is Pride 2020, which usually fills Trafalgar Square. This year it has gone virtual. When I was at school 45 years ago it was terrifying to be gay. It was the fear of being outed, exposed, ridiculed, the fear that one's deepest feeling was actually a thing of shame and condemnation. In such fear the self divides against the self and supresses the person you were made to be. Thankfully in these 45 years things have changed unalterably in this country, for the better, and we pray that they will continue to change throughout the whole world. We learn who we are by loving. I asked my young niece if there are any LGBTQ+ pupils in her class at school. 'Yes,' she said, 'there's about six.' 'How do people feel about that?' 'Oh, it's really cool.' I rejoice in those who had the courage to be the prophets, to speak out and fight for justice and acceptance and for the rights of those oppressed and discriminated against. On their shoulders and through their courage we stand. Yet liberation is not just the work of the prophet, or the mission of the righteous, it is the work of each one of us called to live the gospel. It is the work of love. I remember a mother coming to me and anxiously confessing how worried she was that her son had told her he was gay and could I pray for him and her. I wondered if she was expecting me to pray a prayer of healing or forgiveness, but I prayed a prayer of thanksgiving for her son and his courage and his acceptance of his sexuality and all that God had made him to be and gave thanks for the trust he had placed in his mother in being able to tell her who he was so that she could share his true self. And it was almost as if I could sense the weight lifting and light flooding in.

It is the recognition that we are all made in God's image and called to share the cup of his love which is not always easy. The discriminated against, the marginalized, the victim, the exile, the lonely, the needy, the isolated are *us*, all of us. Last night I watched a documentary about the way LGBTQ+ people are still being treated in other parts of the world. It was chilling and horrifying. The courage of the LGBTQ+ community in the face of violence, torture and death was astonishing and so filled with love in the face of brutality. It was like watching crucifixion as we saw gay men beaten, kicked in the face and cut, and heard stories of government torture and countless disappearances. Religion has so often been shamefully complicit in this dehumanization and condemnation of people, and complicit in the resulting violence. Too often prejudice, stigma and violence have been normalized.

Real change happened when people began to recognize that LGBTQ+ people are not *other* but *us*: brothers, sisters, children, community, church, schoolteachers, social workers, priests, doctors, nurses, politicians, bus drivers, sons, daughters, parents, friends. Yes, friends. Real change happens when love and trust are allowed to flourish and dissolve fear. From the place of pain and struggle, a greater justice, compassion and empathy can be born.

That's what God's love does. It changes you. It transforms fear into hope and enemies into friends. It changes *me* into *us*. I hope you can see the flower with a thousand petals within those you meet, and within your own body too. And that you will know not only the flower but also the sower.

Letter 20: Perhaps the Earth Can Teach Us

11 *July 2020*

Perhaps a huge silence might interrupt this sadness
of never understanding ourselves.
(Pablo Neruda[1])

Perhaps this stopping can change us and this pause can make us think again about the way we treat one another and the earth. Perhaps this is also a time of rebirth. There are a startling number of people who think that the contemplative life means being cut off from and unconcerned with the world and its needs. Contemplation is not passivity. It is seeking to live the risen life. But in order to live that life, we need a discipline. We often fear disciplines, because we think we will fail or, even worse, be judged for failing; though usually it is ourselves who do the judging. But a spiritual obedience is in fact a deeper listening, and it leads to a greater freedom. Martin Laird has written with such clarity on this subject, and once again has been such a wise spiritual guide. I encourage you to read his books. Here are some insights from his book *An Ocean of Light* that can help us develop our own contemplative practice. Martin Laird has been like a guide to me, especially during this time of lockdown. These are some of the things he has taught me:

Contemplative practice allows for more space to be freed up as our mental clutter is cleared away. God is always there. What contemplative practice does is to allow us to get through the clouds that have obscured God's presence and enter the luminous vastness beyond. 'We discover what it means not to be silent but to be silence.'[2] We begin to discover the eternal now.[3]

Reactive mind.[4] This clings to what it wants and discards what it does not want. Reactive mind looks around at others and decides that, however they are, we must be better. Reactive mind draws its life from two things: comparing itself with others and being the centre of attention. It derives its sense of who it is from what it thinks others think of it. It is bent over itself. Its response to others is defensive, suspicious or hostile. Reactive mind allows suspicion and fear to grow, because the other is always a potential competitor or threat. Reactive mind grasps after ownership, control, territory, but not depth, communion or grace. When we are reactive, our humanity is diminished. Notice the way fear can make us reactive. Fear of criticism, or failing, or being rejected, or of not being adequate. It is an inner paranoia that sees others as threat. It is the fear of having our security taken away, or our inadequacy exposed. It is the fear of dying alone.

Receptive mind.[5] Nothing has been added to reactive mind: it is simply that more mental clutter and fear has been cleared. 'Reactive mind differs from receptive mind in the same way hard, dry soil differs from soft, well-worked soil that is rich in organic material.'[6]

> The sheer generosity of receptive mind continues its expanse, an expanse generous enough to cradle in its arms the joys and burdens of a lifetime. Pain still hurts, joy still gladdens, despair still flattens, but we are less demanding that the present moment – whether pain, boredom or bliss – be other than it happens to be.[7]

The receptive mind no longer sees one's past as judgement or shame but as the way of becoming who we are now; and it no longer sees the future as threat but as the possibility of growing in love.[8]

Vigilant awareness.[9] We cannot stop the thought any more than we can stop a waterfall. Rather we learn to recognize the destructive thoughts and to name them, so that we begin 'to change our relationship with thoughts',[10] seeing them as thoughts rather than the reality that defines us. We turn away from the inner chatter of the reactive. We learn to get our attention out of the interior story. We begin to glimpse an inner spaciousness that is silence. And in this silence, compassion and awareness are born. We awaken to a new intimacy with the created world, a new intimacy of awareness to our neighbour, a new intimacy with God. 'It is common for the contemplative to feel on the edge or periphery of things.'[11] We can often feel quite the misfit. The place on the edge is where we discover our centre and it becomes the place of truth and transformation.

> Out beyond ideas of wrongdoing and rightdoing,
> there is a field. I'll meet you there.
> When the soul lies down in that grass,
> the world is too full to talk about.
> (Rumi)[12]

Letter 21: After the Rain

1 August 2020

The rain falls equally on all things.
(Zen poet)

I have found great wisdom in the teaching and meditations of Tara
Brach.[1] The method she uses is a helpful Buddhist practice that follows
the acronym RAIN. In this meditation I would like to use and adapt her
valuable acronym for our practice. I would like to call this meditation
'After the Rain'[2] – which is a beautiful image in itself. After the rain is
the time when the ground is soaked in life-giving water, the pavements
washed with rain, the air smelling fresh and cleansed of the dust. It is also
the time of rainbows. Just for a moment, imagine you are setting out into
the sunshine after the rain.

After the Rain
Now think of the word 'rain'.

R – Recognize[3]

The first stage in a journey to a deeper awareness of God's presence is
to recognize where we are and what we are experiencing. Recognition is
observing your inner life. What is happening within you now? Imagine
your life with a horizontal line that divides the part of your life which is
visible and revealed – above the line. And recognize the below – the large

part of your life that is hidden below the line. Recognize in your own life what is below the line.[4] It's your inner weather. For example, I am really tired or I am experiencing anxiety, or I am thinking about something I should have done, or something I have done wrong. I am holding anger, hurt, guilt or blame within me. What do you recognize within yourself, beneath your defences? It starts the minute you focus your attention on whatever thoughts, emotions, feelings or sensations are arising right here and now. Recognizing involves seeing the things within us that we may have been denying. As your attention settles and opens, you will discover that some parts of your experience are easier to connect with than others. You can awaken recognition simply by asking yourself: 'What is happening inside me right now?'[5] Try to let go of any preconceived ideas and instead listen in a kind, receptive way to your body and heart.

A – Allow[6]

Allow is a liberating word. It is a word that means you are not under judgement or condemned for being who you are. Allowing says to you (and this is hard to assimilate) that you are loved by God no matter what. You are not under judgement, rather you are held in God's grace. All of you. Allowing means 'letting be' the thoughts, emotions, feelings or sensations you discover. You may feel a natural sense of aversion, of wishing that unpleasant feelings would go away, but as you become more willing to be present with 'what is', a different quality of attention will emerge. Allowing is intrinsic to healing. Its aim is to make peace with the wars or divisions within you. Allowing says 'Yes'. Yes, I'm struggling or, yes, I'm lonely or, yes, I am in need of God's help. I let go of my defences and let the truth be. And in letting be I invite Christ in too. Not to point out the failure but to allow his love to occupy the fearful derelict space. And the first stages of allowing – like the rain – may simply be to soften the soil or to wash away some of the self-accusations, or simply to refresh and rehydrate a part of you that feels forgotten. You can't do this all in one go. It may simply begin with a softening of the edges.

I – Illuminate[7]

This is not an interrogation of self, as though you are on trial before a judge. Much more, the next stage in our contemplation is an illumination, allowing the light in to see what you could not see, and may have feared. It is a seeing within. Allowing the light in means that sometimes we see the things that have made us stumble and fall. We also begin to see that some of these things we fear feel real but are not true. And that alongside all we fear, there is also the story of resurrection that we have failed to realize. Illuminating is like the moment when Thomas sees the wounds of Jesus and begins to realize that the very wounds that destroyed love can become the signs or place of hope and resurrection. When we illuminate what we fear we often find that the place where we thought we would discover condemnation and shame is the very cellar of our soul where the hurt, but also the true treasure in our life, are illuminated. Or to consider another image, the darkness is the very place the seed begins to break open and the tender shoot grows into the light.

N – Nurture[8]

The final stage in this contemplation is to nurture the good. It is the liberating realization of grace and goodness that cannot be overpowered. It is Christ's love for you as a whole person and the realization of his compassion at the very centre of all that you are. It is living in and allowing that goodness and compassion within you to grow. It is paying yourself and your neighbour and the world loving attention. It is allowing yourself to let the compassion in your heart grow, rather than the condemnation. It is the gentle, slow-growing realization that you are not defined by failure, but held in love. 'Among the fruits of our receiving grace is the expansion of our ability to receive.'[9] And grace sets you free, free also to share that same grace with the world. Nurturing is realizing your salvation and your blessing, and that you have blessing to share: it is a new openness. Think of Jesus' words to Peter: 'Do you love me? ... Feed my sheep' (John 21.17).

Letter 22: Contemplation is Revolution

12 September 2020

I am aware of how little we know of the future and how at this particular moment in time all our best-laid plans can, so easily in rapidly changing events, come to nothing. A society that depends on planning and control is now trying to navigate the uncertainty of what will happen next. And yet we know that it is in the wilderness that real change is born. One can feel the forces of the reactive mounting, desiring to invade the vacated space and seize back control. But can we not also feel the wind of God's Spirit? We are not sure where it comes from or where it will take us, but we know, indeed have already seen, that it can lead us into new life. We often fear that Spirit, because it challenges us to let go of our securities and follow the intuitions and truths of our faith. I believe that the renewal of our Christian faith involves just that – a deeper faith, a letting go of our belief that it all depends on us, our plans, our programmes, our events, our control, and the realization of the power of what is beyond us. Here are some words from Rowan Williams that he shared with the bishops in Rome:

Contemplation is very far from being just one kind of thing that Christians do: it is the key to prayer, liturgy, art and ethics, the key to the essence of a renewed humanity that is capable of seeing the world and other subjects in the world with freedom – freedom from self-oriented, acquisitive habits and the distorted understanding that comes from them. To put it boldly, contemplation is the only ultimate answer to the unreal and insane world that our financial systems and our advertising culture and our chaotic and unexamined emotions encourage us to inhabit. To learn contemplative practice is to learn what we need so as to live truthfully and honestly and lovingly. It is a deeply revolutionary matter.[1]

PART THREE

Nazareth the Place of Presence

Letter 23: The Upward Gravity of Love

November 2020

In our darkness there is no darkness with you, O Lord. (Taizé)

Have you noticed that while people get ever more tangled up in their plans and projections the inner clock of God's world around us continues so effortlessly that we scarcely notice the wonder or the miracle? How easy it is to be so distracted that we cease to lift our eyes to the heavens. A tree cannot cling to its leaves, a flower cannot cling to petals. In all of us there will be an autumn – a dying and a rising. Can we discover in this shedding not just the fear of diminishment but also the wonder of greater spaciousness within? Not an 'I want' but the '*I am*.'

I listen to Joe Biden's first speech. He spoke of healing the soul of the nation. He said:

> Let's give each other a chance. It's time to put away the harsh rhetoric. To lower the temperature. To see each other again. To listen to each other again. To make progress, we must stop treating our opponents as our enemy. We are not enemies.

I am moved by his words. I don't think he just spoke for Americans, he speaks for all of us.

We seek the healing of our souls and we know that the healing of our own soul also means the soul of our neighbour and ultimately the healing of our nation and our world. Have you ever seen pictures of an oil spill that clogs the wings of birds and the gills of fish? Have we not all felt the weight and the darkness of that oil that shuts out the light and the oxygen of goodness. We too need to be set free from all that chokes us and discover again the ocean of God's life.

It is perhaps only in our losing that we truly recognize our finding; it is only in our falling that we recognize our rising; and when stripped of self that we discover our true self. Meister Eckhart talks of the 'upward gravity of love'. Listen to his words:

> There where I fall
> is where you wait
> and how you call
> O fall with me
> all the long way down
> and so reach me
> through the call
> that rises impossibly
> as the upward gravity of love.[1]

For we do not proclaim ourselves; we proclaim Jesus Christ as Lord and ourselves as your slaves for Jesus' sake. For it is the God who said, 'Let light shine out of darkness', who has shone in our hearts to give the light of the knowledge of the glory of God in the face of Jesus Christ.

But we have this treasure in clay jars, so that it may be made clear that this extraordinary power belongs to God and does not come from us. We are afflicted in every way but not crushed; perplexed but not driven to despair; persecuted but not forsaken; struck down but not destroyed; always carrying in the body the death of Jesus, so that the life of Jesus may also be made visible in our bodies. For while we live, we are always being given up to death for Jesus' sake, so that the life of Jesus may be made visible in our mortal flesh. So death is at work in us, but life in you. (2 Corinthians 4.5–12)

Wonderings

I wonder what is dying within and what is rising.
What hope does the future hold for you?
What do you understand by the upward gravity of love?

Letter 24: The Boulder in Your Path is Your Path

January 2021

I have read a Buddhist teaching that when we are wounded by an arrow it is often not only the first arrow that causes the wound or the pain but the arrows that come after. The second arrow may be the fear of personal loss and the experience of victimhood. Why me? I need attention! I'm hurting! I'm frightened! I'm alone! Or the third arrow, the experience of bitterness and resentment and blame, like a poison within, an anger or hatred towards others. Then the fourth arrow, the arrow of despair: things will never get better; there is no hope only a catalogue of ills. And then of course there is the fifth arrow of guilt: how could I have done better? Is this in some ways my fault that I am feeling like this and so unable to do anything?

But perhaps we have all noticed that this present time has also been a time of change – of the widening and deepening of our gaze. At the moment it is much more difficult to be indifferent. Again I remember hearing these words: 'The boulder in your path *is* your path.' It is not something we can escape. Like it or not, across the world, we are all involved in this. Now is the time to seek a greater truth. The Greek word for truth, *aletheia*, means what reveals itself, what is unveiled, or begins to be seen. Truth is a connection to fidelity that does not deceive or disappoint. It is something we can hold fast to but is always in the becoming.

If we think we have the truth as our own possession we deny the truth; it is always beyond us. Jesus says, 'Follow me,' and later, 'the Spirit ... will guide you into all the truth' (John 16.13). There is a sense of recognizing and yet still discovering – a movement, a beckoning. We are invited into an unknown space, beyond our boundaries, beyond our comfort zones, beyond the territory that we can know and control or own.

When schools can no longer safely educate children, when health services we have always depended on get overwhelmed, when we can no longer depend on homes or care providers to look after our elderly or even us, when our leaders seem unreliable and deceptive, when people are dying and when we too recognize the vulnerability and fragility of our own lives – we begin to see the world as millions of others already see it, not as a national birthright but as a gift we need to cherish, to honour and value, not something *out there* but our body in need of a healing. Perhaps we will learn to live without such expectations of privilege and entitlement, but more provisionally, acknowledging our dependency and our lives as gift.

Pope Francis writes, 'Let us dream':

Just as what separates me from my brother and sister is my and their spirit of self-sufficiency and superiority, what unites is our shared insufficiency, our mutual dependence on one another and on God. We are no longer rivals but members of the same family. We are no longer caught in the mutual spiral of mutual antagonism. We may not think the same but we are part of the same Body moving together. To dream of a different future we need to choose fraternity over individualism as our organizing principle. Fraternity – our sense of belonging to each other and the whole of humanity. It's a unity that allows people to serve as a body despite difference of viewpoint, physical separation and human ego. We have a common home.[1]

We are learning once more that the elderly are not expendable and neither can they simply be farmed out into the underfunded care of others. Our young people need not only education towards examinations but community, friendship and to learn ways of helping and caring for the world. The NHS is not something out there, it's our NHS, and it is made up of people from around our world. The way we behave and respond impacts. We are learning to recognize the wider implications of this body of ours – our planet, our common good, our mutual dependency. There will be those who want to polarize and separate. We have been discovering the opposite – we need each other more than ever and cannot manage alone.

It is the time of *metanoia*. I wonder how many of you could say with me that at this time, 'I have learnt to see the mistakes of the past and to discover again the things that hold my life together, and long for the healing of the soul of the world.'

Love
Compassion
Friendship
The wonder and beauty of creation
The gifts I have taken for granted
The wonder and creativity of the imagination
The hunger for real relationship, presence, community.
The intimacy and beauty of human relationship with all the
    senses awake
The healing power of touch
The path of humility
And the wonder of our Christian faith and words of life which
    Christ has given to us
This is what we have space to discover and make room for
A time to listen with the whole body to the whole body and to
    see again.

Wonderings

I wonder what are the truths that are being disclosed to you.
I wonder what is the beauty of the present.
I wonder what you dream of for the future.

Letter 25: Nazareth the Journey and the Hope

February 2021

I want to begin by describing a moment of revelation I had. I was walking in Chiswick Gardens, which many see as the birthplace of the English Landscape Movement, with its rolling lawn leading to the lake and its bridge and groves of trees, the formal leading us into the informal, the natural and then the wild. Chiswick House and Gardens were the vision of Lord Burlington and William Kent in 1729. Now here I was, nearly 300 years later, being filled with the wonder of all that they had planted. The formal gardens, the lawn, the placed trees, the sculpted lake, the woods and undergrowth beyond – and the thing I loved most is that now it belongs to everyone. Here you could see so many different people, often with their dogs, enjoying this garden. I realized we are the custodians of such amazing gifts and yet so often we have scarcely realized this. But the revelation was more than this, it was that we are all mortal, and it has taken me 61 years to reach this point of awareness of how precious and wonderful life is and to become so vividly aware that God has entrusted all this to us. And somehow each moment is precious, it will not come again. I am getting older, time is running out, and so this revelation is more important than ever. Each moment is sacred. It was like realizing the wonder of something that has been with me all my life but which only now am I beginning to see fully and recognize.

So much stuff gets in the way. But Nazareth is teaching me to let go of the stuff and seek the space, find the opening out, see the wonder of now despite the struggle, even within it. It is the discovery of what John Keats called 'the realms of gold', or R. S. Thomas 'the eternity that awaits you', or Gerard Manley Hopkins the 'immortal diamond'.[1] How much of God's presence can we soak up?

Here are some of the things I am learning:

Proverbs for our time

Nazareth gave me my journey.
Lockdown is the time for opening up.
It is generosity that can open our hearts.
Prayer can be our path through the unknown.
I'm learning …
How much beauty there is in every weather and in every season.
The gift of friendship and to be so thankful for the true friends I have.
To be alone but not alone and rejoice in the joy of that.
To notice the beauty of trees.
To resist the things that injure the spirit.
I'm learning that there will always be times of desolation.
I'm learning that most of my fears are untrue.
Beyond the fear there is the place of discovery.
Life is not improved by quick fixes and escapes.
And that which may taste good at first can leave you more hungry.
I am learning the joy of space, of decluttering all that fills but does
    not satisfy.
How good it is to be free just for a while of appointment
    or expectation.
I'm realizing that the greatest gifts are often overlooked.
I see that the beauty of the pattern you see from a distance often
    depends on the smallest particle.
There is no such thing as the small life, every life is filled with wonder.
The taste of sparkling water can be better than champagne.
I was asked which of our seven Ss reflect our care for creation and I
    responded: *all* of them.
I have learnt that prayer is movement.
God is the gift we give and the gift we receive.
I am beginning to understand that the healing that prayer brings is
    simply love.
We need to learn the wisdom of humility:
'humility is endless.' (Eliot[2])

V. S. Naipaul once asked a woman in a tropical garden about a flower scent. He knew the smell but he did not know the name. 'We call it Jasmine,' she said. He knew the word of course but had never related it to the reality of the smell.[3] How often our faith is like that. We have heard the words but have never really related them to the experience. Now Word must become flesh.

Letter 26: Living Presence

6 March 2021

On the retreat last weekend we reflected on the words of Madeleine Delbrêl. This is what she wrote, which I think captures what I am trying to say:

> Our Lord talked about a life; he did not speak of a program of studies you would have to take in order to pass an exam. He did not speak of a political system for organizing life in society; he did not speak of a philosophical doctrine contrived to give an objective view of the world. He did not even speak of a treatise on God devised to delight our minds. He spoke to us of a life that, if we accepted it, would allow us to live by it. He spoke to us of a life in which knowing that God loved us and being able to love him in turn was one and the same; of a life lived by each person with all people, and with all people for God and by God.[1]

In the practice of this contemplative presence, we are no longer observers. We are entering into a relationship that is always moving back and forth.

> We, the ordinary people of the streets, believe with all our might that this street, this world, where God has placed us, is our place of holiness. We believe that we lack nothing here that we need … In the streets, crushed by the crowd, we make our souls into so many caves of silence wherein the Word of God can dwell and resound … Encountering [God] in all places is what creates our solitude.[2]

We are coming to God not by agenda or intellect or knowledge but by our experience of the gospel, the experience of compassion, kindness, generosity and humility of spirit, joy. We come to God 'not by navigation but by love', as St Augustine said. And this love leads to action because it can be no other way. It is a stepping aside from the competitive, ego-driven self and allowing ourselves to be the clay water jars of God's blessing that can be filled to overflowing with his life – life to be shared.

'My religion is kindness,' said the Dalai Lama. I would say for myself my religion is Jesus Christ. Or St Francis de Sales would say, 'Live Jesus.' So often religion has been a means of controlling and judging, preoccupied with telling people what they should know. 'I came', says Jesus, 'that they may have life, and have it abundantly' (John 10.10).

Madeleine Delbrêl wrote: 'Each tiny act is an extraordinary event, in which heaven is given to us, in which we are able to give heaven to others.'[3]

Letter 27: Sharing

April 2021

I want to write to you to wish you all a time of blessing this Eastertide. We have followed Christ through the darkness of betrayal and death into the awakening of Easter Morning. This is the time, like those first disciples, we realize once again that the life and love of Jesus that we believed had been taken away is in truth with us for ever.

These last few months have been an isolating time. Some of us have felt that loneliness acutely, others have enjoyed a sense of spaciousness and solitude, and for most of us there has been something of both of these – desolation and also consolation in these times. I believe that for all of us it has been a transforming journey in which we have come face to face with hopes and fears and in so doing longed to see the face of Christ. But while our spiritual path is one that we often feel we begin alone or in solitude, it is also one that leads us back into community.

What is it that we seek to learn from our spiritual practice, our silence, our prayer, our attentiveness to God? It is not to be more independent and self-sufficient. It is rather to recognize the gifts we receive from God and one another. I have heard that the poet Rumi said that if you say you can't create a work of art, then simply create a cup from clay from which your brothers and sisters can drink, and that will be your work of art. This is what we are called to do in the Nazareth community, to recognize the gifts of the other and to create the means by which we all can drink. I have been moved by the way you share and pray for one another and the way the needs of one of our community become the needs of all. This is the work of God's Spirit. If we wish to be in communion with Christ then we must see his face in one another.

There is a story of a Jewish rabbi who asked those he taught how they knew the night had become day. One said it was when he could see the shape in the distance was either a dog or a sheep, another said it was when he could see all the lines on the palm of his hand and another said it was when he could see the leaves of the tree in front and know which tree it was. But the rabbi answered, 'It is when you can look into the face of any man or woman and know that they are your true brother or sister; until you can do that it is still night.'

It is often the false practice of those who think they have found God to become more exclusive and separate from others. The opposite is true: the more we know God, the more we must search for the grace of God in each person we meet. Our experience of Christ leads us back into our ordinary everyday life to find the risen Christ there. Notice those fishermen disciples after the resurrection of Christ are still seeking, quite unsuccessfully as it happens, to catch fish, and it is Christ who aids them in filling their nets and helps their daily occupation to become the sign of blessing. We look for the risen Christ not only in beautiful sunsets and moments of heightened prayer but also in the painful difficulties and the tragedies we find it hard to understand. After all, it was the cross that revealed God's love for the world. We also meet God in the ordinary – the phone call, the card we receive, the neighbour we bump into on the stairs, the woman at the bus stop, the supermarket cashier, the member of our family whom we feel disgruntled with, the single man sitting in the pub who begins telling his story of pilgrimage. I heard a story of a man at the supermarket who became increasingly agitated as the woman in front of him in the queue was spending far too long talking to the cashier and talking endlessly about the baby she was holding. He was almost ready to tell her to hurry up but managed to contain himself. When he got to the cashier he said, 'That woman was talking an awfully long time.' 'Yes,' said the cashier. 'The baby she brought in is my son. She's so kind, she lives next door and is looking after him while I am here so I can still work. You see, I'm a single mum and I've needed to hold on to this job to make ends meet.' How easily we can get diverted by our own internal resentments and miss seeing the blessing.

This Easter, I invite you to meditate on Mary and the beloved disciple and Jesus' words to them both. 'Woman, here is your son', and then to the beloved disciple, 'Here is your mother' (John 19.26, 27). The one who gave life to Christ her son is now being invited by Christ to receive back the love of that motherhood through another. Stephen Verney says, 'We give birth to Christ as we see and set him free in each other. We become

94

Christ as we receive Christ from each other into the private depths of ourselves.'[1]

As we learn to see Christ in our neighbour we learn to see Christ in ourselves too. I am discovering there is a collective awakening. It is the way God transforms not the individual but his whole body – each one of us part of the whole.

Thomas Traherne (1636–74), the Anglican poet, priest and mystic, wrote:

> You never enjoy the world aright, till the Sea itself floweth in your veins, till you are clothed with the heavens, and crowned with the stars: and perceive yourself to be the sole heir of the whole world, and more than so, because men and women are in it who are every one sole heirs as well as you … Till your spirit filleth the whole world, and the stars are your jewels; till you are as familiar with the ways of God in all Ages as with your walk and table: till you are intimately acquainted with that shady nothing out of which the world was made: till you love others so as to desire their happiness, with a thirst equal to the zeal of your own: till you delight in God for being good to all: you never enjoy the world.[2]

Wonderings

I wonder what Easter this year has meant to you.

I wonder if in your own life you have experienced this: 'We give birth to Christ as we see and set him free in each other. We become Christ as we receive Christ from each other into the private depths of ourselves.'

I wonder what gifts you offer. I wonder what gifts you receive from others.

Letter 28: Looking Up,
Beside and Beneath

13 May 2021

Why do you weep?
That Source is within you,
and this whole world
is springing up from it.
(Rumi[1])

[Jesus said], 'you will be my witnesses … to the ends of the earth.'
(Acts 1.8)

I write this letter to you all on the day the church celebrates the ascension and waits for the coming of the Holy Spirit. We remember how Jesus left his disciples so that he was no longer with them but became with them even more than ever. Because he is no longer confined to a time or a place or a group of disciples but with us all for eternity – the essence, the source within from which all life springs.

Have we not all at moments glimpsed this when our humanity is lifted up into heaven and when heaven infuses the earth? A realization that Jesus is at the very heart of our lives and yet also the mystery beyond us, to the ends of the earth – eternal – our lover, our saviour, but also the saviour of every human being made in God's image. He is the human who opens up our home in eternity. No divisions, no separation. Nothing so human can be so divine, nothing so divine can be so human.

It is not that God belongs in a different sphere and we belong here. Quite the opposite. Christ – his life, his death, his resurrection – has become the open door that brings heaven to earth and lifts earth to heaven. It is no longer two territories, the above and below, rather the marriage of heaven and earth has begun. We are part of this transformation if we see, hear, touch, taste and live that kingdom – heaven infusing earth with hope.

Look up!

It's what we have been learning to do constantly in our Nazareth Community, looking up to God. Letting God break in. The God who dazzles us with beauty or challenges us with the mystery of all we do not understand. 'What are human beings', asks the psalmist, 'that you are mindful of them, mortals that you care for them' (Psalm 8.4). In this time of the unknown, have not all of us looked up and out and glimpsed an infinite truth, indeed felt our hearts burning within us?

Look who is at your side!

See all those who walk with us and recognize in them your neighbour. Look beside you. The me has become us. Side by side, equal, reciprocal, we discover compassion and love.

Look down!

See the pain and the struggle and how difficult or steep the path is and recognize how often we stumble and fall. But as we look down we also see the earth, the soil, which can become the womb of our new life. The seed falling on the ground and dying yet breaking open, to begin its growth into the light. It is here birth begins. And this looking down is a returning of respect to the earth. 'A flower steps out of its tight bud, gives its nectar, gives its gold. How do we do the same?'[2]

What I am trying to express is a shift in comprehension, 'a new heaven and a new earth' – no longer separate territory but Christ's love infusing the whole of creation. The more empty, the more full. The more open, the more ready for the guest. The poorer, the richer. The greater the darkness, the greater the coming of the light. The greater our humility, the less the barrier to let Christ in. The less we hold on to, the greater our capacity and generosity to give. The more we know our loneliness, the more we welcome the guest. The fewer answers, the more wonder and astonishment at the beauty of all that lies beyond. The more we know our mortality, the more we know the immortal. The more I realize I cannot manage alone, the more God. This is the meaning of grace – an unearned gift from beyond us, and yet deep within the core of our being.

Wonderings

I wonder what you see above and beyond you.
I wonder what you see when you look who is at your side.
I wonder what you see when you look down.
I wonder what it means for you that God's grace is made perfect in weakness.

   May we be filled with compassion
   May we be forgiving
   May we be filled with loving kindness
   May we be filled with grace
   May we bear the fruits of the Spirit – love, joy, peace, patience,
      kindness, goodness, faithfulness, gentleness and self-control.
   Come Holy Spirit. Come.

Letter 29: The Journey into Simplicity

June 2021

Last week I spent a time of prayer on Holy Island in Northumberland. It is the island made famous by those great northern saints, Aidan and Cuthbert, who spread the gospel through the actions of their lives. It is an island scoured by the wind and sea. It is a healing place for me and the place where I came to write *In Search of the Lost* to remember and give thanks for the seven Melanesian Brothers who had died in the conflict in the Solomon Islands and who had been such close brothers to me.

I remember walking round this island in the winter of 2005–06, feeling totally bereft. Grief when it is shared with others is painful but more bearable, but grief experienced alone is like a silent cry that no one hears. I remember walking through the sand dunes, buffeted by the icy wind that seemed to strip away the skin and cage of my ribs and blow my heart ragged. I don't want to be here. I want to be with them. And yet the more I become aware of that need the more I am filled with the realization that I am not with them any more, nor ever will be – the more longing, the more absence; the more emptiness, the more pain. You cannot return to the past, and thus the memory haunts you, like an open wound that cannot be closed. Each morning on the island I wrote. Each afternoon I stumbled along the beach and through windswept dunes and across vast expanses of sand and shallow ice-cold water as the tide sucked me out, or made me run back to flee its advance, as it washed in across the vast beach threatening to leave me stranded in sinking sunset-lit sand. It is an elemental landscape, not soft and fertile like the Pacific Islands, which envelop you like compost. No, Holy Island scours you like shell and shingle, like pumice, and infuses everything with eastern light. I realize now how Holy Island cleansed and sutured the wound of my heart. It was like plunging into icy water. It woke me up to here and now. You can only live now. And you are not the centre of creation. Your lagoon is sucked out into a mighty ocean. Your grain of sand is one among billions pounded by the sea both now and for millennia to come. Looking back on this time, I realize how cathartic it was. The story of the seven martyred Brothers pouring out of me into words; the wind, the sea, the light breaking me open, shaping me like a pebble that becomes smooth and polished, reflecting myriad colours as the waves throw it up on the beach.

Last week I returned to Holy Island. It was breathtakingly beautiful. We followed the pilgrim path across the sands at low tide, with the sound of the seabirds and seals honking and the wide horizon filled with light where the sky meets the sea – like walking into eternity. It is as though the veil between heaven and earth is very thin here. There is something wonderfully holistic about the way these first monks lived, so stripped of all excesses, so in harmony with the rhythm of creation. It is said that, as Cuthbert prayed, the seals in the sea came to warm his feet, and the ravens who had stolen the grasses from his roof came to ask his forgiveness, bringing him a piece of pig's lard as a peace offering. Yet how unaware our own world often seems. While there I heard stories of how each year impatient motorists think they can beat the tide and how even four-wheel drives can end up abandoned on the causeway because the tide has come in too quickly and left them stranded. This time for us is a time to recognize the mystery of our unknowing. Growing older and wiser is not about learning more but realizing all that we have already but have never realized.

I believe the call of our Nazareth Community is to strip away all that clutters us and weighs us down; to come, as it were, free before God. We are seeking the unencumbered truth of Christ's love for us.

In our community we recognize the tides of our lives. There is the tide that sweeps in around our feet, encircling us, destabilizing our foothold, pulling us into deep water and threatening to drown us. We recognize the full tide, those moments filled by God or battered by the waves. We also recognize the tide going out, leaving the sheen of silver, joining sand and sky, earth and heaven. We recognize a mystery beyond our understanding and yet one that we are called to enter into. Our community is standing with one another in the tide of God's love and trusting in that love when the tide comes in and when the tide goes out. I wonder what will be revealed in the breathing in and breathing out of God's mighty ocean.

Part of our fear is always that we are not able – we have got things wrong, made mistakes, failed even now to live as we would want to live. Part of our spiritual journey is learning to let go of our own inner cycles of blame or regret. It is also the realization that in God's love all is included. Every seeming injury, injustice, rejection, past, present or future, every blow of fate, becomes an essential note in the music of God, however discordant it may sound. And God accepts the whole of us. In God's forgiveness, all of one's sins and weaknesses are there: it is the darkness that has revealed the light, the falling that has revealed the rising, the rejection that is now the inclusion, the wound that has become the sign of grace.

He who bends to himself a joy
Doth the winged life destroy
But he who kisses the joy as it flies
Dwells in eternities sunrise.[1]

Letter 30: Pause

July 2021

I have been called up for jury service. Twice I have been excused but this third time there is no avoiding the summons. I have cleared two weeks in my diary and apparently it may be more. Now my diary is free I feel free too, to concentrate on something entirely different from my usual job. I cycle along the river to Southwark Crown Court. The first day I simply wait but am not called. The second day I am led into a courtroom with other jurors. The defendant makes no objection to the selection of the jury and after a further briefing and wait the case begins.

I have been expecting not to enjoy being part of this legal process but the opposite is true. As the case unfolds I am drawn into it like a real-life drama being acted out in front of me. I suddenly realize how important it is that I, like other members of the jury, have had to make time for this, to participate in such a crucial way in the justice of the nation. Far from being an interruption and a disturbance, this feels a huge responsibility and the judge reminds us that we have the fate and the future of the defendant in our hands. So often I have been sucked into that frenetic feeling that I can't be away from my job, that they depend on me and that somehow I am indispensable. Of course I can be away. This experience forces me to turn off all the stuff that usually occupies my head from morning until night and give full attention to something completely different – completely specific to this one particular case and the people involved.

The charge against the young defendant in his early twenties is robbery. The judge explains what the charge means: the general elements of robbery are the taking of personal property or money from the person or presence of another, the use of actual or constructive force, the lack of consent on the part of the victim, and the intent to steal on the part of the offender. Neither deliberation nor premeditation is necessary. During the first day the prosecution present their case, bringing forward witnesses and showing us footage from surveillance cameras that they claim confirms a crime had taken place. But even as the case for the prosecution is being presented I am not convinced and the evidence seems far from conclusive. It is a 20-year-old black student who is the accused and because of Covid-19 he has been waiting over a year for this case to come to trial. The arrest took place when he was only 18. When he speaks he speaks with thoughtfulness. He argues that he has no reason to steal and this is something he has never done and simply would never do. He is clear and articulate.

It is when he faces cross-examination that he most impresses me. The prosecution tries to press him hard – almost deliberately trying to antagonize him perhaps so that he will respond with anger or frustration and let his guard down. 'I suggest to you', says the prosecution, after a barrage of questions, 'that you are a thief and a liar and that your whole ...'

'Pause,' says the defendant, holding up his hand to stop the prosecution continuing. And then politely adds, 'In your opinion. But I am not, nor have I ever been.'

'Do not interrupt me!' the prosecuting barrister continues. 'I suggest to this court that everything you have said is a complete pack of lies and, what is more, you have been deliberately misleading ...'

'Pause,' says the defendant politely again, holding up his hand to stop the prosecution continuing his accusation. 'I just want to tell you, sir, that I am not lying, nor would I lie, nor have I ever robbed anyone of something that does not belong to me, nor would I want to, nor have I any reason to take the alleged property. It's just not the person I am.'

By this stage the prosecution is getting increasingly annoyed and testy in his responses to the defendant. It seems to me aggressive, and in contrast the defendant seems calm, and every time the volume and the vehemence of the accusations increases the defendant holds the accusation at bay with 'Pause'. Then, keeping a moment of silence, he responds simply and respectfully. It is this demonstration of calm dignity from this very young defendant that is winning my empathy and I find myself subconsciously willing him on and praying for him. I feel I should remain detached and objective but find intuitively I am totally on the defendant's side. I love his 'Pause' in the face of attack, giving himself the time and calm to respond with authority and without anger. By the end of the cross-examination, I have become so impressed by the defendant's method of stilling the courtroom that I want to tell him how well I think he had answered, facing a fully qualified barrister and courtroom, most of them white and more than twice his age and in such a highly formal setting, especially in contrast to the aggressive, intimidating way he is being questioned. Of course, this is not allowed, and I will never meet him, but his 'Pause' allows him space and the time to think and respond with balance. I am feeling anxious that the members of the jury will disagree with me and I will have a hard fight on my hands, but I believe that he is innocent; certainly there is much reasonable doubt that he is not guilty and I feel more like his mentor than his judge, hoping he will be found innocent. More than that, I feel moved by the dignity and courage with which he has calmed proceedings in what must have felt, after a long wait, a hostile environment, with real fear of punishment. He has answered the case against him without anger or bitterness and with seeming openness and honesty. His defence lawyer in his summing up highlights how poor the case against him is, and suggests that he is being accused not on any real evidence but through association based on his colour and the colour of others who he was with.

The judge in his summary gives us wise advice on how we should conduct our deliberations and I am grateful for the structure, clarity and balance with which he sets out what we are called upon to decide. When the other jurors retire to come to a verdict, we are at first tense and unsure of how each other will respond. The lead juror decides to give everyone the chance to express their opinion, but rather than having to convince anyone I discover that like me every single juror believes the defendant to be innocent. More than this: such was his use of 'Pause' it is as if we are all calm and centred too in our deliberations. Many speak up about how poor the evidence against him has been, how the police case does not add up, how much evidence has not been properly looked into, how much they are not only not convinced beyond reasonable doubt but not convinced at all that he has robbed anyone. One juror expresses still more that this case should never have been brought to court and says she thinks it's completely wrong that he should have had to go through this trial. After only 20 minutes we return a unanimous verdict of 'Not guilty'.

I return, impressed by the jury, impressed by this court system and the judge and the detail and time given to the evidence, and most of all impressed by the defendant and his 'Pause' and his refusal to respond with anger or aggression. I carry this 'Pause' away with me, having learnt from it and having been given a real pause from my own compulsions and working habits. Every time now I feel that I might lose my patience or respond with irritation or anger, making a situation worse, I remember in my head and in my heart that simple word our defendant has taught us – 'Pause' – and his calm dignity at the centre of this trial.

Letter 31: Acedia

August 2021

I wonder if you have found it difficult to concentrate or give your full attention to things during these last months. It's easy to grow tired of Zoom, to find yourself flitting between emails, messages, WhatsApp or other forms of social media, distracted and finding them increasingly unsatisfying. I have a pile of unread books but find it hard to concentrate. I find my eyes glazing over and my head filled with other thoughts. I turn on an audiobook but find I am not listening or it has sent me to sleep. Have you felt unfocused? Have you found it difficult to decide things and make the right choices? I have heard that many people are experiencing these feelings at this time.

What is this feeling?

John Cassian, a monk and theologian, wrote in the early fifth century about an ancient Greek emotion called *acedia*. A mind 'seized' by this emotion is dissatisfied, frustrated, unable to settle, restless, as though the batteries are flat, unable to make any significant change. He feels:

> such bodily listlessness and yawning hunger as though he were worn by a long journey or a prolonged fast ... Next he glances about and sighs that no one is coming to see him. Constantly in and out of his cell, he looks at the sun as if it were too slow in setting.[1]

One of the clearest descriptions of acedia is given by Evagrius of Ponticus to those embarking on the monastic life. In this passage he describes the dangers of acedia tempting the monk to abandon his life of prayer and leave the monastery:

The demon of acedia, also called the noonday demon, is the most oppressive of all the demons. He attacks the monk about the fourth hour and besieges his soul until the eighth hour. First of all, he makes it appear that the sun moves slowly or not at all, and that the day seems to be fifty hours long. Then he compels the monk to look constantly towards the windows, to jump out of the cell, to watch the sun to see how far it is from the ninth hour, to look this way and that lest one of the brothers ... And further, he instils in him a dislike for the place and for his state of life itself, for manual labour, and also the idea that love has disappeared from among the brothers and there is no one to console him. And should there be someone during those days who has offended the monk, this too the demon uses to add further to his dislike (of the place). He leads him on to a desire for other places where he can easily find the wherewithal to meet his needs and pursue a trade that is easier and more productive; he adds that pleasing the Lord is not a question of being in a particular place: for scripture says that the divinity can be worshipped everywhere (cf. John 4:21–4). He joins to these suggestions the memory of his close relations and of his former life; he depicts for him the long course of his lifetime, while bringing the burdens of asceticism before his eyes; and, as the saying has it, he deploys every device in order to have the monk leave his cell and flee the stadium. No other demon follows immediately after this one: a state of peace and ineffable joy ensues in the soul after this struggle.[2]

How much I can identify with some of those moans of the soul. The feeling that something else beyond is so much better and more fulfilling than what we have now, that other lives are so much better than our own. And within the wound of love – that we have never loved or been loved as we should – the memory that leaves us empty and hungry in a way that yearns for what never comes. Now, the pandemic has at times created social conditions that approximate those of desert monks

So how do we respond to acedia and overcome the temptations to give up? Well, first of all recognize these symptoms and how common they are. Know that this is not unusual in the spiritual life but also part of our path. And just like other temptations that need to be faced, so does this inner lassitude and tiredness. More rigorously than ever we need to hold fast to our simple, contemporary rule of life:

Silence. This must regularly root us in the mystery of God. Without those roots the tree dries up. You can't keep digging up the roots and expect growth or flourishing. The more we enter into the regularity of contemplative prayer the better we pray. It's like one of those athletes preparing for an uncertain Olympics. Each training session can at times be a struggle against the temptation to give up but each time we complete the discipline, so each time we feel more free, less confined. Silence is an obedience but this kind of obedience does not limit or contain, rather it frees – just like exercise frees the athlete to run.

Service. This requires that we look up and out. How easily we can become bent over ourselves, trapped by our own needs, disappointments, failures and worries. Our faith is a faith of costly relationship and engagement. In loving your neighbour you are also learning to love yourself. In accepting your neighbour you are also learning to accept yourself and open wide your heart. This is the movement away from isolation into compassion, kindness and care.

Sacrament. Sacrament reminds us that we do not have the strength to do this alone. We depend upon the power of God just as a battery depends on the power of the energy with which it is charged. While the temptation is to let one's light grow dim, the call is to allow God to recharge you with God's life-giving presence. This is when Eucharist becomes so important. We need to be fed by Christ and one another.

Scripture and sacred reading. Have you ever noticed how reading the wrong book at the wrong time can drag you into a dark place or a place of agitation or even despair? Or sometimes you reread the page over and over again and it simply refuses to go in. What we need at times of acedia is spiritual or divine reading that can nourish or rehydrate our souls. This can come through scripture, or spiritual wisdom, or poetry or music. Words, wisdom and prayers shared by the Nazareth Community can often bring this nourishment or point us to ways of finding it. Think of words or books read or spoken to you that have consoled or upheld you. Our spiritual path is not like climbing a ladder of perfection; rather, it is the unfolding of truth we live.

Sharing. While we can learn a lot in solitude, human beings were ultimately not created to live alone but to share with one another. We need to create times for meaningful human interaction, and real listening and being with. Just as too much interaction can be exhausting so equally can too little. When we share, we learn how to share who we truly are and receive back through the other the gift of their own sacred self and the discovery of our own sacred self.

Sabbath. Now is the time to give thanks – to recognize all that has been made and all that has been given. It is to reach the point when we can be astonished again by the miracles of life. Sabbath is rest and peace but it involves an awakening to goodness of the gifts around us. The English author and journalist Storm Jameson said that there is only one world: the world pressing against you at this minute. There is only one minute in which you are alive: this minute here and now. The only way to live is by accepting each minute as an unrepeatable miracle. Sabbath time is about wholeness and recognizing the wonder of all that is with us and around us and within us.

Staying with. There are times when the only way of getting through is continuing to put one foot in front of the other. Not giving up. The secret of success is to keep on turning up. Ultimately our spiritual life is not about moods or feelings – its much deeper than that. If you love someone you will keep on watching out for them or turning up no matter what and whatever your feeling or mood at that moment. Staying with is not a contract, it's a covenant of love, a relationship that will be there whatever the weather. It is through staying that the small seed becomes the mighty tree in which many find shelter.

Surprisingly, it's the rhythms and routine disciplines of our lives that free us rather than restrain us. They become the trellis or the lattice where our lives can begin to grow again and blossom. You do not get rid of acedia by condemning yourself for your futility or failure. That simply adds to the heaviness. You free yourself from acedia by planting a garden of love and watching and waiting for the seeds to grow and nurturing all that begins to flourish.

Wonderings

I wonder if you recognize the feelings of acedia.
I wonder how you overcome your own temptation to give up.
I wonder how we nurture God inside our hearts.

Letter 32: Finding Nazareth

Ithaca, September 2021

Don't surrender your loneliness
So quickly.
Let it cut more deep.

Let it ferment and season you
As few human
Or even divine ingredients can.

Something missing in my heart tonight
Has made my eyes so soft,
My voice
So tender,

My need of God
Absolutely
Clear.
(Shams al-Din Hafiz, fourteenth-century Persian poet[1])

While I was away on holiday in Ithaca, I lost my Nazareth cross from around my neck. I went back to all the places I had visited to search for it and looked everywhere but with no success. It felt such a precious and painful thing to lose. Like a loss of part of me. It made me realize how much Nazareth means to me. This simple cross, the painted wood from a refugee boat, the knowledge of Christ's presence with us in all things: in suffering, pain and even death, but also in hope and joy and resurrection. I realize this cross is a symbol of our community, our prayer, our presence with one another through every storm – and extending and widening that sense of generous, life-giving hope and welcome to all those in our world who need it most. I realize how often I lift my hand to feel that cross around my neck and am strengthened by the presence through that cross of Christ himself, the one who stands at the very centre of our boat and commands, 'Peace! Be still!' (Mark 4.39). It is the thing that holds me. The cross calls me to pause, to relocate, to reorientate my life in Christ.

My brother Matthew, who knew how bereft I was without my cross, generously offered his own Nazareth cross for me to wear. 'You can wear mine,' he said. I wore it for the Saturday meditation on the hillside and in the chapel. I am wearing it now. In every loss in Christ there is a finding. In a Christ-centred community every loss can be the opportunity to receive a grace – in this case the generous sharing of my brother. I have worn his cross with such thankfulness and love.

Somehow we have to learn to look beyond our losses and find the one who holds all things together in his love for us and can turn even the cross into a sign of resurrection. As I write this now I reach up and hold the small cross around my neck.

Be kind, for everyone you meet is fighting a hard battle.[2]

Here in Ithaca I have had the joy of being with my brother Matthew, his wife Siobhán and son Jack. Every day Jack comes to my apartment and calls for me and we swim together. Far out beyond the bay there is an island. One day I tell Jack I am going to swim around the island about a kilometre out from the shore. I ask my brother to come but he says another time. I head off alone, the sea between my teeth. I have a stubborn determination to do it anyway. It is very much further than I thought and out in the main channel I am increasingly anxious that I will not be seen by speedboats or jet skis. I begin to realize that this swim is not such a good idea after all, yet I have come too far to turn back now. How often we set out only to lose faith in our plans. I look round and see that far away in the distance someone is swimming after me. I tread water and realize it is my nephew Jack. He is an even stronger and much faster swimmer than I and suddenly all fear is gone because we are swimming together and laughing and joking as we slowly make our way to the island ahead. I am looking after him and he is looking after his uncle. And then I see that a canoe with my brother Matthew and Siobhán has also set off in the distance to join us on this trip around the island. A solo effort has become a community of care. We often set out alone, but when we let go of self-sufficiency we can discover how God intends us to live. We can find Nazareth or, in this case, Ithaca.

> Ithaka gave you the marvellous journey.
> Without her you wouldn't have set out.
> She has nothing left to give you now.
>
> And if you find her poor, Ithaka won't have fooled you.
> Wise as you will have become, so full of experience,
> you'll have understood by then what these Ithakas mean.
> (Constantine Cavafy[3])

Letter 33: Living with Trust

Late September 2021

While many of the restrictions we have been living with have now lifted, all of us are learning to live with uncertainty, no longer completely sure of what the future holds or what the aftermath of these last 18 months will look like. Nothing seems to quite add up. Why, for example, are you required to wear a face mask in an airport and on a plane but then can take it off when the drinks trolley comes round and you are all packed together like sardines?

Our Christian faith is a call to trust.

Trust – I think of a young couple I know waiting to have their first child, unsure of all that that will entail or of the change this child will bring, but trusting and hoping in the promise and joy of that birth.

I think of an 18-year-old setting out for university, living away from home for the first time and all that that entails. I think of his parents dropping him off at the university and him sitting in his new room, and the parents driving home waiting to hear – trusting. I look at the picture his father sends me of their dog sitting by their son's empty bed. I think of this generation for so long locked down, now learning to set off again.

I think of an elderly couple I see in the hospital waiting area. She is holding on to his hand tightly so he doesn't fall, the old man looking very unsteady, as together they shuffle towards the counter. 'Don't worry darling,' I hear her whisper, 'it will be all right. I'm not leaving you.' I see him grip more tightly, fearful, trusting.

I think of my niece beginning her first job, the fear, the uncertainty, the stress and demands and yet excitement of the workplace. 'You're going to be great,' I tell her. I see the uncertainty in her eyes. I also see her talent, the confidence she has yet to discover, her whole life ahead of her. Only trust.

I think of my own uncertainty. The fears that crowd in and threaten to sink me. I turn on the radio with the ever-repeating news of our national anxieties. I turn it off. Only trust.

I cycle up to Hampstead Heath to swim in the ponds. It's a cold but bright day. This pond has been my refuge. It feels a sacred space – a church. The ceiling is the sky. I remember an Iranian refugee telling me that he always tried to remember: 'The sky belongs to everyone.' As I swim, the ducks swim with me. The water is so cold you cannot think of anything else but only now. That huge intake of breath as you enter the water, and in that initial gasp all tensions forgotten. Then, as you swim, the cold makes your skin burn. Afterwards my body feels so awake – ready to face the moment. I walk up the hill to Kenwood House and share a wonderfully hot cup of coffee with Rosalind from the Nazareth Community. She is a great lover of this heath and the women's pond. We decide to try and keep coming – going down with the temperature and swimming through the autumn into winter. Returning on my bicycle I feel fully alive. Somehow, we must not let the fears overwhelm us.

I have been reading a remarkable book called *Apeirogon* by Colum McCann.[1] It is a novel but based on the true friendship of a Jewish Israeli Rami and a Muslim Palestinian Bassam. Both of them are fathers and both of them have lost a daughter tragically and brutally in the Israeli–Palestinian conflict, which brings these fathers together across the divide. Out of the enormity of their grief and pain both of them come to the same realization that there can never be an answer in hatred, brutality and the escalation of revenge. It is a book made up of many fragments, like a collage or tapestry of many voices, and through those many fragments we come to glimpse the complex interweaving of the stories and memories we experience and tell in our search for truth. To read *Apeirogon* is like experiencing a tragedy that keeps spiralling round and round, because the whole of Bassam and Rami's lives are a reminder of the death of their daughters – an ever-present moment of loss – forever repeating like a constantly rewinding video within. This is the trauma of horrifying violence but also, because nothing can ever be the same again, the realization that this is the defining moment of their lives.

Yet there is something deeply redemptive about this book. In his *Guardian* review of *Apeirogon*, Alex Preston wrote:

For all its grief, *Apeirogon* is a novel that buoys the heart. The friendship of Bassam and Rami is a thing of great and sustaining beauty.

There's a picture of the two of them, asleep on a train in Germany, travelling from one speaking engagement to the next. They lean against each another, Rami – the older man – supporting the smaller Bassam as he sleeps. This, the novel suggests, is the solution to the conflict: something as simple and easy as friendship, as the acknowledgement of a shared experience, as love.[2]

These two, who should according to prejudice be sworn enemies, discover a tenderness and grace born of shared suffering that moves outwards. We do not know when or how but ultimately it is this humanity that is the only thing that will overcome the violence. 'This will not be over until we learn to talk to one another and understand one another.' And they keep on telling their stories again and again – stories that cross all that divides because they tell of our common humanity, the horror of violence that destroys lives, and two fathers' longing for an end to the hatred and prejudice: the agony of their grief has removed all the barriers between them.

In one of the fragments we read of an exchange of letters between Albert Einstein and Sigmund Freud. In 1932 Einstein wrote to Freud with a question that must still be within all our hearts. He wrote that, despite the profound hope of the greatest moral and spiritual leaders from Christ to Goethe and Kant, no one has been able to stem the war and savagery of human beings. The essential question Einstein wanted to ask was 'Why?' Is it possible for humankind ever to become resistant to the psychosis of hate and destruction, thereby delivering civilization from the constant fear and menace of war and violence? In September 1932 Einstein received a reply from Sigmund Freud. Freud wrote that he doubted that anyone would be able ever to supress humanity's most aggressive tendencies. He wrote: 'It is easy to infect humankind with war fever, and humanity has an active instinct for hatred and destruction.' What was needed was 'to establish, by common consent, a central authority that would have the last word in every conflict of interest'. Beyond that he said that 'anything that creates emotional human ties between human beings, inevitably counteracts war.' What had to be sought was 'a community of feeling and a mythology of the instincts'.[3]

This is what we must continue to work towards. A community of feeling and a mythology of our instincts – a community of compassion and empathy.

Letter 34: The Guest House

October 2021

This being human is a guest house.
Every morning a new arrival …

Be grateful for whoever comes,
because each has been sent
as a guide from beyond.
(Rumi[1])

Have you ever felt used up, as though your inner life is like a battery that has used up all its power? In the Solomon Islands, where it was hard to buy batteries, they used to put flat batteries out in the direct sun and the warmth would recharge them enough to light their torches again. How can we recharge our inner lives, especially on the days when the sun has gone in?

No one wants to be a fair-weather friend. We know how important it is in times of struggle or loss to try to be unconditional in our support for those we care deeply about. But I wonder if we are not at times fair-weather friends to ourselves. Rumi's poem calls on us to treat each guest within our lives honourably, as though we were a guest house welcoming each guest with gratitude.

I wonder who or what are the unexpected visitors coming to you today? Perhaps joy, hope, wonder, laughter, love. But if we are honest, perhaps lurking in our house are our fears, our resentments, our inner loneliness, our despair, our dread. These are guests too in our house that we would often rather lock away. They are not easy or beautiful but jagged and often ugly: some frighten us, some are like an ulcer within. Some of this pain is physical too because we feel it in our body – it aches within our back or joints, it can make our stomach ache or head throb. It hurts, it knots us up and makes us wonder how we will ever cope. And these guests, we imagine, whisper our deepest fears about ourselves and tell us we are unacceptable.

I have been reading the story of Jesus and Zacchaeus and I realize this is how Zacchaeus must have felt: despised. Perhaps worse, despising himself, isolated from others, knowing his failings even better than others know them. I wonder if Zacchaeus' inner shame is reflected in the way he feels about his body – small, insignificant, unable to see, but not wanting to be seen or exposed. And yet he wants to see Jesus. In this wanting there is hope. In this longing is our healing. I love the way he runs. In that running he is present to the moment, the now, the hope beyond all that has imprisoned him. At that moment of running he is not thinking about himself, he is thinking about seeing Jesus. He climbs a sycamore tree, a tree that can grow 20 metres tall, a symbol of protection but also of life. Zacchaeus wants to see without being seen, to know while remaining hidden. But Jesus sees him. He looks up at him and sees all of him, fully revealed. Caught in the act, the tree is not a hiding place but the place where he may be exposed to public shame. But the opposite happens. Jesus honours him. He calls him by name:

'Zacchaeus, hurry and come down; for I must stay at your house today.'
(Luke 19.5)

I invite you to imagine those words addressed to you. Your name. Jesus speaking to you. 'N, hurry and come down; for I must stay at your house today.'

Jesus, entering your own door, which you have opened for him. Jesus coming into your own home or homelessness. He has chosen to be your guest and you have chosen to be the host of Jesus. He visits the familiar places of your life. Notice the way he does it, with grace not judgement. Jesus also visits the hidden places, the places of sadness, loss, failure and shame, and he does it not despising but with recognition and honour. He sees you. He sees all of you. He sees your woundedness and he sees your eternal life in the wound – your resurrection – God's love for you, in you and in your body. You too are the beloved of God. This radical, unconditional acceptance is not avoidance or denial. It is the love that knows the cross, the pain and brutality of the world, but it is the love that knows God's forgiveness, a healing from beyond us and the call to life in all its fullness. You are called into this meeting. You are now the one receiving the light and the energy and the Spirit of Christ who visits you. You too can be recharged with that light and love. Remember how Christ himself will be revealed on a tree. Remember the words again found in Luke's Gospel: 'Jesus, remember me when you come into your kingdom.' And Jesus' reply, which echoes his words to Zacchaeus: 'Today you will be with me in Paradise' (Luke 23.42–43).

Rumi writes:

Don't turn your head.
Keep looking at the bandaged place.
That's where
the Light enters you.[2]

There is a well-known story of Mohini, a white tiger from the Washington DC National Zoo. For many years she lived in a cage 16ft by 16ft where she would pace backwards and forwards all day. After years of pacing, the zoo, realizing the cruelty of keeping her caged like this, created a purpose-built park for this white tiger, with acres of space and a pool and a hill to climb. Yet Mohini stayed close to the bars and continued to walk backwards and forwards wearing the grass away in a small strip 16ft by 16ft. Christ comes to us so that we may have life abundantly. Christ visits us to set us free. I wonder if we do not sometimes remain in the cage pacing and re-pacing the same land where all the grass is bare, imprisoning ourselves even after Christ has set us free to enjoy the whole.

Wonderings

I wonder who is inside your guest house and how you respond.
I wonder how you can recharge your soul.
I wonder how salvation comes to you today.

Letter 35: Love is a Moment
Eternally Overflowing

Pitlochry, November 2021

At the end of the conference one of the priests said, 'What you have shared this week about the Nazareth Community sounds really counter-cultural.' 'What do you mean?' I asked. We had shared about the importance of silence, service, scripture, sacrament, staying with – not what I would have thought of as counter-cultural for a group of 50 priests and ministers: a simple stripped-back message of opening ourselves and allowing the space for Christ's Beatitudes to live within us. 'Well,' he said, 'often at church conferences we discuss methods of church growth, strategic plans for church development, mission action plans, management and resource development, leadership development skills. In these last few days we have been invited to pray, to keep silence, to enter into scripture, to share our faith with one another. It's been different to what I was expecting. To share with one another in this way has been life-giving.'

Isn't this the way we grow like seeds that fall upon the ground and break open and shoot and grow and become the trees in which others find shelter? What we are seeking is organic growth, allowing God in us to do God's work. Growth from the bottom up. Allowing the light of God to warm and then slowly crack open the shell of our defences, to allow the breath of God in, so that we are no longer dormant but begin to become filled by that breath, expanded into life. As we grow, we thirst and discover the water of life. The Spirit that becomes our sap, our osmosis, our flourishing. We unfold, and as we unfold we realize that this growth is not something we do alone. We are in a field of those growing together, each one of us protecting, sheltering, giving light and shade and nourishing the others. We are not seeking genetic modification for ourselves to make one variant grow taller, stronger and more dominant. We are seeking God's miracle of biodiversity in us and in communion with one another and with the world.

I am convinced that this is the path to church growth – God's growth in us. I remember, before the beginning of a 30-day silent retreat, I asked the gardener if during the retreat I could help in the garden. He answered me, 'The real question is, can the garden help you?' His meaning slowly became clear. It was not what I was doing to, it was what I was making space for, in order to participate in. I remember distinctly that as I began to dig the earth it was as though my action scared away creation. I was the source and the end of the action. But slowly as I watched the skilled gardener I learnt to let the fork do the work, and I became more attentive to the soil, its colour, its texture, the worms and insects within, the birds that began to join me. I remember distinctly each day as I worked in the garden the way a robin visited me and each day came closer. It was no longer me against nature. It was us. It was Communion.

I write this from Annie's Bothy in Castle Weary, not far from Pitlochry in Scotland, where I am staying for a few days to write. I am looking out of the window and there is a blue tit coming to eat the nuts from a small hanging feeder, its little head bobbing backwards and forwards as it pecks, until a larger great tit displaces him. A robin redbreast is sitting quietly on a silver birch tree. A red squirrel has just appeared in the bracken, among the mossy boulders, grass and dry leaves. The light is forever changing. It is like God's theatre before me: a leaning gate, a grassy path bending to the left, and beyond the flaming bronzes and oranges of autumn trees, and beyond that, smooth-backed hills against a grey sky. You think there is silence until you listen. Then of course you realize that creation is alive with its own music. I can hear the birds, the constant sound of the stream 100 metres away and a very soft wind in the trees. I am completely alone. But today I am not alone. I am very aware of all of you, our Nazareth Community, and the way prayers cross distances when we are attentive to them. They too are like the wings of birds upholding you or a bird's sudden song calling you. They are like the seeds that you can almost hear growing around you – listen. Prayer too is palpable without and within. And I am also acutely aware that prayers traverse this world and beyond.

I am staying in this small bothy among silver birch trees. It is lit with warm autumnal light. Its long glass window, through which I look as I write, opens up the wonder of the landscape that surrounds me. Although it is cold I have the door wide open because I want to breathe fresh air, which smells of earth, leaves, damp ferns and autumn. It's like a small warm hermitage here. In front of me is the house where Annie lived whenever she came to Scotland before she died this year. I have come here many times to write. In fact I wrote parts of *The City is My Monastery* when I was last here in Spring 2019. In the afternoon Annie would come over and ask if I wanted to go for a walk. She loved her wild garden with its many hidden bulbs blooming in spring, the landscape, the narrow bridge across the burn, scrambling up the steep banks to the top where you walk through trees to see the sheep with their new lambs. In the evening she would call me over to her house for delicious, simple, local food, home-grown vegetables, fish from the local smokery and the warmth of a log fire. She is no longer here. I keep on expecting to see her coming up the path. But her house is shut up now. No lights. No fire. And I feel her loss in the pit of my stomach painfully like a knot. But her Spirit pervades this place. When our hearts are attentive we are awake both to the living and to the spirit of those we love who have gone before us. I thought I did not want to come back here as I would miss her too much. But being here I can feel her pleasure within me. She did not plant this garden for it to be forgotten or unseen. Why do we turn away from the sorrow of our love? It is here the light shines through. In Christ we meet the whole of our lives now – not as loss but as blessing, as though held together by him, transfigured by his love. He opens the grave and calls us to see even the cross and tomb as signs of love and resurrection. In the missing there is also a finding. In the solitude of loss there is also the memory of a friendship that has not ended and calls me back. I see that the seed that falls on the ground and dies does indeed shoot and grow and can become this silver birch tree in which today I find shelter. Andrew, the estate manager, came over to my hermitage last night. 'I'm still planting Annie's vegetable garden,' he said. 'Couldn't not do that. She would have wanted those vegetables planted each year for everyone to share. So I am going to keep on doing just that.'

In the afternoon Charlie visits for a walk and we pass through the garden and trees that Annie and he planned and planted together. The Bothy where I am staying had been Charlie's gift to Annie. He has her same gift of kindness and generous hospitality. In the evening he poaches smokies in milk with leeks and we drink red wine together. Annie feels very present. No rush, no deadline, just stories and memories circling – the past, the present, the grace continuing.

Wonderings

I wonder if you have experienced prayer upholding you.

I wonder if and when you have experienced a sense of communion between heaven and earth.

I wonder how the love of those who are departed from you upholds you.

I wonder how something you planted, or was planted for you, continues to bear fruit now.

Letter 36: Making Room for Christ

December 2021

After the taste of opening up after Covid-19 there is now a closing down again and many must be asking how long this will go on. Will there ever be a clear end in sight? It is hard to make plans and hard not to make plans. All day I have been trying to think of wise words to share. And I have none. Words themselves are inadequate – like papering the unknown. And then I came upon these words in a poem:

> Not to make sense, inside the keel of sweating ribs,
> not to make sense but room.[1]

Not sweating ribs perhaps in winter, rather cold brittle ribs but still constricted by all the fears that inflict our world. The tightening chest, the shallow breath, the cry for ventilation. I thought of myself within my own keel of ribs like an upturned boat – and the desire to make not sense but room, room within me, room for the other, room for Christ.

Room to breathe deeply, to expand from the inside out. Room to breathe Christ's life-giving breath. God's breath within us.

Room to give the Christ-child life.

Room from the anxieties that hold us captive in the unsocial gatherings of our fears.

Room for those facing the dark waves and cold cruelty of the English Channel, clinging to their children, only flimsy life jackets to keep them warm, fearing the cruelty of our modern Herods and the death of innocence, but still courageously dreaming of salvation.

Room for all those who find in this country that there is no room at the inn; rather, they with Christ are the outcasts. Room to come into his stable to discover that our salvation begins here among the humble and the forgotten, with animals and a cold night lit up by the stars. Room to open our senses to the meaning of our humanity and see both our birth and death side by side cradled in eternity.

Room within the stable of our lives amid all the mess and dung. Room for Christ to be born, the one who makes trampled straw golden and turns social isolation into communion with angels. Here our very poverty is transformed into the place of beauty, because we have made the space for this child to fill this emptiness with the warmth of his precious body.

Room to wonder at the enormity of creation and our own insignificance: 'What are human beings, that you are mindful of them, mortals that you care for them' (Psalm 8.4). This mighty yet intimate God present in the stars, but also this newborn child held in our hands – cheek to cheek, dependent on us and yet all of life dependent on him. Close yet cosmic, as gentle as the heartbeat that separates your mortal life from eternity.

Room to discover that as we make room for God, God has already made room for us. The one we make room for is our room, our resting place, our eternal dwelling. The one who will stay with us no matter what and no matter how bad things get. That's the message of Bethlehem. God is with us.

This time is an elemental time. It's a time of stripping away all the pretences and hypocrisies and seeing the face of God.

Room to be born.

And then in Nazareth to find the place in which to ponder this birth and to nurture this incarnation – to become the bearers of Christ. Immanuel the God who stays with us. Neil MacGregor sends me a copy of Ruth Padel's poem she has written to celebrate John Keats. I love it.

Night Singing in a Time of Plague

> Here there is no light
>> Keats, 'Ode to a Nightingale'

Can't you sleep either? After a dark year,
many old friends gone, I thought I heard you sing
in the empty street outside the window,
inches from my ear. Who are you singing for
this time of night? Did I dream you?

Even if I did, I'm with you, robin,
the only ones awake at half-past two
under a full December moon
in city air the colour of spat-out liquorice.
Again. You really are here. One chirrup,

then a song I've heard in better times
and other countries. An olive grove on Crete –
where I'd love, love to be right now –
and a snowstorm in North Wales,
challenging the gods of loneliness and ice.

Take me to a new world! No. You've turned
the music off. And someone else can't sleep,
a light comes on between those green-
lit stairwells, in flats across the road.
But you, I bet, are perky as a Christmas card

among thorns of that shaggy creeper.
Another trill, rich as day. Now a carol,
a wild cantata. What do you know
of months penned in, not seeing anyone,
a hundred thousand people dead,

this country alone? Or the larger thing,
poisoned seas, whole pristine forests burned,
a dying planet? Your little tribe has learned
to stay up close and use what humans bring.
Come morning you'll be on the sill

waiting for crumbs. We're in this together,
this Stations of the Cross situation,
and you are the Advent hymn.
Bonkers but brilliant.
Let sleep come softly. Let the heart return.[2]

Letter 37: Staying with Love

January 2022

Love waits for you at the station
Filled with joy at your coming
Or outside the doctor's surgery
In the car to drive you home
It frustrates, irritates, gets in the way, longs, hopes, worries, wants to
    do it for you, knows jealousy, protects, confronts, defends, flashes
    with anger at your selfishness or neglect
Longs for your successes
And yet loves you exactly as you are
Through years of imperfections
Love waits at the door for your return
Under the hanging basket of flowers you gave them years before
And welcomes the whole of you
The bed is already prepared with towel
The endless cooking of the food you like
The room which you painted is waiting
The photo by the bedside from twenty years ago
And the thousand memories that pierce your heart
with affection and concern
and fear of loss
This love is home
To which you will return in search again and again
For this one who is watching and waiting
Whose eyes you know better than your own

And clothes you with the carefully folded clothes they have kept in
   your drawer for your return
The pyjamas smelling of washing powder
And the clock on the wall already aching with the tick of departure.[1]

I am aware how powerful our memories are and how these winter times
of long shadows and contrasts of light and darkness often evoke them so
strongly. Perhaps it is January that is the 'cruellest month', stirring up our
senses of remembering and longing more than other months. What happens when everyone separates? When those who gathered at the crib go
their different ways? What happens as people get older and the witnesses
of birth and childhood become the witnesses of death and mortality?

After New Year I go to visit the garden of remembrance where my
father's ashes were scattered. The winter sun comes out. It is the church
where I grew up. The path leading to the gate I remember going through
so often. The church is so familiar it is like turning back 50 years. And
following the path I come to the locked-up church hall where, long ago,
each Christmas and New Year we performed pantomimes with the church
youth club. These memories, so vivid, begin playing out in my head. I still
remember the smell of the newly painted sets, the hessian flats, the songs,
the costumes, the dressing room and grease paint, the excitement, the
characters colourful and larger than my life – a life still ahead of me.

They've taken the bench away where each anniversary of my father's
death my family gather to sit. Apparently the local *youth* used to congre-
gate there to smoke. I used to sit there and watch my nephew and niece
dance on the grass where his ashes were buried because we thought their
grandfather would love that. My dad always said he could not imagine
heaven being more beautiful than this world. He loved life with an artist's
eye and did not want to be parted from us. 'I want to see what happens to
you all,' I remember him saying. I know I am blessed to have such good
memories of him but it does not stop the twisting of the heart in grief
even more than 20 years after he left us. How much I would still love to
ask him, 'Are we nearly there?' He always seemed to know such things.

Then on the train to Dorset last week I passed through Wareham
which is where Mum and Dad used to live in their retirement. So familiar
yet now just rushing past on a train to somewhere else. Whoosh … gone.
I remember my mother when widowed waiting at the station when I was
coming home to visit. So excited. Her little white car parked in the car
park I can still see from the train as we draw in and out. Her small figure
waiting there full of expectation. The ride home in her automatic. My
brothers and I used to call it 'the white-knuckle ride'. The car lurching
forward at speed, the automatic gearbox trying to catch up with her foot

on the accelerator. And then from the windows the wet fields and river where we used to walk the dog. Again, that painful knot of love between my ribs inside me, as the train I am in speeds on. These memories so vivid and yet so transitory. We are very fortunate to have my mother still with us, still so loved. But because of her dementia, how I miss now those conversations and the engagement that wanted to know all about my life, and how aware I am of old age where the body and mind you took for granted are breaking down. I remember helping her move to her new house with my brother. So many boxes of memories that there was no room for in the new house, even after the small garage had been stuffed full. But how do you throw away the memories of someone's life – the photo albums, the letters, cards, school exercise books, old address books and diaries, gifts and Christmas presents, and things collected on mantel pieces for the last 60 years? I remember an argument in which I told my mother that she had to be ruthless in throwing out things she no longer needed and my mother saying angrily, 'You don't know what it's like to have a home and what it feels like for someone else to be telling you to throw your memories away.' And me shouting back at her, 'I do know. I've lost those I love too!'

The secret of course is how we learn to live now. The great contemplatives tell us about this now. The only life you can live is the now. You can't hold on to the past, nor can you ever know the future. The now is all that we have. And yet that of course feels incredibly difficult, it is not the reality inside us. All of us are filled with memories. To be so detached, like my mother expressed so vehemently, would be to deny what it is to live and love a world that is a physical, palpable, material, living thing. Love brings us into that physical world. You can't love without getting your hands dirty or feeling the pain. You can't love without your mind being able to remember the things that touched you so deeply – they will remain inside you for ever.

Living the now is not negation or a careless abandonment. Living the now is not social isolation from the memories of your body. Living the now is the realization that the memories of the past have made you what you are now. Desire, hope, fear, longing, sorrow, grief are all part of your humanity – the love and the pain and the struggle are in your flesh and blood. Christ does not abandon that flesh and blood – he too lives it fully even unto death. But he also redeems memory by allowing us to recognize the love that is eternal, which reaches into our past and gives hope to our future, a love that is not an added thing but infuses all we are and will become. This is a movement from holding on to a memory as a material possession to living out of the Spirit of that grace received. Jesus says this to his disciples: 'I am with you always' (Matthew 28.20). This steadfast love, this eternal love, is that which lives on after the fleeting disappears. I will love you always – for better or worse. And somehow even when we feel the pain of the past, our love, the love of Christ, must be given the space to disentangle us and help us live and love now. Our prayer does not aim to switch off the past or turn out our future dreams; rather, it seeks to illuminate and transfigure and to heal with the Spirit of the love that is everlasting and will never, ever leave us.

Sometimes I think we are frightened of pain or grief, rather than acknowledging it or treating it compassionately. Allow for seasons of sadness. *You* are not sad, you are only experiencing sadness and you will pass through this changing season. This knot inside is the seed of love. Do not let it remain hard and dormant inside you. Release it, nurture it, and let it grow and dance. I hear Christ saying, 'This is the Spirit of love I have put inside you.' Yes, it is wounded by the world, yes it cries out and thirsts and longs to be embraced, but it is also this love that leads us all beyond the grave to the place where all our memories find not only healing but also a home.

Letter 38: The Heart of God

February 2022

Let Thy wish become my desire,
Let Thy will become my deed,
Let Thy word become my speech, Beloved,
And let Thy love become my creed.
Let my plant bring forth Thy flowers,
Let my fruits produce Thy seed,
Let my heart become Thy lute, Beloved,
And my body Thy flute of reed.
(Hazrat Inayat Khan[1])

I was given a wonderful invitation by a priest, Ayla, who works at the National Gallery, to come inside the gallery early one morning each week before the doors have opened to meditate and pray in front of one of the pictures. In a conversation I had told her how I had always longed not just to look at the pictures in the Sainsbury Wing but to kneel down and pray in front of these altarpieces and reredoses. 'Well, come in and we'll do it together,' she said. On the first early morning, Ayla asked me which painting I wanted to pray in front of. Without hesitation I said, '*The Baptism of Christ* by Piero della Francesca'.[2] If you have never seen it, this astonishing painting is only a hundred metres away from St Martin's church in the National Gallery. If you have seen it, go and see it again and be silenced by it.

It's as though in this picture Piero has captured a moment of eternity. The whole picture is leading us to the figure of Christ: tall, luminous, poised, upright and yet at the same time his body is peaceful, tender, soft, without rigidity. His posture is a lesson in how we too should pray with our whole bodies, not simply with words. His eyes are slightly downcast, centred, grounded, deep in a meditation into which we too are called. So on my prayer stool, I knelt there, the two of us together in front of this picture, hearing the distant clip of footsteps of those who work in the gallery coming and going in other rooms, but slowly being stilled, breathing in the Spirit of the dove of peace hovering over the figure of Christ, our self-consciousness dissolving as we are taken up in the picture. It is a moment in time captured for ever by the artist, and within I hear the words, 'This is my Son, the Beloved, with whom I am well pleased' (Matthew 3.17). We are drawn to the face of Christ – everything seems to lead us there. The bending figure behind him, stripping away his clothes in preparation for his own baptism, lead us, as do the three angel witnesses. He is framed by the tree on one side and John the Baptist on the other, pouring water on to the crown of his head, the water caught in mid-flow. The Baptist's raised arm is like an arch through which Christ enters and takes centre stage. In the words of John the Baptist, words I remember my father saying at my own ordination, 'He must increase, but I must decrease' (John 3.30). Christ's own hands, palms and tips of fingers joined, lead us up to his still face. This figure accentuates the vertical relationship from heaven to earth, from earth to heaven – nothing so human, nothing so divine. The Word made flesh. The whole of creation in this painting is part of this revelation. It radiates outwards from Christ and it radiates inwards towards his face. Christ, stripped and transparent before us, centred. He knows who he is. He is accepting his role, the weight, the implication, the sacred heart of all that is to come – total self-knowledge. Here is the man full of grace and truth.

And as I pray I search for the words that this picture is speaking to me and I hear in my heart the words of John the Baptist: 'Here is the lamb of God who takes away the sin of the world!' (John 1.29). And I am acutely aware that the turmoil inside my own heart is not dissimilar to the words Peter uses when Jesus calls him: 'Go away from me, Lord, for I am a sinful man' (Luke 5.8). So often as we pray our minds fill with the stuff that turns us away, that makes us feel unworthy, that tempts us to believe that we are not capable or good enough, or to believe that all of this is just a delusion and the reality of our world is filled up with struggle and deceit and pretence. This Christ is the peace we cannot ourselves enter, the miracle in which we cannot trust, the transparency and purity we cannot share. I wonder how many of us share Peter's sense of unworthiness – not good enough, not able, on the edge, outsiders not able to come in, too trapped in self-fear.

This perfect Christ reveals our own imperfections: his own incorruptible, perfect body in comparison to our mortal imperfect bodies. How could we ever be as perfect and as at peace as this? Yet on this day, as I kneel here, a simple revelation: 'Here is the Lamb of God who takes away the sin of the world. It is not you that must redeem yourself.' Christ speaks: 'Courage, it is I. It is I who come to you. It is I who am the Saviour – it is the water of my baptism which also flows through your baptism and you. It is I who call you.'

I become aware of how Jesus' hands are shaped. The palms are open as though holding space within them. It strikes me that the shape of that space is the shape of a heart. Christ is offering in his hands his heart to us, his heart to those who behold. The heart that Christ offers is a heart that seems great enough to contain all. It is all compassion, all forgiveness, all love – his heart has no limit, no cut-off point. This heart is a heart ready to risk all on us. It is not saying, 'Do these things and I will love you for it.' It is rather saying, 'Come into my heart and you too will become the heart of God.' Your fear of all you lack is the space into which God comes. Your failure is the very place of your healing and his gift of grace. Your emptiness is the offering that he longs to fill. This recognition is the beginning of trust – not trust in self, not self-righteousness, but trusting in the loving sacred heart of God.

Let us for a moment imagine that gift, held in our praying hands – the heart of Christ.

In this heart there is no division
All is contained
All is redeemed
This is the heart of unrestricted love
The heart that is porous
And contains all the sins and wounds of the world
And yet in that heart there is only forgiveness.
Christ's love – the lifeblood of the world
And as we receive the heart of Christ it is our refuge, our life,
    our becoming.
It transfuses us with the blood of his healing and forgiveness
We lift up our hearts
We open our hearts
We are humble of heart
We know generosity of heart
We receive our heart's desire
There is lightness of heart
And yet our hearts are filled and overflowing
Our hearts are broken open

Our hearts will feel the pain
Our hearts will become hearts of flesh
A sword will pierce our hearts
Becoming sacrificial hearts
We too will discover a heart for the world
A heart wide and deep enough to love one another as Christ has loved us.
This is the meaning of prayer.
Not words
Not a list of requests
But entering into the heart of God
without fear or reservation
Because that is where Christ has called us to be
At the very heart of God.

I am so aware of how different this is from the games of intrigue and deception we have been witnessing in our national life, the meaningless apologies, words used to manipulate and justify and escape consequence, apologies with no repentance. In our twenty-first century, armies are still lining up along borders with the weapons of war and destruction that can kill, maim and destroy, with missiles aimed at cities. Children are still going hungry and thirsty, emaciated by malnutrition caused by sanctions, and refugees are still being deported to countries they have risked their lives to escape. Our creation is groaning for salvation. Have we learnt nothing in the last 2,000 years? And in our own hearts, inconsistencies too, and the fears and failures we hide or run from: the preservation of self rather than the recognition of God. Here we come face to face with the one who stands before us and pours out his heart for our redemption.

Henri Nouwen, when facing his own experience of a broken heart, wrote this prayer:

It is so hard for me to believe fully in the love that flows from your heart. I am so insecure, so fearful, so doubtful and so distrustful ...

But your Father's love was so unlimited that he wanted us to know that love and to find in it the fulfilment of our deepest desires. So, he sent us you, with a human heart big enough to hold all human loneliness and all human anguish. Your heart is not a heart of stone, but a heart of flesh; your heart of flesh is not narrowed by human sin and unfaithfulness, but is as wide and deep as divine love itself. Your heart does not distinguish between rich and poor, friend and enemy, female and male, slave and free, sinner and saint. Your heart is open to receive anyone with total, unrestricted love. For anyone who wants to come to you, there is room.[3]

O Lord, all you ask of us is a simple 'yes', a simple act of trust.

I will remove from your body the *heart* of stone and give you a heart of flesh. (Ezekiel 36.26)

Blessed are the pure in *heart*, for they will see God. (Matthew 5.8)

For where your treasure is, there your *heart* will be also.
(Matthew 6.21)

Take *heart*, son; your sins are forgiven. (Matthew 9.2)

Take *heart*, daughter; your faith has made you well. (Matthew 9.22)

Take my yoke upon you and learn from me; for I am gentle and humble in *heart*, and you will find rest for your souls. (Matthew 11.29)

But immediately Jesus spoke to them and said, 'Take *heart*, it is I; do not be afraid.' (Matthew 14.27)

Forgive your brother or sister from your *heart*. (Matthew 18.35)

You shall love the Lord your God with all your *heart*, and with all your soul, and with all your mind. (Matthew 22.37)

He looked around at them with anger; he was grieved at their hardness of *heart* and said to the man, 'Stretch out your hand.' He stretched it out, and his hand was restored. (Mark 3.5)

Take *heart*; it is I; do not be afraid. (Mark 6.50)

But as for [the seed] in good soil, these are the ones who, when they hear the word, hold it fast in an honest and good *heart*, and bear fruit with patient endurance. (Luke 8.15)

Jesus told them a parable about their need to pray always and not to lose *heart*. (Luke 18.1)

No one has ever seen God. It is God the only Son, who is close to the Father's *heart*, who has made him known. (John 1.18)

Heart speaks to *heart*. (St Francis de Sales)

Out of the believer's *heart* shall flow rivers of living water. (John 7.38)

Letter 39: You Shall Not be Confounded

March 2022

It's impossible not to be disturbed by the news at the moment, with the events in Ukraine filling us with such sorrow and fear for the people there. Lent this year begins at a bleak time for Europe – the sign of ashes, the reminder of our mortality, so tragically made present for us in news of explosions, destruction and the sound of sirens warning of air raids in a way that has not been heard in Europe since the Second World War. 'Remember that you are dust and to dust you will return.'[1] We are filled by the horror of what is happening to so many innocent people. An image I hold in my mind is that from the news of an underground bomb shelter in Kyiv where little children have been taken for safety – each child, so very small and frightened, waiting in the darkness, stacked one above the other on the shelves of the wall. This invasion has filled our minds, hearts and prayers.

I write this letter to you from the Royal Foundation of St Katherine's in the East End of London, where I have come for the Companions of Nazareth retreat. On the altar in front of which I am praying I read these words inscribed into the stone:

Behold, I lay in Sion a chief corner stone, elect, precious: and he that believeth on him shall not be confounded. (1 Peter 2.6)

And I am very aware of how much we need this cornerstone at this very time and the promise of God that we will not be confounded.

'Behold'

It is the time to behold this chief cornerstone – to be and to hold on to this chosen one, Christ, the one who did not seize power but emptied himself to be with us in the world.

It is in the battlefield of our lives that we long for the liberator, but the promise of God is that the liberator, the precious chosen one, is already with us now.

It is here we discover Jesus, often among the rubble of our lives. Rejected by mortals, but chosen by God, precious and true. Precious. I wonder what the things are in your life that are most precious. We often do not discover how precious they are until we have lost them or fear losing them. Jesus Christ is precious. It took Calvary to discover how precious he was. They thought they could pull down the Temple. Little did they know he would build it again in three days. They thought they could do away with him, snuff him out. Little did they realize the power of his love. They thought he was dead. Little did they realize he would be with us until the end of time. It is now that all need to build on this cornerstone:

> Wherefore laying aside all malice, and all guile, and hypocrisies, and envies, and all evil speakings,
> As newborn babes, desire the sincere milk of the word, that ye may grow thereby:
> If so be ye have tasted that the Lord is gracious.
> To whom coming, as unto a living stone, disallowed indeed of men, but chosen of God, and precious,
> Ye also, as lively stones, are built up a spiritual house, an holy priesthood, to offer up spiritual sacrifices, acceptable to God by Jesus Christ.
> Wherefore also it is contained in the scripture, Behold, I lay in Sion a chief corner stone, elect, precious: and he that believeth on him shall not be confounded. (1 Peter 2.1–6, KJV)

It is not hard to see the escalation of malice, guilt, deceit, envy and slander at this time. We are not promised here an instant solution or miraculous remedies to the tragedy our world is facing. We are, however, offered something infinitely more precious: the promise that we will not be confounded. What does this word hold for us? It means, even in the midst of turmoil, you will not be overcome, you will not be shamed, or swept away in confusion, you will not be lost. You have a cornerstone, one that holds you fast even in the storms of your life, upon which, through God's grace, our lives can be built. This living stone, this living Christ, will hold you fast. He was the one who was rejected and condemned and put to death but was never confounded. And he will never ever reject you. This cornerstone is there, present and ready to become our chief foundation even in the very bombsites of our lives.

In the midst of the Hundred Years' War, during a time of plague that killed thousands, a woman named Julian of Norwich, living a life of prayer, had a vision of this love of Christ:

And this word: Thou shalt not be overcome, was said full clearly and full mightily, for assuredness and comfort against all tribulations that may come. He said not: Thou shalt not be tempested, thou shalt not be travailed, thou shalt not be afflicted; but He said: Thou shalt not be overcome. God willeth that we take heed to these words, and that we be ever strong in sure trust, in weal and woe. For He loveth and enjoyeth us, and so willeth He that we love and enjoy Him and mightily trust in Him; and all shall be well.[2]

The cornerstone is the very base, the first stone in place from which all other stones will take their reference and orientation. We find Christ at the very bottom of our lives. Look for him in the same places he was found in his lifetime, in the stable, among the rejected, at the bedside of the sick, searching for the lost, welcoming the sinner home, releasing the captive, on Calvary. It is often in the fallen, derelict places of our lives that he finds us. It is weeping outside an empty tomb that Mary meets the risen Christ. And the risen Christ raises. He raises her up. He calls this rising the Beatitudes:

'Blessed are the poor in spirit, for theirs is the kingdom of heaven.
'Blessed are those who mourn, for they will be comforted.
'Blessed are the meek, for they will inherit the earth.
'Blessed are those who hunger and thirst for righteousness, for they will be filled.
'Blessed are the merciful, for they will receive mercy.
'Blessed are the pure in heart, for they will see God.
'Blessed are the peacemakers, for they will be called children of God.
'Blessed are those who are persecuted for righteousness' sake, for theirs is the kingdom of heaven.' (Matthew 5.3–10)

You see, this is where the kingdom of heaven is born. It can never be created with bombs or tanks or missiles. It can never be seized or invaded or snuffed out. They think they have destroyed Christ's kingdom and that is the very place where resurrection begins.

This kingdom is being born down in bomb shelters under the city of Kyiv as people huddle together so courageously in the dark in love and hope for their nation. It's being born among the courage of reporters like Lyse Doucet and Clive Myrie and many others risking their own lives so that the truth of the story can be told. It's being born in hospital cellars where, amid the air raids, doctors work tirelessly to save lives. It's being witnessed in the generosity of neighbours, sharing what little they have, and in the welcome of other nations like Moldova, Poland, Slovakia and Germany as they reach out to those who arrive with nothing. It's witnessed by those businesses who are ready to put people and humanity before their own profit and gain. It's witnessed in the unity of those praying throughout the world for justice and peace. It is in this outpouring of love and compassion that we see the hope for the world and the healing of the nations. I wrote these words below after the conflict we went through in the Solomon Islands in which seven members of my community were murdered:

What can we learn?
We can learn that God is real
He spans the void
His cross from top to bottom
From side to side
From God to flesh,
From flesh to flesh
And so we dare to follow
Risking all
Our vulnerable lives
Following the vulnerable life giver
There is a precious goodness
A greater beauty
A hope beyond despair
A bold humility
A Courageous love
A cornerstone of hope
God with us.[3]

Behold, I lay in Sion a chief corner stone, elect, precious: and he that believeth on him shall not be confounded. (1 Peter 2.6, KJV)

Wonderings

I wonder where you have found Christ in your life.
I wonder what we can do when we feel confounded.
I wonder what the point of prayer is.
I wonder what you have learnt from the people of Ukraine.

Prayer

For the People of Ukraine

God of peace, your prophet Isaiah promised
swords would be turned into ploughshares,
and your son's mother Mary proclaimed
the mighty would be put down and the humble exalted:
visit the people of Ukraine;
deliver them from fear, violence,
attack, injury, destruction, death;
and give them courage, solidarity and allies
in their hour of vulnerability and sorrow.
Turn the hearts of those bent on war and invasion.
Strengthen the hand of all seeking to halt conflict,
restore order, and pursue justice.
And make this moment of peril
an occasion for your Holy Spirit to show your world
the cost of conflict and our dependence on one another.
In Christ our Lord, who went to his death because of our hatred,
and rose again because our hatred
is never stronger than your indomitable love. Amen.[4]

Letter 40: Prayer

April 2022

I once asked members of our Nazareth Community what prayer is and Jamie answered very simply and wisely, 'Prayer is loving.' He was right of course. Our practice of prayer is the practice of loving and that love will take on all moods, contexts and the events of self, neighbourhood, nation and world. Our prayer is both intimate and cosmic. It is both within the individual heart and within the heart of God that contains all creation.

When we talk about prayer many people seek a system or practice that can unlock the mystery of our relationship with God and take us to the place we want to reach. Perhaps there have been times when we have tasted a sweetness so beautiful it felt our hearts would overflow, and each time we pray we have wanted to reach and taste that same place again. However, the more I pray the more I realize that prayer is like love: it contains all moods and all seasons.

When we pray, we are turning towards the beloved, face to face. Our attitude or orientation in prayer is most receptive when it is one of complete openness and acceptance, a readiness to let ourselves become mirrors of Christ. In this practice of prayer there is nothing formulaic, no rules carved in stone. Yet there is a trellis of the Spirit that helps the life of God to grow within and helps guide and nurture all that seeks the light and waits to bloom where it is planted.

The trellis of the Spirit of Prayer

Stay faithful

As when we love a person, so when we love God. Love needs time, presence and perseverance. There are heady moments of infatuation but there is also most importantly a constancy: a returning again and again to the beloved and a making space to be with. That faithfulness will involve moments of beauty and transformation but will also involve a faithfulness in the ordinary – the washing-up, the laundry, the mistakes and humiliations, those moments of our lives we would rather hide away.

The more we pray the easier it becomes. Prayer is as essential as breathing. We may think that breathing is boring but stick your head under the water and you will quickly realize that this faithfulness to the breath is life itself. Our prayer is not an optional extra. It is life itself.

Slow down and give time to prayer

If we don't give time our love can easily become crowded out or choked. It needs a place and a space in our lives. We often think we have no time. When we are busy contemplative prayer is often the first thing we sacrifice in a way we would not miss an arranged meeting or a planned event. We may think, 'It's only silent prayer. What does it matter if I miss?' But would you miss picking up your son or daughter or grandchild from school? Would you miss the date with a person you love? To pray, we need to give a generous space to God, a priority booking, a time when we leave the hundred different alternatives at the door and come, just as we are, pause … and enter into wakefulness.

Be attentive

Our minds are like waterfalls of thoughts that never cease. Recognize the diversions and compulsions gently. Our practice recognizes the weather within us, be it restlessness or anxiety or fear or longing or anger or uncertainty. Whatever the weather, we try to hold our course – open and receptive to the light beyond those clouds. The way to the light is often through the cloud. As St Francis is quoted as saying, 'It is no use walking anywhere to preach if this walking were not our preaching.' This is a call to be awake to this present moment. It is a way of living intimately. When buffeted by those thoughts that overcome you, become like the tree that bends but does not blow over. But also aim for a lightness of being, that sense that you have put down the suitcases you have travelled with and now are simply open and receptive to live here. I saw I woman the other day, carrying bags and trying to answer a text message one-handed in the middle of the road. I politely reminded her to be careful as there were cars coming.

Be generous and kind in your practice

This is not a competition or a process of acquisition, it is a very generous offering of self – a willingness to give oneself away, and then discovering in that offering that we have welcomed the most wonderful guest. This is an emptying that allows oneself to be filled. When we pray, we open up all that we long to offer and share and all we long to receive. When you pray, remember the Beatitudes: 'Blessed are the poor in spirit, for theirs is the kingdom of heaven' (Matthew 5.3).

Allow compassion to expand within you

As you pray more deeply you will often feel the wounds and pain of the world more acutely. Do not fear this. You are learning to live the Beatitudes. Our hearts are tenderized by prayer. The more we love, the more we feel the pain and humiliations of the beloved. We are not the solution to need. We are not the ones who can save single-handedly. But we are those who share the journey and help carry the load. Like Simon of Cyrene, we may carry the cross with no solutions to avert Calvary. Sometimes the only thing we can do is just be there. You may fear the suffering of others because you can do nothing to stop it, thus it judges you and finds you lacking. But when you recognize in your prayer that you are among the poor in heart, among the grieving, among the peacemakers, you are no longer the judge but one who is alongside and with. Perhaps you are carrying the pain of Christ's death in your own body just as you will also be the bearer of his risen life.

Allow the Beloved space to grow

How quickly we can become controlling and possessive, and the way becomes *my* way. Remember our prayer always reaches beyond what I want for myself. It leads into the mystery of difference and wonder. Prayer is not narcissistic, it lets go of self to discover self. It lets go of certainty and self-interest to discover the beauty and uniqueness of the other. Prayer is a pilgrimage of the soul, bringing transformation in the way we experience and relate to the world.

St Francis is said to have spent his whole nights in prayer, and he prayed:

Who are you, O God?
And who am I?

Evelyn Underhill claims this is the most perfect prayer. It allows infinite space for growth and discovery. In this question we are not proposing answers, we are open to revelation.

Wait patiently in your prayer and wait with open hands

Think of the father of the Prodigal. He does not know if his son will return but he is watching and waiting. It is the memory of that steadfast love which will, in a foreign land, bring his son to his senses. There are times in our prayer when we simply do not know the answers. There are times when we will walk through the valley of the shadow of death. At such times our prayer is simply to keep the love of God alive in us. When God can't help us, perhaps, as Etty Hillesum said, we need to help God. Etty writes to God in her journal:

> We must help You to help ourselves. That is all we can manage these days and also all that really matters: that we safeguard that little piece of You, God, in ourselves ... There must be someone to live through it all and bear witness to the fact that God lived, even in these times.[1]

In helping God, God does help us. Our posture in prayer is one of readiness and openness to become God's sanctuary.

Forgive and be forgiven

Forgiveness is at the very heart of our prayer. Resentments confine us, the judgements of others and most of all of self, imprison our becoming. Sometimes it is pride that makes us think our own sins display such personal failure or weakness that we cannot be forgiven. God's forgiveness begins in the dust. It is from the dust that he breathes new life. It is in the dust that Jesus writes in front of all those who condemn: 'Let anyone among you who is without sin be the first to throw a stone ...' And then, rising from the dust again, those words that set free: 'Neither do I condemn you. Go your way, and from now on do not sin again' (John 8.3–11). In our prayer we recognize our deep need of redemption, and in our own woundedness the woundedness of the world. Sin is not a stain that needs to be scrubbed out, it is a wound that needs to be healed. The place of encounter with my God is the place of my wound and where I have wounded others. It is here in the love revealed on the cross that my resurrection begins. It is here that we begin to discover why it is the broken who show us Christ. For Christ's grace is enough for us and his power is made perfect in our weakness (2 Corinthians 12.9). Or in the famous words of the poet Alexander Pope, 'To err is human, to forgive divine.'

Remember the story of the two soldiers who had been Far Eastern prisoners of war. Fifty years after the end of the war one said to the other, 'I don't know how you can ever forgive the Japanese after all they did to us. I never can.' 'Ah,' said the other, 'because I have been set free. It sounds as if you are still in prison.'

Let your life itself become your prayer

Remember always that prayer is not just the words you say – it is the prayer of the 'Word made flesh'. It is your seeing, your hearing, your touch, your taste, the fragrance of your world, your movement, your breathing out and your breathing in. It is your relationship to all that is around you and each person you will encounter. Each encounter is your prayer with God who is incarnate here and now. Remember that you pray not only with your head but with every sense of your body and in the beat of your heart and through the pores of your skin.

Your prayer is your love for God and the way you love your neighbour as yourself

Take your prayer from the church or off the prayer stool into the street, the shop, the workplace, the underground, the email, the impossible meeting, the problem that has no resolution. Find God not just in the sunset but on the battlefield, among the dying and at the hospital bedside. Live your prayer. Let your prayer not just be reserved for the sacred place but be at the very moment when you feel that even God has abandoned you. And let your prayer be for all, not just the like-minded and those who are easy to love, but for those whom you may find difficult, and for those who need God's healing and peace.

Wonderings

I wonder how you pray best.
I wonder where you pray best.
I wonder why you pray.
I wonder how contemplative prayer has changed you.
I wonder if God answers your prayer, and how.

Letter 41: Abiding in Love

21 *April 2022*

On 21 April I was privileged to be asked to share a reflection during the Solemnization of the Civil Partnership of Felix and Francesco. Francesco is a member of our Nazareth Community and Felix was confirmed by the Bishop of London at St Martin's in 2018. They have both given me permission to include my words to them here that I shared with all those who gathered on that wonderful day of celebration. I hope they can be a faith story for us all.

Felix and Francesco

You have chosen the most beautiful passage of John's Gospel for today: 'As the Father has loved me, so I have loved you; abide in my love' (John 15.9).

That word 'abide' is a deep and beautiful word. It is not just an action of the moment. It is a calling that will last for ever. Abide means to make a home with, to dwell with, to stay with, to be with in faithfulness, companionship, presence, solidarity, steadfastness. It is to pitch one tent together, for ever, and that tent is God's dwelling. It is an awesome call.

Abiding with God

One of the most exciting things about your love for each other, Francesco and Felix, is that it has also been the story of a journey into faith. From those first heady days of constant romantic text messages and discovery, which began in 2017 on Boxing Day, and those nervous meetings-up, it was difficult to keep God out of the relationship, although Francesco did at first tell Felix he was a charity worker, frightened that being a prospective ordinand might put off any sensible, possible partner. Similarly, Felix did not disclose until a later date that he was the proud father of two large rabbits. They remember meeting in the rain in Camden – bread and butter and onion soup in Côte – how the conversation flowed, how they saw kindred gentle spirits in each other, how they wanted to see each other again and again and hoped the other did too. It was not until date three that Francesco came out about the church. Felix was still unsure of Christianity. He had been hurt by religion and its harsh judgements and was understandably tentative about a faith he feared might condemn him again. Yet beneath those fears they discovered in each other something so much deeper, the call of the Word made flesh: 'Just as I have loved you, you also should love one another', says Jesus (John 13.34). What they began to discover was not fire and brimstone and ugly repression but a love that could set them both free. 'As the father has loved me, so I have loved you; abide in my love' (John 15.9). 'In Francesco I saw a man who was deeply seeking the love of God and that search was creative, alive, kind, gentle, infectious.'

Felix describes their first holiday together:

Our first holiday together, during my journey to rediscover God, was to a remote part of Devon, where there was a very small, very unused hilltop church called St Peter's that Francesco and I visited every day for morning prayer. We also visited that church one evening to sit in the churchyard among the graves and look up contemplating the stars. Francesco and I argued – in the way we did then, and still do – about creation and existence; me, at that time, about the meaninglessness of it all, Francesco about the meaning which God offers us. It was the first of many times since when I have secretly conceded to myself, in my mind, that in fact Francesco might just be right, and I wrong – although then, as now, I probably never admitted it to him. I think he already knows that was a very special moment for which I'll never be able to thank him enough. It was even perhaps the first moment when I imagined that I could try to make it as a vicar's wife, if it was God's calling for me. I tried to imagine what it would be like living with a person who disappeared at odd times of the day and night to visit sick old ladies while he tried to get his head around being hitched up to a Tory Councillor campaigning for Teresa May with rabbits in his bedroom.

But the Christian faith had taken deep root in Felix. Francesco and he shared a love for all the same favourite characters in novels, like Dorothea in George Elliot's *Middlemarch* and Jane in Charlotte Brontë's *Jane Eyre*. Felix said that he began to notice how every character he loved best in fiction shared true Christian virtues – compassion, integrity, kindness. It was hypocrisy he found so hard to tolerate. It was the empathy and kindness towards others that he saw in Francesco that drew Felix into the Christian church, and when Francesco was pastoral assistant at St Martin's, Felix began to come along to our informal midweek communion, Bread for the World. Felix speaks of falling in love with the service and the way it included him and Francesco and left him feeling as if his inner spirit had been filled. In this learning to trust and abide in God and one another there is a deep sense of healing, healing from the wounds religion has for so long inflicted in the name of God upon God's LGBTQ+ children, all of us also made in the image of God. Felix, encouraged by Francesco, but never forced, began confirmation classes at St Martin's. I remember his gentle perceptiveness and exacting questions. 'My fear', admitted Francesco, 'is not that he will never find holiness but that he was far more righteous than me already.' In May 2018 Felix was confirmed at St Martin's, much to the joy of Francesco and all of us.

In June 2019, on his thirtieth birthday, Felix proposed to Francesco on the steps of St Martin's and the answer as we celebrate today was 'YES!' In the same year they visited the Holy Land. Felix described this as synchronizing their spiritual lives together. He wrote to me, 'We encountered God anew giving us both sincere and intimate feelings that drew us closer together than any holiday before had.'

They were abiding in each other's love, and more and more discovering together that this meant abiding ever more deeply in God's love.

Abiding in faithful love

This abiding love of which Christ speaks is not something passive but active. It has the quality of a free and most amazing gift. What do we give when we love? We give of ourselves, we give the most precious thing we have, we give of our life, we give what is most alive in us, our joy, our interest, our understanding, our humour, our senses, our hopes and fears, our struggles and sadness, our dreams, our talents, our laughter. Christ's love is the essence of who you are and who you will become.

This abiding love is named in Hebrew, *hesed* – faithful love, unconditional love, steadfast love, love which, as Shakespeare wrote, does not alter 'when it alteration finds'.[1] It is described in the New Testament as *agape* – sacrificial love, which sounds painful, and actually it is because it is not just a theory but something that offers the whole of you, and comes from the head, the heart, the body and the very guts of your personhood. Love risks all. Real love will mean that you will also bear each other's struggles and pain and losses. It is not something static or that is signed and sealed and delivered today; it is something that will need the rest of your lives.

Abiding in the body

The abiding of which Jesus Christ speaks also involves the body. The church has always been a bit wary of bodies, fearing the anarchy of immorality. One of the most beautiful signs of change I have seen in our society is the fact that young men and women are no longer ashamed or fearful of their genuine love and sexual orientation. It is so good to be here, where we are today, to celebrate the joy of your love. Today we stand on the shoulders of those who fought for this liberation, but as we know, the struggle is far from over, especially in the church, and today we hold in our prayers all who still suffer violence and discrimination and live in fear because of their sexuality. Abiding in the body means realizing that we communicate and realize our full personhood and humanity, not just with words but with our whole bodies, our eyes, our touch, our taste, our senses. We communicate through the senses of our skin and from the depths of our humanity. Abiding means learning to listen deeply not just with our ears but with the ears of our hearts. It means learning to honour and trust in faithful love, and the beauty and tenderness of intimacy. Today we celebrate the fact that God's love is made flesh and abides in your bodies – your full humanity – a unity and beauty of body, mind and spirit. Your bodies are of course the temple of God's Spirit breathed into and filled with the life of God, who longs for you to have life in all its fullness.

Abiding in the mind

I remember the first time Francesco preached at St Martin's. I told him to prepare for his first sermon carefully, and remember my alarm when I looked over his shoulder and saw just three brief notes on an otherwise blank piece of paper. This seemed to be taking Italian spontaneity to an extreme. I need not have worried because with Francesco the ideas just flowed out of him. I saw his love of the classics, philosophy, theology, the interplay of ideas and his gift of Augustinian oratory. I believe, however, in Felix he has met his match. They love sparring – discussing and arguing, trying to put the world to rights. While Felix's political conversion is perhaps still some way off (though I have been working at it at St Martin's!), I have to say, alongside my wonderful grandmother, he is one of the kindest Tories I have ever met. I think these two, though very different, will continue to challenge each other in an exciting dialogue about issues that really matter. Both will need the humility to listen and to admit that they can at times get things wrong, and be ready to grow and learn from each other with forgiving hearts.

Abiding in struggle

Of course, no relationship is ever plain sailing. We often learn most about the things we value when we mess up or face struggle. 'Look towards the wounded place, it is there the light enters you', says the poet Rumi. You already know the pain and struggle of life and the suffering and divisions caused by abandonment and betrayal. Forgiveness is at the very heart of our gospel, our good news. This will need you to forgive not seven times but seventy times seven and always do unto others what you would have them do unto you. Hold fast to that which is good. Learn from your mistakes and weaknesses. Remember you learn most about love in times of struggle. It was from the dust we were given life. It is also from the dust that we receive new life. This is what Meister Eckhart called 'the upward gravity of love'.[2] 'Do not let the sun go down on your anger' (Ephesians 4.26).

Abiding in peace

Peace is Christ's resurrection gift. Forgive me for preaching at you. You know this stuff better than me. I share this message with you because I care and have seen all that is possible in this relationship and how deeply blessed you are to have found each other. The fact that you have already got through a lockdown together and still wanted to live in partnership bodes very well for the future. After such a lockdown many would be frantic to escape! Today we celebrate your love. It is a tender and gentle love, full of humour, deep affection, care for each other and care for the world. It has already allowed you both to flourish and your rabbits to flourish. Love one another as Christ has loved you and love others as you have loved one another, with the same truthfulness, fun, generosity and grace.

I want to end with a prayer that encapsulates all I have wanted to share:

Felix and Francesco,
Go forth into the world together in peace;
be of good courage;
hold fast that which is good;
render to no one evil for evil;
strengthen the fainthearted;
support the weak;
help the afflicted;
honour all people;
love and serve the Lord,
rejoicing and filled with the power of the Holy Spirit.

PART FOUR

Nazareth the Place of Pilgrimage

Letters from the Holy Land

Letter 42: Letter from Jerusalem – *Inshallah*

29 April 2022

Many of us will have heard the Arabic expression *inshallah*.

It means 'if it is God's will', or in short 'God willing'.

It expresses the belief that nothing happens unless God wills it, that everything is in God's hands. This phrase is used by Muslims but also by Arab Christians and Arab speakers of other religions.

'Thy will be done', we say in the prayer that Jesus taught us. The will of God. Each of us stands on the edge of the unknown seeking the will of God. Our prayer is our means of discovering the will of God and being transformed by it.

I had wanted to stay in the Old City of Jerusalem when I planned my trip to the Holy Land, where I have just been for 12 days. But we never know in advance how God will be at work in the events of our lives. *Inshallah*. To get to the hotel I had booked I needed to trust in God. The Israeli taxi driver had told me he could not enter the Old City. He would drop me at the Damascus Gate and I could walk through. 'Which way do I go?' I ask. 'I don't know,' he replies. 'I have lived in Jerusalem all my life but never been through the Damascus gate. I am a Jew and this is the Muslim Quarter. It is a divided city.'

There I was, like an innocent abroad, pulling a large suitcase and trying to limp my way through the Damascus Gate in a sea of people as dense as a football crowd on cup-final day, but all these people were trying to get to prayer. There are, they say, 250,000 Muslims who are here for the last week of Ramadan, many pilgrims from around the world, and most of them at the time I arrive at the Damascus Gate are trying to get to the mosque to answer the call to midday prayer.

In the sea of people a man in a high visibility jacket grabs my suitcase. 'Where are you going?' he asks. 'The Hashimi Hotel,' I answer. 'Yes, the Hashimi.' And he is off in front of me with my suitcase and all I have brought with me to the Holy Land. I try to keep up with him but it is very difficult to move. *Inshallah*. I am having to trust God. I can do nothing else. The man with a florescent jacket is my saviour and within minutes he has threaded his way through the crowds and down alleyways to the Hashimi Hotel. I am delighted and, still unfamiliar with the currency, I give him a note which is far too much and he is delighted too, which makes me glad.

When I booked the hotel I had asked for a room with a view. Sister Kerry, dressed totally in black with a black hijab covering her head and neck, welcomes me in a very kindly way. I am given a key to my room on the second floor. I go up and find a small cell of a room, just about big enough for a bed and nothing more and no windows at all. I go back downstairs to ask if I can change it for a different room at least with a window.

'I am so sorry,' says Sister Kerry, 'that is our only room left. At this time we are full of pilgrims for the end of Ramadan and Eid. All our larger rooms have whole families or groups sharing. Forgive me for offering advice but just follow God's will and accept. When I first came here I was given a room with no view too, but it ended up being the right place God had provided. It has privacy and if you want to see the city go up to the fourth floor, where you will meet other pilgrims and you will see the whole city from the rooftop.' I decide to accept the room graciously and feel better for doing so – *inshallah*.

I set off into the old city, scared I will get lost, but I'm hungry. The Muslim quarter is alive with its market and alleyways filled with people. Night has fallen and people are out to order food after the fast. There is excitement in the air. Ramadan is a real community time. There are hot flatbreads on the grills, with sizzling lamb and chicken shawarmas and chickens being roasted on spits. But the queues are long and I wander into the Coptic area and then find my way down into the outer court-yard of the Holy Sepulchre. The Christian quarter is much quieter. I'm hungry and find a place that is serving hot falafel, salad and flatbreads. Noah, who runs the place, says they are the best falafels in Jerusalem and freshly cooked. I watch him scoop out the chickpeas and lower them into the boiling oil. We sit down. He brings me a plate full of salad and five falafels and a huge heap of delicious houmous which he also says it is the best and I assure him that I think it is too. As I eat he opens up and tells me he's only been running the place for a week. They closed down because of Covid. I ask him if he is keeping the fast. He looks embarrassed and tells me he has managed to give up smoking cannabis, that he's had a drugs problem and his head has felt all clouded up. He's grown forgetful and has been unable to keep the full Ramadan fast, like his brothers. His brothers are away breaking the fast now. Then he asks me direct personal questions about what it's like to be single and how he couldn't live without a woman and needs a wife, because he's not married but his religion says premarital sex is wrong. I tell him there can be a freedom and openness in being single: 'Try and see it as a blessing.' He does not seem very convinced.

I tell him about my work in London and we discuss drug addiction. I like him, he's honest and open about the troubles he's faced and really seeking to make good. He's also proud of his cooking and his salads and I compliment him on the food he cooks, which is delicious. Before I leave he makes me a cup of Arabic coffee, which he gives me for free. I say I will visit again but when I go back the following day I cannot find which alleyway the cafe is in.

Back at the Hashimi Hotel I go up to the fourth floor, which has a roof-top view of the whole city, and I write my diary. The Dome of the Rock is lit up and golden. As I gaze over the city I meet Ali from Walthamstow who is leading a tour party of Muslims around the holy sites. He tells me about the religious tours he leads and how he comes to Jerusalem about six times a year. 'It's such a peaceful place,' he says. It doesn't feel so peaceful at the moment with Ramadan. He is warm and friendly and talkative and I feel totally at home. Some of his Muslim friends come and join us and we sit talking late into the night. The owner of the hotel's two sons come and chat away too. Here I am on my first night, already with a group of Muslim friends who have made me so welcome to this holy city. It's good to be here at this time of pilgrimage.

I'm beginning to love my room. It feels peaceful and I am able to sleep quite deeply. I am learning to discern the will of God. *Inshallah*. Two days before leaving for the Holy Land I twisted my knee. I could hardly walk and needed a walking stick. But strangely too even the painful knee has a lesson – 'Slow down,' it says. 'You are trying to do too much. Just spend time in a single place. Just spend time with God.' I do just that. I am learning from my Muslim brothers. Five times a day they pray, tidal waves of people coming through the Damascus Gate for the midday prayer. But my place of prayer is this Holy Sepulchre where I slowly climb up to what they believe is the rock of Calvary, and there I spend time each day in silent prayer. My knee has turned into a blessing, reminding me to be still and know God. I realize I am not seeking to do everything but seeking the space between. Not further onwards but deeper. Each moment is precious. Do not fill it. Open it.

In the morning I make my way along the covered market passageways to the Holy Sepulchre. It's straight through the Muslim quarter and then a right turn. As soon as you turn right you leave the Arab quarter behind and enter into the Christian area, where there are a lot of shopkeepers trying to sell you religious artefacts. Jerome Murphy-O'Connor writes:

> One expects the central shrine of Christendom to stand out in majestic isolation but anonymous buildings cling to it like barnacles. One looks for numinous light but it is dark and cramped. One hopes for peace but the ear is assailed by a cacophony of warring chants. One desires holiness only to encounter a jealous possessiveness: the six groups of occupants – Latin Catholics, Greek Orthodox, Armenian Orthodox, Syrians, Copts, Ethiopians – watch each other suspiciously for any infringements of rights. The frailty of humanity is nowhere more apparent than here; it epitomizes the human condition. The empty who come to be filled will leave desolate; those who permit the church to question them may begin to understand why hundreds of thousands thought it worthwhile to risk death or slavery in order to pray here.[1]

This place is real, lived in, sweated over, touched, kissed, prayed in, argued and fought for. It makes me realize why we need Christ now just as much as they did then. Not Christ who is an escape from the world but Jesus who loved the world so much that he died for us.

I enter the Church of the Holy Sepulchre and straight away see the slab where they lay Jesus' body. People are venerating it, kissing it, placing their cheeks against the stone. Prayer is palpable. I remember the last time I was here and prayed touching that slab too. It was before I returned to Melanesia, the conflict and the death of the seven brothers who were members of my community. Somehow praying in this place in 2001, I had had some kind of premonition that a time of suffering was coming. Praying there had reminded me that Christ himself had been through suffering and somehow all the way through those dark days the image of that slab stayed with me. St Martin-in-the-Fields' altar is very like this slab of stone, with its contours and the cracks of time like wounds. The altar at St Martin's during our passion play has become the place where we too lay the body of Jesus. It's a powerful symbol of the real meaning of an altar – Christ visibly giving his body for us. I kneel and pray again, feeling the suffering of Christ is with me and with our world, like the wounded body that was once laid on this very stone. Religion is very palpable in this place: you touch it and smell it in the incense. The mystery of God is all round you, people bending over in prayer, placing their crucifixes upon the place where Jesus' body lay to bring them closer or bring new blessings and protection. I kneel too and kiss the stone, my lips touching the cold slab.

At the top of these steep stairs many tourists are taking photos, taking it in turns to kneel in front of the altar and reach down and touch the rock of Calvary. In the corner, an Ethiopian monk is praying, wrapped in a simple white piece of cotton cloth. I open my prayer stool and kneel down beside him, feeling the cold hard stone under my knees and realizing my knee is not as painful as before. I sense the monk next to me is a very holy presence in this place. Waves of pilgrims and visitors come here. I love watching the way they respond. Some just take photos, others take selfies of themselves in front of the altar and others just follow the guides, who often seem to fail to communicate quite the enormity of where they have brought their tour groups. 'This is where Jesus died between two thieves,' and then off they go to visit some other site – as though that death is just one line in a story and not the story of the one who dies for the sins of the whole world, including our own. Many want to pose in front of the silver cross for more photos. Through all the hanging lamps I can see Christ's legs and feet unobstructed. Mary on his left. John on his right. Then there are the pilgrims who are deeply devout. They come and kneel at the foot of the cross and reach down to touch the stone of Calvary, visibly moved, their lips whispering prayers. I am stopped by this place. I would love to spend my whole holiday coming here to pray. I already have a plan to come back this evening and tomorrow early. My knees are on the cold marble floor, now hurting. The security person comes by wearing a black cap and speaks to me but I can't understand. I hope he is not ordering me to move. I keep quiet, silent and still. I pray the Jesus Prayer over and over again. I notice it is mostly the older people who show the greatest devotion, kneeling and praying as if their lives depended on it. They do. But I love it when I see young people showing devotion, kneeling to touch or kiss the rock of Calvary. Palpable faith, knowing Christ within you, not a museum of faith but sacrament – real presence.

I am praying next to the Ethiopian monk. He has become my example of staying with God. He is holding in his hands a small, very old Bible, and every so often he stands up, opens it and quietly chants to himself. I follow his example – staying and praying. After several hours of prayer I move forward to the altar and kneel down and touch the rock of Calvary – God's will be done, the will that gives all, in love for the world. Suddenly I am prompted within to ask the Ethiopian monk for a blessing. I think he'll just think I am another crazy tourist. But I ask him. At first I think he has not understood. But then he places his hand gently on my head and moves his hand so that it feels like wind ruffling the hair on the crown of my head. Then he takes his small Bible and taps me on the head with it – gently, but over and over again, rhythmically. He is gently and compassionately admonishing me and reminding me to live the word of God, in my head, to follow it, to allow that Word to be incarnated in my life. The will of God; my will. And now the Ethiopian monk blows on me, three big, long breaths he blows into my face. I am filled by that blessing, and when I leave the Holy Sepulchre I am carrying that Spirit and blessing within me. His whispered prayer continues within me even now – Lord Jesus Christ, Son of God, by your holy cross, you have redeemed me and redeemed the world.

I am learning how to follow God's will. The Muslim pilgrims are so very kind to me, full of excitement about their pilgrimage to this holy city. They sit with me in the evening on the rooftop and we chat for hours. Hasan tells me about what the Dome of the Rock and what the Al-Aqsa Mosque mean to them, and I tell them about the Church of the Holy Sepulchre. Hasan is from Manchester. He is totally in love with his faith and this his first pilgrimage to Jerusalem. He tells me about the excitement of a week of prayer in the Al-Aqsa Mosque, the sharing, the generosity, the special chants of the imam for the final week of Ramadan. He tells me that he has even been going to the extra prayers in the middle of the night from 1.00 a.m. to 3.00 a.m. He's even slept in the mosque and shows me the pictures. He is a man opened up with compassion. He tells me that Muslims are called to live in peace; he says that you will find conflict and violence if you go looking for it. But he is disturbed by what happened today. He said he saw an Israeli policeman hitting an old man with his baton outside the mosque and when he tried to defend the old man from being hit, he too got hit in the ribs. He tells me about when he arrived a week ago at the airport and was kept waiting in immigration for six hours before they let him go through. He said you just have to stay patient because they are waiting for you to show signs of aggression. His friend tells me of a trip they have made to Hebron – the concrete, the barbed wire, the kids trapped in this bleak compound. He tells me about a Palestinian kid playing there with some kittens. 'They were all he had.' Yet he is amazed at the warmth and friendliness of these kids. 'They have nothing but they made us so welcome.' He tells me a story of Muhammad and the woman who gave him three dates, which was the most precious gift of all because it was all she had. Here with Hasan and his friends I see a passion for prayer and a deep generosity and humanity – it's as if they are overflowing with love for God. He tells me it is good to speak to me because, as important as prayer, is the sharing with others of one's love for God. I ask Hasan if he wants to be an imam. 'No,' he says, 'too much responsibility ... I am just open to the will of God. I try to say, "yes" to whatever the Spirit Of God wills – *inshallah*.'

It is holy ground, this city where pilgrim journeys meet. Later Hasan and his fellow pilgrims share with me bread and houmous to break the day's fasting, and birthday cake. They tell me that Sister Kerry, the receptionist, is a kind and very holy woman: 'We always take her advice, she is a wise guide.' Three days later when I leave the hotel I thank Sister Kerry for her kindness. I have presumed by her dress and the care she shows to all the Muslim guests that she too is a Muslim. I have seen her working through the night, as the guests must eat before daybreak. 'No,' she says, 'I am a Christian.' Here in this hidden humble way she is living out her Christian vocation. God's will takes the humblest part. She is living Jesus in such a way as Charles de Foucauld wrote: 'If such is the servant what must the master be like?'² Or in the words of Jesus himself: 'By this everyone will know that you are my disciples, if you have love for one another' (John 13.35).

On Saturday morning I record a conversation with Hasan on the rooftop for our livestreamed Nazareth Contemplative Prayer. He says he does not find it hard to believe in God. Although there have been times in his life when he has perhaps left God, God cannot leave us. He says that he finds it hard to understand not how people believe but how anyone cannot believe in God. He says he thinks that it is an amazing thing that two people like him and me, who would walk past each other in England, can spend three hours talking to each other in Jerusalem. He tells me he has told all his group about his long conversations with me, a Christian priest, and how happy they are that we have shared our faith together. It's his first time in Jerusalem: 'What's not to love?' This is the place where all our faiths meet. People of faith and the prophets have been walking here before us ... these same streets these holy people have walked we are walking now. What's not to love?

Hasan tells me of the mystical visionary experience of how the prophet Muhammad was conveyed miraculously from Kabah to Jerusalem's Temple Mount. In this visionary journey, Muhammad spoke to Moses, Aaron, Enoch, Jesus and John the Baptist. Respect for other faiths is part of our faith. The Caliph Umar refused to pray in the Holy Sepulchre in 638 when he was shown around the city by the Greek Orthodox Patriarch. If he had done so the Muslims would have wanted to build a mosque there. Instead the mosque was built close by. Here is Jerusalem – the three Abrahamic faiths have always existed side by side. 'There is no blessing in conflict or fighting. When I go back to Manchester I will be leaving my heart in Jerusalem. The month of Ramadan is the month of being a blessed guest. And when I leave this place I will take a shot of humbleness and gratitude back.' He tells me that in the UK everything is a click away on his smartphone or tablet but here he has seen a deep goodness, hospitality and gratitude among people who have far less in material terms. 'Hopefully, I will take the spontaneous back with me, and gratitude for life – life as a gift, Richard.' I ask him to say a prayer. He says a prayer, giving thanks that Allah has given us this blessing of bringing us together to this Holy City. 'Send your blessings down upon us. Send down your protection upon this city. Whatever your plans for us, Allah, you are the best planner, we accept it gratefully.'

I offer to take Hasan with me to the Holy Sepulchre because he has never been. To my surprise he eagerly accepts. He comes and asks many questions and seems awed that we too are in the very place where Jesus walked. He keeps telling me how much Muslims respect Jesus. Then he buys me a prayer rope from where a Franciscan monk is selling them, as a gift. 'Like we also used to pray,' he says.

Inshallah – God's will, breaking down barriers, expanding our souls.

I realize faith is not a private thing
About ownership or territory
Not a means of control or a hierarchy of authority
It is something much deeper and wider
It seeks eternity
It seeks an open heart
It includes generously
It seeks a light that belongs to everyone
It gathers us – children of all colour, race, age, and faiths
And it says:
'You are all my family
What I desire is to remove the heart of stone
And all that hates and spreads prejudice and bitterness
I will discover again in you,
The heart of flesh I have put in you
I will welcome you – from the very least to the very most
All you need is that heart of infinite compassion
And eyes to recognize and see the meaning of God's love.
Your religions which defend themselves so often shut me out.
I am the one who longs for you to live without defences
With simplicity, joy, gentleness, mercy and peace.
I am the one who longs for you to hold in your heart all humanity.'

In the evening I come back to visit the tomb. As we queue up to enter, a man in front of me reaches up to the hanging lamp and dips a piece of paper into the oil and then he rubs the oil on his head and hair and rubs it on to the woman's head next to him. He reaches up again to get more but this time an Orthodox priest in black sees him and shouts angrily at him to stop what he is doing. I have seen Orthodox priests doing the same action, using the oil from the lamps to anoint the pilgrims. This man's fault is he has done it without permission. The Orthodox priest is furious and orders both the man and the woman to leave the place immediately – he literally drives them out. 'Out! Out!' I realize how much I fear religions of judgement and humiliation, always imagining myself among the outcasts and sinners, longing for redemption and inclusion. I stand meekly in the queue, looking down, not daring to say anything. I wonder what it feels like to be driven out in that manner from the empty tomb, the place of resurrection. When my time comes, I duck down through the first arch and then bend down even further to enter the inner sanctum and kneel on the stone floor in the candlelight. But as I kneel here, praying, I know that Jesus has already gone before me. Why am I looking for Jesus among the dead? I will meet him not in this cold tomb but in Nazareth and by the Sea of Galilee.

Letter 43: Part 1: Nazareth – Can Anything Good Come Out of Nazareth?

1 May 2022

I have chosen the wrong day to travel to Nazareth. No buses are travelling there as it is the Jewish Shabbat. I have already booked and paid for my place to stay so I have to leave by taxi. But it is good to be in Nazareth. My room at the top of the city looks out over the rooftops. It's a lovely room with a veranda and a place to write.

This is a busy city too often gridlocked with traffic. For most of the night the mosque has been calling the town to prayer, another mosque in the distance, like an echo, answering the call. It has been the last week of Ramadan and now the festival of Eid as Muslims break their fast and celebrate with fireworks and loud firecrackers. At the same time there is the sound of bells ringing out from churches and the beautiful Basilica of the Annunciation where this morning I went for the Mass. They too on Saturday night, not to be outdone, were booming out their celebration of the consecration of a new bishop on megaphones across the valley. It is an eclectic and exciting cacophony of religious sounds. The buskers of Trafalgar Square have nothing on these noise levels. And of course it is Saturday – the Jewish Shabbat. I am made very aware of the meeting and significance of faith in our lives. The whole city is our monastery.

In the morning I wind my way down through the narrow, covered market walkways to the Basilica of the Annunciation. There is an upper vast basilica and a lower church, preserving the outline of the post-1170

Crusader church. The Byzantine remains are conserved in an octagon whose floor level is lower than that of the Crusader church. You descend the steps and behind a gate there is a cave that has been venerated as the place of the annunciation since early times. I sit inside this basilica for many hours watching the coach parties arrive. I wait for a gap in the visitors to make my own devotions. Each time the lower church clears, another coach party arrives. I notice how most of those who come spend so little time. I am glad I am not on one of these tours. Most of the visitors are looking at this place through their smartphone screens, taking photos or films. I suppose it is the way we try to hold on to the moment in our world today and pass it on. I am the same, for I too am also waiting to film a message for the Nazareth Community. We all seek God in the midst of distraction and disturbance. How little time most people stay before their tour guides wave them onwards – five minutes of photos, and then off. We carry so much of the paraphernalia of the world – our bags, phones, water bottles, chatter, timetables and programmes, all our modern addictions – and one thing only is really needed: to make space, a simplicity, a stripping back, an opening beyond the agenda. How can we ourselves clear the space where our lives themselves can hold the imprint of your footmarks, the fresh living imprint of your presence? We cannot photograph revelation. It is a lived moment. Hold on to nothing, only live this space and recognize Christ's presence in it.

We hunger for what we do not have or to hold on to experiences like possessions. But what we have is here and more able to satisfy our hunger than what we do not have or seek to possess.

Within me this morning, as I sit here, there is joy. Modern technology is a great gift too, for I have received news that Catherine Duce, who has been so much part of the life of our Nazareth Community and Companions of Nazareth, has just given birth to a baby daughter. Her wonderful husband Matt has sent me a photo. The child is so beautiful and seems filled with light, like an icon of love and blessing. Every birth, in so many ways, is a miraculous conception. We come face to face with the wonder of God and life itself. This child, like Christ himself, has been infused with prayer. She was longed for and dreamed of, and prayed, prayer-walked and loved into birth. I know the reality will involve nappies and sleepless nights and a whole new way of life, and responsibilities that will last a lifetime, but there is no mistaking the wonder of birth. The miracles of God continue. As I pray today I believe the hopes and fears of all the years continue to be met in Jesus of Nazareth and his mother Mary, beginning that journey of faith then and now with us. In this basilica above the ancient home of Mary I can hear a group of pilgrims praying together: 'Hail Mary, full of grace, the Lord is with thee. Blessed art thou amongst women and blessed is the fruit of thy womb, Jesus. Holy Mary, Mother of God, pray for us sinners, now and at the hour of our death.'

Finally, I find a space between the coach parties. I walk down the steps to the cave beneath and pray the same pray for Cath and Matt and Jennifer Joy:

> Hail, Mary, full of grace,
> the Lord is with thee.
> Blessed art thou amongst women
> and blessed is the fruit of thy womb, Jesus.
> Holy Mary, Mother of God,
> pray for us sinners,
> now and at the hour of our death.
> Pour your grace into our hearts
> that we too may be made worthy of the promises of Christ.

The scripture readings from the lectionary, as often happens, have a deep and particular resonance for me today in this Basilica of the Annunciation. The reading from Isaiah is this:

> For thus said the Lord GOD, the Holy One of Israel:
> In returning and rest you shall be saved;
>   in quietness and in trust shall be your strength.
> (Isaiah 30.15)

The reading has the quality of a true homecoming.

The next morning, I go to the Eucharist in this lower church, looking down into the sanctuary where religious brothers and sisters in their vestments have gathered around this sacred altar in the womb of this basilica. It is very beautiful. This celebration of Mass is not a performance. It is a getting out of the way, a standing aside so that all of us see the incarnation for ourselves. We too must get out of the way. We are not the light; Christ is the light within each one of us. We are not the water of life; we are the bucket. We are not the flame of the lamp; we fill the lamp with oil ready and waiting so that when the lamp is lit it will be the lamp to our feet.

> It is good to be here in Nazareth
> To unpack my life.
> To go down to Nazareth.
> I am always searching for this still empty place
> And the temptation is to leave it behind as soon as I have found it

Onwards rather than inwards
Like a thirst that can never be quenched
In each arrival there is a struggle against the restlessness of departure
Down in Nazareth
In this still, open place there is nothing and everything.
I spend so much of my time losing and looking
That I no longer have enough time to stay with the finding
And be found
And here I find what I was looking for
And of course it was there all along.
In Sha Allah
If God wills
And God does will
If I say yes ...
And I do – with all my heart
What a wonderful thing
Nazareth
Home with God.

Letter 44: Part 2: Nazareth is Our Home with God

We are grounded in contemplative prayer both alone and together. It is a calling to be people of prayer, praying for one another and for the world. It is a calling that is centred on Christ's presence and love here and now with us. We learn to depend on God and to listen for his guidance in all things. The resurrection gift of peace is the greatest gift we seek – Christ's peace at the very centre of our lives. It is life-giving and not life-denying. We aim to create a sense of space for one another and time to become aware of a world far beyond us in which we are on the edge of a vast unknowing.

We are discovering through Christ all that gives life and sustains life, life in all its fullness. We look to discover God's blessing even in the shadows, darkness, pain and failures of our lives.

We embrace humility. Nazareth is taking the last place at the table, the place Christ took. It is a stripping way of all that keeps us from acts of genuine love. It will mean living at a grass-roots level, revealing 'the upward gravity of love' and being ready to care because we care, rather than for recognition or reward. Our mission is not to be above or separate from but to be among others as those who serve with joy, especially those whose needs are greatest. We seek God's presence in the ordinary, manual and humblest of duties.

We aim to share our lives, with hearts open to the lives of others. It is a calling to treat others with great respect, not just with a sense of controlled tolerance but with God's respect for that person's goodness and

God's presence in their lives. Our calling is to show no discrimination and prejudice but to seek God in all, recognizing the grace and love of God in people of different races, colour, faith, sexuality, age, gender and mental and physical ability. And recognizing God's presence in our own particularities too. This recognition of diversity is not a recognition of *them* but *us*. In Nazareth, the *me* becomes *us*. We support and encourage the mutual flourishing of others without jealousy or pride. We aim to recognize and help others to bloom where they are planted, without prejudice or interference. We rejoice in the gifts of others regardless of age, position or status. We feast or famine with the wider community, rejoicing with those who rejoice, weeping with those who weep. We try always to be ready to welcome strangers and to show a particular care for those who are elderly, vulnerable, sick, lonely, grieving, suffering or with any particular need. Our calling is to live Jesus in the hidden and forgotten places and to realize that every encounter and action can make Christ present. To live Jesus in such a way that people may think: 'If such is the servant what must the master be like?' In Christ we are called to be universal brothers and sisters, brothers and sisters to all.

We depend on faithfulness to God and a simple obedience to our rule of life. This will take time and perseverance. There will be moments of great beauty and revelation but also moments when we are tempted to lose heart because of a sense of personal failure, futility and doubt. Together and through Christ's love for us we hold fast to all that is good. We try to count blessings rather than faults or failings.

Our community has a sense of humour and joy. It realizes that we get stuff wrong and need to be able to laugh. It aims to smile even in adversity and we try to live joyfully and with kindness. We try not to get self-obsessed in our way of life or take ourselves too seriously. It is God's will we seek not our own. We remember that true discernment often involves an openness and a freedom of spirit. It is like dew falling on a sponge rather than a sledgehammer pounding concrete. We make space for creativity, free time, relaxation, learning and fun. We try to live with our whole bodies the smile of God.

We are called upon to create home, through reciprocal relationships, for others – the home and belonging we have always longed for ourselves. We welcome Christ as our guest in all those who come to us or call upon us. We make space and time for one another, for both independence and company. We try to welcome and embrace both solitude and togetherness.

There is an ability to both give and receive. There is no sense of entitlement, just a generous offering and receiving, without counting the cost or counting on the recognition or response for validation.

We speak the truth with kindness, compassion and sensitivity, always recognizing that others may have a different truth to tell. We reject the divisiveness of moaning and gossip while recognizing the right time and way to get stuff off our chests and having the courage to speak difficult truths and to listen to the truths of others. We try to live out of love for God and neighbour, rejecting all that leads to hatred, bitterness and division. We remember Christ's words that we should not let the sun set on our anger (Ephesians 4.26).

We are forgiven and forgiving. We redeem our history only through the mercy of God. We remain humble about ourselves, recognizing that the successes and faults of all will be experienced by all, that all have feet of clay and all of us need God's grace. This is a God who does not turn away, and waits for our return. This is a community that seeks the best in the other but does not abandon the staying with when sometimes it discovers the worst. This is a community that always seeks God's grace in the other, and a community that recognizes that it is often in the wounded place that God's grace shines through.

Wonderings

I wonder which sentence or words from this passage from Isaiah are the words that you reflect upon:

> For thus said the Lord GOD, the Holy One of Israel:
> In returning and rest you shall be saved;
>   in quietness and in trust shall be your strength ...
> Therefore the LORD waits to be gracious to you;
>   therefore he will rise up to show mercy to you.
> For the LORD is a God of justice;
>   blessed are all those who wait for him ...

Though the Lord may give you the bread of adversity and the water of affliction, yet your Teacher will not hide himself any more, but your eyes shall see your Teacher. And when you turn to the right or when you turn to the left, your ears shall hear a word behind you, saying, 'This is the way; walk in it.' (Isaiah 30.15, 18, 20–21)

Letter 45: The Prayer of Abandonment to God's Providence

The Chapel of Charles de Foucauld in Nazareth
2–3 May 2022

I am convinced that the way of Charles de Foucauld has much to teach us in our own path, for he discovered the meaning of Nazareth and desired that brothers and sisters like us would share this path. In seeking his true vocation, which would eventually lead to his life as a monk in the Algerian desert, Charles de Foucauld twice spent time in Nazareth. The first time in 1888–89, aged 30, he went on a pilgrimage to the Holy Land, staying with the Franciscans. It was here that he discovered the humble and hidden life of Jesus. He wrote: 'You know the pilgrimage to the Holy Land has done me infinite and incomparable good. What an influence it has been on my life.'[1] Charles returned to Nazareth from 1897 to 1900, this time, however, not as a pilgrim. He arrived after seven years spent as a Trappist in France and Syria. But he dreamed of an even poorer, more hidden life, like that of Jesus of Nazareth. He offered himself as a servant to the Monastery of the Poor Clares, without revealing his true identity. On a plot of land next to the monastery he was assigned a poor abandoned hut. He passed his time doing manual jobs but whenever possible he would go to the chapel to pray. In 1899 he wrote:

It is the good God himself who has brought me by the hand to this nest which seems to have been prepared for me. I have found here a place of recollection, a retreat for which I cannot bless him enough, with this poverty, this lowliness of a worker so long desired.[2]

In a life that was never straightforward, Nazareth remained for him the stable place, the place of discernment. He found a synthesis for his life in the words, 'Go down to Nazareth', the place where Jesus 'grew'. He wrote:

> His whole life long Jesus did nothing other than go down – go down by his incarnation, go down by becoming a little child, go down by obeying, go down by becoming poor, exiled, forsaken, persecuted, tortured, placing himself always at the last place.[3]

The new covenant began in the lowest place: it is up to us to discover the glory of God in the hidden, ordinary things of our lives. The incarnation made daily human reality a sacred space – each action, each person an encounter with God. It was walking the streets of Nazareth that Charles experienced God. Nazareth was the name he gave to his life *with* God. To find God we too must find that simple home of Nazareth within.

This contemplative humility is also a coming close to others. When Charles founded his monastery he was to find himself overwhelmed with visitors and guests: 'I have 60–100 visitors each day.' But the inner voice Charles heard was this: 'It's love that must recollect you interiorly in me, and not distancing yourself from my children. See me in them and like me in Nazareth live close to them, lost in God.'[4] A contemplative life that drew its inspiration directly from the incarnation. Nazareth where you learn to listen and live. Today I went to where Br Charles prayed for many hours in front of the blessed sacrament during his stay in Nazareth from 1897 to 1900 at the sisters of the Poor Clares. When I went first it was midday but the door was locked. The notice on the door said to ring if you wanted to come in and pray. I rang many times and knocked too but no one came to the door. I walked away and then came back and rang again but still no one came. Then I saw that on the notice it also said that there was a time of adoration of the sacrament at 6.00 p.m. I remember that Br Charles of Jesus believed in three guiding rules:

To live the hidden life of Jesus.
To live with those who are most forgotten.
To spend time in contemplative adoration.

I would be there at 6.00 p.m. to keep this hour of adoration with them.
When I went back shortly before 6.00 p.m., the door was ajar. As I

entered in I realized I was coming home to somewhere that was very close to my heart. The door opened into a courtyard of soft warm stone, with trees and shrubs and climbing plants around the window.

I go inside the chapel, an outer area for guests leading to a sanctuary. There is a deep stillness here. There are two priests saying the evening office together – one young and handsome, the other elderly, bent forward and deeply devout with a kind face. I sit hushed as if welcomed into a deep peace. They read the prayers in such harmony that although I do not understand the words they nevertheless speak to me. They are dressed in bleached white cotton cassocks, with hoods and leather belts.

When the office is over, with a harmony now of movement, for I am sure they have carried this out many times together, they light three candles and place them in small olive-wood bowls on the altar. Behind them is a simple wooden tabernacle with silver doors and the impressionistic repousse of an angel messenger on one door and Mary kneeling on the other. The younger priest takes the sacrament with gentle reverence and slips it into a very simple olive-wood monstrance – slowly turning it to face us. Then, coming round in front of the altar, he kneels to add incense to a clay pot with charcoal on the floor. The fragrance of our prayer rises. The young priest on one side of the altar kneels on cushions, the older priest, on the other side, sits quietly on a chair leaning forward. At the back of the chapel I too find a cushion and prayer stool as if waiting for me, and I also kneel. I feel I want to stay here for ever. In that moment everything is balanced and makes sense. Our prayer is stripped back of all that is superfluous, and I am led to the centre of all that I seek. It is being held in the heart of God. It is peace. It is coming home. It is Nazareth.

Each icon in this chapel I know already intimately: on the right of the altar the Greek icon of Christus Rex; on the left of the altar the Madonna and Child; above the altar, the St Damiano Cross that spoke to St Francis, which I have prayed in front of in Assisi and at Hilfield Friary – in fact all my life – the cross that said to Francis, 'Rebuild my church'. To my left there is a candle burning and an icon of the risen Christ reaching out and raising the dead with his hand. I am drawn into a meeting in this silence, which is both deeply human and deeply of God. The hour seems to disappear – I want it to last much longer. I remember the time I prayed in the Melanesian Brothers chapel I felt the same, as though I never wanted to leave. I have arrived in this silence. I have come home to Nazareth. At the back of the church there are some prayer cards. I take one. It is the prayer of Charles de Foucauld:

Father,
I abandon myself into your hands;
do with me what you will.
Whatever you may do,
I thank you.
I am ready for all,
I accept all.
Let only your will be done in me,
And in all your creatures.
I wish no more than that, O Lord.

Into your hands I commend my soul;
I offer it to you
with all the love of my heart,
for I love you Lord,
and so need to give myself,
to surrender myself into your hands,
without reserve,
and with boundless confidence,
for you are my Father.[5]

For the first time in my life I feel able to pray that prayer without reserve and with boundless confidence, 'for I love you, Lord', and I no longer wish to hold anything back. I do not know how long I will be able to say this, but I know today, here in this chapel, I surrender my life to you again, without reserve. I realize I could not and cannot live in any other way apart from you.

The sign of this community of Charles de Foucauld is a heart pierced with a cross. The cross and the heart together, the sign of total love and sacrifice. It is when the cross pierces the human heart that the blood of Jesus' love and forgiveness flows.

There is something so beautiful here, and within me the longing to give more fully and yet at the same time to remain open-handed, as open-handed as the hands of this priest, without pretension or pride or fear, as natural and open as grace.

In our lives there are so many temptations to leave this all behind. Good temptations to settle for something else, to believe that you are somehow missing out, that there is something better, that this sacrifice of love is not worth it, that what you really need is what everyone else has got. Yet I want to call out:

Do not abandon this path
Abandon yourself to the love of God.
Yes there will be struggles and sins and disillusionment
But there is goodness beyond all your imaginings
There is the revelation of God's love in so many people and places
This love will pierce your heart too and make it bigger
Is your own heart broken-open enough to become the heart of Jesus?
This heart is the only heart that can heal the world.

I come back for the Eucharist the following day. If I could, I would come
here every day for ever.

The Eucharist is not a performance
It is not the reading of words
Or the completing of actions
It is a getting out of the way
It is an opening of the door
It is a taking off of your shoes because you are standing on holy ground
It is seeing the burning bush

It is not in your power to light the fire
You are not the light
You are the lighthouse keeper
Simpler still
You are not the water of life
It is enough simply to provide the bucket

You are not the bread of life yourself
But you are the one who takes and eats
And becomes Christ's body

You are not the wine
But you are the one who drinks and shares
The cup of Christ's blood
Which can take away the sins of the world.

So come back time and time again
With great devotion
With great simplicity
With great love
Make space
Give all
Become what you truly are.

Letter 46: Tiberias – Learning
to Walk on Water

3–5 May 2022

Dear Brothers and Sisters,

I am learning what it is like to be a foreigner in a foreign land. I am having to depend on the kindness and patience of strangers. I needed a bus card to get to Tiberias from Nazareth. It's called a Rav-Kav, like Israel's version of an Oyster card. Everyone told me I needed one but no one knows where to get one during the Muslim festival of Eid with nearly every shop closed. Eventually I am directed to a small travel office on the third floor of a building that looks closed. Everyone in the office stops what they are doing to discuss my need of a Rav-Kav for the next 15 minutes and they make several phone calls. I am finally directed down the road to the third floor of another building. I ring the bell outside and nothing happens. Finally a passer-by who stops to help me reveals that the door I am ringing on is open and I should just go in. On the third floor of this seemingly deserted building I find three people in an office who all stop what they are doing to sort out my travel card and how much credit I need to put on it to cover the cost of all my travels in Israel. They also find out where I will need to catch the bus and the various times of departure. All this takes at least half an hour of their time, with a young girl gazing at a computer for what seems like a long time before she says, 'Computer slow'. Finally I emerge, clutching the precious Rav-Kav. I am aware of how often members of our International Group are in need of help that can sometimes seem to take for ever. But when you are helped like this, I realize I will carry these acts of kindness always. It's like saying, 'I am prepared to give my time to you even though I don't have to.' It's like saying, 'Even though I don't know you, yet you still matter to me.' It's a simple but such a wonderful gift, this gift of someone's time and care. I think of Sophie leading the Sunday International Group – a different place but the same message. We are saying, 'You matter to me.'

I did my research for this simple journey the day before, remembering Loren's edict: 'It's all in the pre-production.' Just as well, because the bus stop was not easy to find, and I had not realized you had to flag the bus down or it would just roar past you at 60 mph. When I had successfully stopped the bus, the driver indicated that I could not get on the bus with a suitcase, and I was flummoxed. He shouted at me excitedly but I could not understand a word and thought he was going to drive off. Until he climbed down, smiling, and indicted the side locker underneath the bus to stow my bag away. Then the Rav-Kav worked a treat and we were off. How many of our social interactions we take for granted and how easy to be impatient with those who are lost in the complexities we ourselves take for granted. A simple smile and a moment of help means so much.

When I arrive at Tiberias bus station, I wheel my suitcase down towards the Sea of Galilee. My first impression is that the seafront is like a cross between Bognor Regis and an Arab market. There is a smell of hot cooking oil in the air, but from shawarma and falafels rather than fish and chips. The tourist restaurants on the seafront are selling St Peter's fish for a high price for a lot of bones and unfortunately no coin in the fish's mouth for paying your taxes. My footpath leads me into a huge car park in which everyone is honking their horns at the same time. There is no visible layout plan, so the place is in gridlock. A car behind me almost knocks me flying and the driver shouts angrily out of the window because I have knocked his wing mirror out of place, or rather he has knocked his wing mirror out of place on my shoulder. There is road rage in every part of the world. To drive with consideration for the welfare of others on the road is a great modern virtue. Cars are like modern tabernacles. To damage a car is sacrilege. In England perhaps fluorescent Lycra garments in all liturgical colours are a cyclist's modern vestments.

But the Casa Nova Pilgrim Hotel is wonderful and I am staying here for four nights. It is a cross between what feels like an ancient monastery, youth hostel, holiday fellowship seaside guesthouse and pilgrimage centre. Andrej, whom I have been emailing to arrange this stay, welcomes me warmly and calls me 'Father' and leads me to the end of a long tiled corridor to room 122. Unfortunately, despite my attempts at mindfulness, I do not pay enough attention and later in the day will burst into room 102 at the end of a different corridor where two people are having a siesta and I apologize profusely.

Mine is a big room with both a single and a double bed and a balcony with a small table and a metal chair. 'You wanted a sea view, Father', Andrej says. I get a view out past the Arab coffee shop to the sea of Galilee. Later he asks me if I would like to celebrate Mass with him on Friday. I fear they have mistaken me for a Catholic priest and perhaps I have been given the balcony under false pretences. I don't have the heart to tell him I am only an Anglican! I simply reply I would love to come and for him to celebrate the Mass for us.

In search of the calm of things above

It's the heat of the day but I am eager to explore. It's so different from Nazareth and Jerusalem. The place is crowded with people celebrating Eid. There are about 400 metres of Galilee seafront promenade, places to hire jet skis and speedboats, cafes and many Christian tourists. There is also, sadly, litter everywhere, like Trafalgar Square after St Patrick's Day. I decide not to eat but instead set off in search of a place to swim. Some Palestinian lads have climbed over a fence and are swimming from a high wall, diving and jumping into the sea, but if I were to do the same I don't think I would be able to climb back out again. I am looking for a proper beach. It's a long hot road out of town. One path leading down to the waterfront seems hopeful but when I get to the bottom it's just some steps into the water and some rocks, and the shallows are full of plastic bottles and plastic bags. There are some people camped on the steps and swimming among the garbage but it doesn't look very inviting. It's definitely not, 'O Sabbath rest by Galilee, O calm of hills above, where Jesus knelt to share with thee the silence of eternity, interpreted by love.'[1] I feel a bit disappointed. I walk further along the road out of town hoping to find a better place. There is one hotel with a notice that reads 'Jaguars only', beside a limited number of parking spaces. I think it must be a joke. Everywhere there are notices with red crosses over the illustration or the icon of the swimmer, so it seems swimming is forbidden, at least if you are poor, because there are a number of very posh hotels along here with swimming pools and exclusive Galilee seafront access. I go into one that has a flashy looking pool, advertising spa treatments, but the man on the door does not give me a very warm welcome and says, 'This pool is for residents only.' 'And the sea?' I ask. He shrugs. 'Plenty of public places out of the town', he responds dismissively.

Further along the road I'm getting hotter. I turn round and see an

Orthodox Jew in black waistcoat, trousers and with tassels hanging down from his tallit katan. I had admired the kipas, clothes, hats and hat boxes of all those on the aeroplane with me when I flew to Tel Aviv, and their care and devotion to prayer during the journey, with their tefillah (prayer boxes) strapped to their foreheads and upper arms and tallitot prayer shawls with their special twined and knotted fringes. How faithful many Jews and Muslims are to their life of prayer. But this person following me down the road looks as hot and as lost as me. He speaks to me but I'm unable to understand. I tell him that I'm from London but he too is unable to understand me. He pulls out a smartphone and starts typing into Google translate and then holds up the phone for me to see. 'Where is the beach?' the message reads. I shrug. He's asked the wrong man. He hurries off and I see him getting into his car and driving off. Perhaps we are both in the same way searching for the promised land.

Over the fence there is a beach and there is a large noticing saying, 'Designated Swimming Area', and a very green lawn. Outside, a young man is trying to load a very expensive-looking jet ski on to a trailer. He calls me over to help him. In seconds there I am trying to hold the whole weight of a jet ski while he winches on a handle, but the winch seems to be slipping so the operation makes no progress and after about ten minutes I indicate I have had enough supporting the weight of a jet ski, apologize and put it down. I get no thank you. Inside the hotel there is a notice saying that to swim costs 70 shekels, which is about £18, and anyway they tell me that they are closed.

Not to be defeated, I make my way back to the first swimming place I tried, with the steps and floating bottles. When I arrive the police have also arrived and are talking to the Africans who are in two pop-up tents camped on the steps. The police drive away and I speak to the Africans and find out they're from Ethiopia. One of them, who seems to be looking after the rest of the family, and reminds me of members of our International Group, especially Ebenezer, tells me the police have told them to clear up their rubbish and go. I tell him his English is very good, which it is, and he responds quite rightly, 'I know'. I watch all of them as they carefully pack up the tents and their bags and possessions. The one who spoke to me seems to be in charge and taking great care of the young ones – two young girls, about 12 and 14, perhaps his sisters, and a very young boy with wonderfully big hair, about 9 years old. I go over and say, 'This is to buy you all a meal tonight', and give him 100 shekels hoping they will not feel insulted but wanting to help this family trying to have a holiday in the pop-up tents and a swim like me. He's not insulted at all and grins and thanks me and bows touching his heart. I smile back and touch my heart too and go back to where I've been sitting, but when

I look back the whole family is smiling towards me and waving at me and the young man gives me a thumbs up. I then notice him taking some bread over to two older men who look pretty destitute to me. They thank him and the family move off. Share and share alike. Like the feeding of the 5,000 – when we share the little we have, there is enough for all.

I ask a young man who has just come out of the water if we are allowed to swim here, pointing as I do so at a large notice with an icon of a swimmer with a red cross. 'Yes,' he says, 'No swimming!' and jumps in again. His big Israeli friend with spectacles who has been wading in the water smiles and says, 'This is Israel.' They come out of the water and sit on the steps, smoking, and indicate they will look after my clothes if I want to go for a swim too. I do. It's cool and feels fresh. I swim out into deep water, swimming in the same sea that Jesus walked on. The same sea where Jesus told disciples to put out into deep water and let down their nets for a catch. This lake is 12 miles long, 6 miles wide and over 200 feet deep. I am surrounded by hills on all sides. I think of Peter jumping into this water when he saw the risen Christ, and their nets filled with 153 fish, and Jesus sharing breakfast with them. Today it has not been quite the living water of my dreams but I realize I too have jumped into the water and shared a breakfast of sorts on these steps. I walk back to my balcony, drying in the sun and feeling that, somehow, I too have celebrated communion and somehow God has transformed swimming apartheid into a time of blessing. I am glad I swam in Galilee and pleased I decided to swim with this lot, not in the posh hotel for £18. Yes, a memory of baptism echoing those words from above: 'These are also my beloved sons and daughters, with whom I am well pleased' (Matthew 3.17).

Turning water into wine

Tonight I wandered around trying to find somewhere to eat and kept on finding myself getting nowhere and having to retrace my steps. All the cafes and restaurants are now closed because in two days it's going to be Israeli Independence Day and there are flags everywhere. The Muslims are also still celebrating Eid and for them it's already holiday time. I'm hungry as I have not eaten all day. I end up going to the Scots Hotel, which I figure will stay open. It's very 5 star and out of my league, listing the cheapest room at £355 a night. I wander around and eventually find a bar with no barman. I go in search of him and, when I find him downstairs, he is very friendly and gives me some peanuts and a glass of Italian beer. He tells me they are not doing bar snacks but I could join the buffet downstairs. 'It is very expensive, but you can eat as much as you like', he tells me honestly. I hum and ha but when I look at the numerous dishes set out, I decide to go for it, justifying the extravagance as an interesting cultural experience. I am sitting at my own table. Next to me is a table of two young women, whom I notice standing up and holding hands and praying together after they have finished their crèmes brûlée. There is a large group of American Christian tourists on the table opposite. One lady is talking animatedly and loudly about how she loves a rare beef salad and she's going to get a second helping.

To make sure I enjoy the full value of the buffet, I stock up in the way I learnt to do from the Melanesian Brothers, when we were invited to a bishop or politician's birthday party or a feast day. Following Joseph's example, we always ate enough for the seven years of famine! It's not difficult. The buffet is delicious fish, prawns, mussels, squid and every type of salad imaginable, and there is the rare roast beef that the woman loved, carved for you by the waiter. There is duck with oranges, roasted chicken and the most wonderful selection of vegetables, roasted broccoli, dates, nuts, seeds, chillies, tomatoes, olives, fresh breads, and then a sweet of apple cream cake, followed by bread and cheese and coffee. 'Feast or famine with the community', we used to say in the Melanesian Brotherhood. In other words, when you're at the Scots Hotel don't try to diet, think more of the feeding of the 5,000 and enjoy God's abundance.

After I have filled my plate with food, I am brought the wine list that seems to have nothing under £75. The waiter asks me if I would like wine and I ask him if they do it by the glass. He asks me what kind of wine I like and I say, 'The cheapest'. He laughs and says he will find me a delicious wine. I thank him. After all you can't be in Galilee and not drink red wine, can you? He brings a new bottle and opens it. 'Just one glass,' I say. 'Yes,' he replies. 'This wine is a very delicious wine from Galilee made from three different types of grape.' He gives me a drop to taste. He is right, it is delicious. He tells me he has studied winemaking for two years in Israel. I ask him where he is from, and he says that his mother is from Tunisia and that he wants to go and live in Australia. 'What's wrong with staying in Israel?' I ask. 'National Service,' he replies. He says that he's just completed three years and it was very tough. He was in the Golan Heights at the front end of things, and it was dangerous and unhappy. I reply cautiously that it must have been very hard for the Palestinians too, not knowing how he will respond, but he agrees and tells me that he felt so very sorry for them. Then he said that he knew what it was like to be put in prison too. During his time of National Service his mother had been taken very ill and he went home to visit her without permission and when he got back he was put in military prison for 14 days as a punishment. I notice how thin he looks, his collarbone and neck, and how sad he looks as he tells me this, as if he is still living it. I can see that he is a very gentle, kind man. I think of my own mother. I think of the very young Israelis I have seen everywhere carrying those dangerous-looking machine guns. I remember in the Solomons feeling that holding a gun was like touching evil. I say to him, 'I think you made the right decision, going home to visit your mother who was ill and needed you. To me that seems worth 14 days in prison.' He smiles and seems pleased and gives me another glass of wine for free and I say to him, 'It's over now.' I mean the National Service is over. 'Now you can go and make delicious wine.' 'Yes,' he says, and smiles, 'but if there is trouble, I know they will send me back again.' 'I do understand', I say, 'how difficult it must be to be in the army. I myself would hate to have to do it too.' I think of the wall, the checkpoints, the occupied territories, the number of men and women in uniform looking so young carrying machine guns. I feel the division, the fear and threat of violence. It feels so wrong, this segregation. A nation locked in, divided by fences and this wall, living in fear. We have all seen the pictures. The stones being thrown, the sound of rubber bullets, then bullets, then buildings being demolished. Stretchers and cries of the terrified and grieving. Fear and hatred spreading like poison. Blessed are the peacemakers. For they shall be called the sons and daughters of God. 'Do not let the olive branch fall from my hand.'[2]

When I leave, I say to him, 'God bless you. I've enjoyed talking to you very much.' 'God bless you too,' he says and it sounds like he really means it. As I sit in the hotel gardens, which are very lush and beautiful smelling of flowering jasmine, I realize Jesus is still turning water into wine. I am eating a very sweet orange that I took from the overflowing fruit basket as I left.

I went to Mass on Wednesday night. It was in English and there were only about seven people there plus me. They were a young American group, obviously on a tour with their priest around the Holy Land. The priest spoke in an animated way telling the story of Peter and the catch of fish, how Peter had chosen to return to his old ways and then how strange it must have been to be told to cast his nets on the other side, he a professional fisherman. God is calling us to let go of the things we know, and trust in his ways. How often we return, said the priest, to our old ways of doing things, failing to trust in the call of God. He spoke well. But the Mass was conducted at such speed. And he did not look at me once in the whole service or say anything to me when I left. Even when he gave me the bread he did not look at me. I am learning how important it is that we who have the privilege of representing Christ at the altar show warmth and welcome to those who come. Carlo Carretto says, 'What is the use of saying the Divine Office or sharing the Eucharist if one is not impelled by love?' But the question he asks himself, 'Are you capable of an act of perfect love?'[3] is a hard question for me to answer.

Desolation and consolation

After the spiritual depth and passion of Jerusalem and the religious intensity of Nazareth, Tiberias over these last few days feels so secular, so thin. The kids below my balcony have been hired electric cars by their parents and are whizzing round and round in circles honking their toy horns. Out on the Sea of Galilee jet skis are revving their engines and ploughing up the water, racing each other in constant arcs. No wonder everyone is prohibited from swimming. There are cars blocking everywhere with boom boxes thumping out music in competition with one another. And there is rubbish and litter absolutely everywhere, the hedges and fences are clogged with it. There are places to discard rubbish but no one seems to use them. There are loads of bits of plastic, plastic bottles, the discarded remnants of barbecues, and greasy foil trays floating in the sea and lurking everywhere you look in the bushes. I wake early in the morning, thinking that at least 6.30 a.m. will be a time that is peaceful. But down by the water's edge the young men look distant and stoned. I try to be friendly but there is no response and the seafront is like a tip. Then a car arrives, and all the doors are thrown open and out comes thumping music. And the occupants of the car tumble out and start a drunk, stumbling dance, oblivious of me or anyone else present. It's like the worst kind of modern hangover. Like a modern purgatory. 'Peace be still.' Shut the mouth of this modern storm that regurgitates everywhere the plastic and waste it feeds on.

I turn away from Galilee. Later in the day I walk out of the town, as far as I can go, in search of peace and beauty. The rain is falling gently and dampening the dust and it feels refreshing to walk through the rain. Everywhere along the road there are notices with red crosses over the illustration of a swimmer. About three miles out of town after the signs that say 'No entry' there is a path down to the sea. A man speaks to me in English and asks me if I am looking for a beach. 'Yes,' I say. He points down the road. At the bottom, on a beach covered in garbage, a rotten discarded sofa and rusty bottomless chair in the water, there in front of me is the most beautiful Sea of Galilee, its waters shimmering in the sunshine after the rain. While I am standing there peacefully a group of young people arrive with tents. 'Shalom,' I say and we talk. They have come to camp. 'It's beautiful here,' the girl says to me. 'Yes, very,' I reply, 'but I feel so sad to see so much rubbish.' 'Me too,' she says, 'but we will clear it up.' The group divides and while the men set up camp the women bring out bin bags and start clearing up the whole beach. Three big bin bags full. I help them. It feels such a very good thing to do, as good as Jesus driving out an evil spirit. After half an hour the beach is clean again, and we sit smiling, pleased with ourselves. It is not long, however, before carloads of people start arriving with new rubbish and take over the space, seemingly completely or deliberately unaware of the fact that we are already here. I thank one of the girls whom I helped clear up. She thanks me too and I take my leave. Clearing up was so deeply satisfying. It felt like a prayer answered, as though we were on God's side.

The Casa Nova, where I am staying, is like a bastion against the tide of modern consumerism. It's quiet and cool and the staff are so thoughtful and kind. There is no excess here. Even the prices are so very reasonable and considerate in comparison to everywhere else. My room is spacious and my balcony beautiful. I like it best sitting out there in my pyjamas in the middle of the night when everyone has gone home. This morning I went down to the chapel to pray. It's called the chapel of St Peter and it was one of the Crusaders' chapels that has been here since 1100. The shape of the ceiling is like the shape of the hull of an upturned boat. The chapel is cool and peaceful and feels like a solid defence against the assaults of the modern world. On the curved wall above the altar there is a wonderful mosaic of Peter in a boat by himself holding on to the tiller with both hands. His face is looking up and out into the distance. It's as if he's remembering the storm on the lake when Jesus was in his boat. It's as if he's holding on to that memory to give him courage to face any storm that may come now. It's as if with both hands he is steadfastly holding on to his course – Jesus' course. And it's as though, through that memory, he has become the fisherman that Christ called him to become. It gives me great strength looking up above this altar. Christ does not promise that our lives will be easy, but Christ does promise that we will not be overcome.

Again I am reminded that each time the world turns my head away, I must return to prayer. It is the silence of contemplative prayer that can replenish, that can enter one's whole being and pour into the soul new strength. How many times must I learn this to realize that it is true? I unroll my mat on my balcony, take out my prayer stool and pray silently as the sun sets. Then on the balcony I take out my handmade notebook and write this:

O Galilee
I need a space within me
Uncover all that has marred your presence
How do we become like clean wet sand
Holding the imprint of your footmarks
Until the sea washes them away
And you make a fresh imprint of your presence?

Help me to strip myself back in prayer
To put myself once again in front of Jesus
I know I can't reach God with my own understanding
Or with my own judgements
I can only reach you in silence
Or rather let you reach me
Because your love has never ceased.

The next day, after leaving Casa Nova, I discover I have lost my note-book: all my reflections and thoughts since arriving in the Holy Land lost – days of writing. I search everywhere. I go back to the Casa Nova and retrace all my steps, go back to the Scots Hotel – it's nowhere to be found. I feel gutted. All those hours of meditating and writing in Jerusalem, Nazareth and here in Tiberius, lost. I phone my brother, as he always understands, and he does. I pray that St Anthony will inter-cede for me. He does. The following day, after I have left Tiberias and travelled on to Tabgha, I receive a phone call from the priest at the Casa Nova to say he has found my notebook on the balcony of room 122. I am so thankful. Without those notes I could not have written these letters to you my sisters and brothers. Sometimes you have to lose things and find them again to realize the blessings of God.

Letter 47: Heading Out into Deep Waters

Tabgha and the Mount of Beatitudes
6–8 May 2022

I spent a lot of time searching in Tiberias for the place of peace. I feared it was an illusion and I would not find the place of Sabbath rest and calm of things above or the silence of eternity. But it was here all along. How often we wear ourselves out looking, only to discover we have been looking in the wrong place. And God, in God's time, discloses what we have been looking for all along, and more.

In Tiberias, it was both Israeli Independence and Muslim Eid, and the result was like a town full of football supporters with no football match. So many young people wearing the same identikit black T-shirts with gold-embossed horizontal logos and the same haircut – shaved sides with crew-cut strips on top – all dressed up and nowhere to go, except those who had the money for jet skis or speedboat rides or to build barbeque camps and discard their plastic rubbish in wasteland.

But now the national and religious holiday is over and the jet skis are back on their trailers and the white four-wheel drives have gone home, and I have moved on to Tabgha. I am staying at Pilgerhaus, which is a German pilgrim house and run immaculately as only Germans can. The litter ends as soon as you walk through the gates. The German Association of the Holy Land have been welcoming pilgrims here since 1889. It is next to a German Benedictine monastery and convent and the

Church of the Multiplication of Loaves and Fish, and on the other side of this beautiful church is St Peter's Church, where the Primacy of Peter the Rock is remembered.

I swim in the Sea of Galilee very early in the morning. It must be about 6.00 a.m. There is a very soft early-morning light here, so different from the light of the Mediterranean. There is a sandy, warm haze where the land meets the sky, as if the top edges of the mountains that surround us have been smudged into the sky, with pastel colours of gentle pinks and oranges. It makes these mountains that surround the lake have an ethereal crown-like quality, like a halo warming the sky. Both the sea and the sky have the same colour of pale misty-blue. Entering into the quiet of this place feels like a total immersion, as if being gently held. The contours of my own life are softening too. All around there are bright bursts of colour: the reds, whites and crimsons of rambling roses; the 'be still' tree, yellow oleander; and the 'mill' tree, white oleander. There is purple and red bougainvillea and the yellow blaze of Jerusalem thorns. And trees – palms, purple orchid trees and banana trees with their splitting huge leaves, eucalyptus, ancient terebinth trees, and the most amazing sacred fig trees with great twisted trunks. There are thorns and purple thistles and bullrushes, bamboos and dry grass, and the sea-spindly black willow and bald cypress growing in quite deep water, inviting me, through the spaces, into the open light of Galilee. All around me I hear the sound of birds and as I swim I see them too – thin black cormorants, grey herons, gulls, cranes, egrets and even pelicans. There is something prehistoric about the birdlife here, as they swoop over the water as they must have done for thousands of years.

After all the noise and restlessness of Tiberias and the discarded plastic, I have now found a place to swim. It's as if the landscape, the trees, the birds and most of all this bowl of freshwater sea – they are all themselves the meditation. It's as if the whole of Galilee is now speaking to me and saying:

Peace – be still,
You have been rushing too much
Your mind has been in overdrive
You have walked, run, organized, worked in the belief that if not
    things would fail.
Frenzied activity, fearing letting anything fall.
Trying to make sense in your head of your life,
church, family, friends, community, past and future –
The needs of all who are searching for home,
The lost, the displaced, the rejected, the pain of the world.

Trying to remember so much that you have sometimes missed the truth.
This life does not depend on you. It depends on God.
Now practise what you preach.
Now seek the balance of which you speak.
The weight of the world is not yours to bear –
'Come unto me all who travail and are heavy laden and I will
   refresh you.'
Now, here and now, put yourself in front of Jesus,
it's not you yourself doing the work of redemption – let Jesus do it.
And let him begin with you.

Stop trying to be the meditation yourself
Let Christ be the meditation
Let Christ be the prayer
Let the waters of Galilee in which you swim be the waters on which
   he walks
And raises you from death to life.

It's strange how in this place I react against sound. As I was swimming in Galilee, swimming out into deep water, I heard the engine of a fishing boat. They came close and I realized they were pulling in fishing nets, metres of fine mesh. Caught by the gills were a number of fish, not 153, but a good number, some of them several pounds in weight, and also plenty of the St Peter's fish I have seen people eating in restaurants. In fact, I was fortunate I was not caught in the net myself. But as they sorted the net and tossed their catch into a large container, they turned on loud pop music. The calm was broken. It was the sound of the modern world breaking in. This whole lake is an amphitheatre – it is the stage for God's presence, God's action in the world. It is here that the incarnation takes place, it is here that Word becomes flesh; here is the place of intimate encounter, of revelation, of prayer, of healing. This is the place Christ meets us in his resurrection. The whole place, this whole bowl of this sea, is the crucible of Jesus' love for us – it's a vast church, a cathedral, a monastery for our encounter with the incarnate God. He is the one who here seems to be walking so simply before us, stripping me back to the essence of all that I am and all that I long to be. Here God is amplified in the silence and I can't understand why everyone is not hushed by this holiness.

That's what I had felt in Tiberias, that we are trashing God's home. We are driving jet skis through a timeless miracle of his intimate presence. We are turning the house of God into the plastic bags, the bottles, the food containers, the plates, the straws, the filth that clogs the beaches, and the wasteful consumerism of a marketplace that is ultimately empty of value. We are turning the truth of God's kingdom into a lie. This is not just here in Galilee. This is what we are doing to our world. We are trashing it, turning the intimate miracles of God into such waste and exploitation – while alongside there is so much poverty, so much need. We are killing the planet. We are wrecking the homes of our neighbours. All over the world people are being oppressed. This nation is still divided by such terrible injustice and prejudice. There is a wall dividing this nation. The apartheid continues, within every nation and between nations, divided between the rich and powerful and the poorest of our world. Galilee is within the world as it is. Nazareth is not some idealized kingdom of peace. It's in the world. A world that as I write is being blasted with missiles and bullets and cluster bombs. 'My house shall be called a house of prayer; but you are making it a den of robbers', said Jesus as he overturned the money-changers' tables (Matthew 21.13).

I realize I too am culpable with my own refuse bags full of non-biodegradables and caught up in the addictions of our times. I too have been sucked into the delusion. It's just that here in this place my eyes are open to God's miracle – an endangered miracle of divine love that is still being crucified. I just want the world to stop what it's doing, to stop like it did during Covid-19 and wake up to the horror of the blasphemy. The incarnation is taking place in our midst and so many have not noticed, hearing only the endless song of self-interest blaring in our ears. We are all part of the amphitheatre of God's incarnation. This is God's creation and we are in danger of losing it. This is planetary vandalism. We search to spin ever faster in the fairgrounds of futility and the manufacture of what can never ultimately satisfy. We are like diabetics feeding ourselves with the sugars of our addictions.

I no longer want to be fed addictions. I realize my own sin and failures of the past and present are like the garbage by the lake and the plastic discarded in the sea. It's so non-biodegradable. You think you can hide your sins. They last for ever. They clog up the places of natural goodness and the arteries of beauty. Yet the recognition of human destructiveness begins with the longing of the soul for redemption. It is when we clear away the debris of our compulsions and addictions that we discover that Christ is still there waiting. It's like discovering living water in the place where nothing would grow. It's the heart of flesh in the valley of dry bones. It is the One who does not even need our apology that we have been eating with the pigs. He knows the experience of pain and desolation was enough to bring us home. He raises us. He restores us. He washes away our shame and clothes us and gives back to us again the inheritance that we ourselves squandered.

Here in Tabgha, on this lake, I realize that the most miraculous drama of God's love is still taking place here and now – down here among us. God is with us now. God's love is now. Jesus is still speaking. He is still walking on water, calling to us across the lake. If only we can hear him. If only we come and see and stay with him. 'Come and have breakfast' (John 21.12).

When we discover again Christ's presence we realize that the wounds we cause can indeed become signs of resurrection. When we open ourselves to the grace of God it's as if we too have come home. We don't need to go on hurting and hating, because we have entered the light. Like these mountains around Galilee, we are softened by that light and encircled by the same golden halo. We carry a peace within us that is pure gift.

I am swimming in this baptismal water
You know when you float you have to be very still
If you thrash around or panic you will drown
Just be still feeling the water holding you
Holding the water as you float with open hands
Looking up at the vastness of the sky.
To walk on water you do just the same
You look towards Jesus
You tread the water very gently with your feet
You keep trusting
And if you start sinking Christ will take you by the hand.

I must return from here. But I don't want to go back bringing with me an experience that will slowly be depleted or lost in the rush of a greater reality.
No, I want to continue to live in the same amphitheatre of grace.
Knowing that the city too is God's monastery
God's peace
Christ's resurrection is the reality
Eternity is already here.

The image of Nazareth and Galilee I will hold on to is the image
    of a mother
Mary pregnant with God
And like a mother waiting to give birth to a miracle
Our bodies are the womb of all we are,
Filled with this life within
Each action is an act of love nurturing that life

The life that gives us life
And just like a mother would not want to do anything to risk harming
   this child within
So we are all called to give attentive love and life
That is what Nazareth is:
Discovering here and now that we are the dwelling place of God
The God who longs to abide
If only we can make room
We need to discover again his breath within
The heartbeat inside us
The love that we have been given to tabernacle
The peace that is his eternal gift.

In Sha Allah
God's Will

At the Pilgerhaus they serve the most beautiful food and in the evening
the Palestinian manager, seeing I am sitting alone, introduces me to a
fellow pilgrim, Philip, who, though I have never met him before, just
happens to live less than five minutes away from me up St Martin's Lane
in London and has sung at St Martin's. What a blessing it is to have his
company. Galilee opens us and we share deeply about our lives and all
that has brought us here, and after only one meal it feels as if we have
known each other a long time. He is a spiritual director, loves the Holy
Land, has a real centredness and is so easy to talk to. What a blessing
to meet him here. At the morning prayers at the Benedictine monastery,
he sings with a wonderful tenor voice. He is going to Tiberias so offers
to pick up my notebook for me from Casa Nova. God is good and I
am so thankful. Over the next few days, Philip asks me many questions
about the Nazareth Community and when we return to London decides
to become a member. 'I met Philip by the Sea of Galilee,' I tell everyone
when he joins our community, and that same tenor voice fills St Martin's.

   It's Sunday, and I follow the sound of a bell through a gate and
along a path. Today the Mass is being celebrated not in the Benedictine
monastery but down by the Sea of Galilee, a large rock the altar. I watch
as the Filipino sisters decorate it with fresh wild flowers. Around the
altar are wooden logs for those who come to sit. There is a cross draped
with a white linen cloth blowing in the wind. You cannot improve on the
Eucharist. It's life stripped back to the primordial encounter. No produc-
tion, no artifice, no performance, just presence – face to face with the one
who created all this and chose to be with us just as he was. And me, just
as I am.

After the Mass I sit here by the sea for a long time as the others depart.

And then I decide I must find the mount of Beatitudes and follow Christ up. I am walking slowly and it's the heat of the day, walking stick in one hand and Bible in the other. And my phone to picture this. Somehow I want to hold on to this for ever. I follow the road. I make my way down to the Church of the Primacy of Peter. I contemplate the rock upon which Jesus will build his church, each crack stuffed with prayer requests and spotted with melted candle wax, and then I set off up into nature, the buzz of crickets and the singing of birds. I have brought no water and it is very hot and I wonder if I will dehydrate. It's a steep climb but I take it slowly. Every few minutes I stop, turn and look out across Galilee and read:

When Jesus saw the crowds, he went up the mountain; and after he sat down, his disciples came to him. Then he began to speak, and taught them, saying:

'Blessed are the poor in spirit, for theirs is the kingdom of heaven.
'Blessed are those who mourn, for they will be comforted.
'Blessed are the meek, for they will inherit the earth.
'Blessed are those who hunger and thirst for righteousness, for they will be filled.
'Blessed are the merciful, for they will receive mercy.
'Blessed are the pure in heart, for they will see God.
'Blessed are the peacemakers, for they will be called children of God.
'Blessed are those who are persecuted for righteousness' sake, for theirs is the kingdom of heaven.
'Blessed are you when people revile you and persecute you and utter all kinds of evil against you falsely on my account. Rejoice and be glad, for your reward is great in heaven, for in the same way they persecuted the prophets who were before you.' (Matthew 5.1–12)

These are still the most exciting words I have read, and the most challenging; still unfolding, still revealing, still saying to me: 'Have the courage to let go, have the courage to trust – the poorer you are the more you will make room; the more you mourn, the more your heart will be broken open to receive; the more you hunger, the more you will be filled; the more your soul expands with a mercy and compassion, the more you too find yourself flooded with the mercy of God. Have the courage to embrace purity, it is so much more beautiful than all that tempts you away. Embody the gift of the resurrection. Carry peace in your very heart, Christ's peace, even at the centre of the storms.'

I am wearing sandals and the stones keep lodging under the soles of my feet and between my toes. I do not rush. I feel the stones and the heat. I balance in the spaces between the potholes and along the edges of the furrows and turn and turn again to see the sea. Around me huge banana plantations are emerging on the side of this hill, swathed in netting with the fragrance of their ripening hands of fruit. I am breathless now, completely alone and yet completely not alone. This whole place breathes, sweats, whispers his presence. And the call is to turn, to look out into the crucible of creation and recognize the living presence of the one who crossed those waters and silenced the storm and called you up the mountain to be with him. 'Do you love me? Yes, Lord you know that I love you.'

Walking attentively so I do not stumble, I climb up and then across. I can see the Church of the Beatitudes above me, and below me, Galilee. The path is banked with rocks and tall grasses and blue thistles. Each time I stop I read a bit more of the Sermon on the Mount, the pages of my Bible flapping in the wind. 'But what I tell you is this ...' Christ's words open up a way of living that never seems possible and yet it is the only way, a way that strips bare and demands nothing less than everything and is so abundantly life-giving – such a song, not of negation but of the fullness of God's love and the utter unconditionality of that love. It is not something narrowing and confining, it's like climbing a mountain and there, breathless on the summit, seeing the incarnation, the wonder of the entire world infused with Jesus.

At the top I negotiate my way round a fence and back on to the road. The tour coaches and taxis follow. I pause in an olive plantation and hang my walking stick on the branch of a tree while I take photos and then set off and have to come all the way back for my hanging walking stick, my shepherd's crook. 'Feed my sheep.' 'What, me?' At the Church of the Beatitudes there are many people arriving. The woman in the gift shop is getting cross because people are touching things they shouldn't be touching, and at the cafe the group of women in front of me are trying to order fancy coffees. 'I'll have a caramel latte,' one woman demands. 'This is not Starbucks,' the man says, and everyone laughs. 'You can have coffee with milk or without milk.' I am searching to get away from the crowds up here, but it's all fenced in. An American tour guide in front of me is explaining to a group in front of me: 'This man Jesus was like a long-haired hippy and he just went all around this place workin' all kinda' miracles.' I need to get away. And then I find a break in the fence and a rough unformed path down into the olive trees, beyond which the whole of the Sea of Galilee is stretched out. And I sit down with a thump in the thistles and dry grasses, the thorns and brambles scratching my arms and legs – the voices of the crowd, distant. I am surrounded by the soft haze of afternoon and the peace that comes from following Jesus up a mountain and holding him in my heart – or rather him holding me in my heart. It is good to be here.

PART FIVE

Nazareth the Place of Struggle and Hope

Letter 48: Catching Covid

June 2022

A month ago I was climbing the Mount of Beatitudes, feeling so full of life and faith, and last week I was lying on my bed feeling so unwell. How strange life is and yet how important that we include both the ups and the downs so that all of life becomes part of our journey and part of the revelation of our faith. The journey into understanding is doing just that, *standing under* – under both the revelation of wonder but also sometimes standing under the fear or the darkness that seems to overwhelm.

Last month in Tabgha by the Sea of Galilee, by the lake that Jesus silenced and walked upon, it felt to me as if I was inside the gospel. I was walking the Beatitudes.

It's now three weeks later and I am in London. I begin to shiver. I've just swum in the Hampstead Heath pond so perhaps I've got too cold. But it's a hot day; perhaps I've got heat stroke, or am I dehydrated as the sun has been hot on my back. And yet in my bones, in the core of my body, I feel cold. I cycle home. I take a lateral flow test. For over two years, somehow I have escaped this virus that has infected the world. Somehow even though active at St Martin's I have stayed healthy, but now as I look at my slide, so used to seeing one stripe, I am surprised to see two red stripes emerging, faint at first but growing darker. I wish the second red line away but it's there, a positive test. I send a text to our clergy team and go to bed and sleep, hot but unable to get warm.

I am so fortunate I do not get Covid-19 badly, but enough to know or glimpse how others must have suffered. Fortunately, despite a cough, my chest remains unconstricted but I can imagine how frightening it must be to fear that you are suffocating, unable to breathe and alone. Alone, perhaps that's the worst of it. This virus can drain your strength. They say it is like flu but to me it feels different. It feels as if the spirit, even the spirit of prayer, is being sucked out of me. It makes me feel heavy, like a flat battery that can no longer retain its charge. Life too feels somehow empty. Empty like a wine skin from which all the joy and celebration has already been sucked out.

I read back what I wrote by the Sea of Galilee, which felt so heartfelt at the time but with Covid sounds like it comes from a different world. I had felt so full of God. Now I am finding it very hard even to pray. A kind of spiritual lethargy is within me. Today the words I wrote in Galilee, when I read them back, sound more like the street evangelist outside my door. Rather than converting me to God they sound more like self-delusion.

St Ignatius talks about consolation and desolation. Martin Laird describes depression or desolation as being like a squatter who turns up and sets up camp within us and we don't know when or if the squatter will depart or how much mess will be made. Desolation can sometimes feel like being inside a mess that you do not have the strength to clear up. My mother, who suffered from depression, told me that it helped her to name the despair – to realize it is not you and to know that it will depart. But I believe there is another learning in emptiness. It is the learning of how much we long for God. We all fear dependence. We all fear at some moments of our lives that we cannot cope. We fear there is no way out. But perhaps, as Martin Laird says: 'The way out is the way in.' We have been taught from an early age to fear our weakness and that to survive we must be self-sufficient. But perhaps when we are unwell, or when we experience powerlessness or emptiness, it is then that we learn how much we depend on God. Sometimes you have to be empty to learn that lesson. We are healed not by pride or our own righteousness. We are healed by grace. We want to know, of course, how long we will remain empty. But it is perhaps only when we are truly empty that we are empty of self, enough to be filled by God. St Augustine believed that there is nothing in our lives, no matter how defeating, that is beyond God's ability to use for the discovery of grace and our good. I am reminded of the words that are sung on Easter morning in the Exsultet: 'O happy fault, O necessary sin of Adam, which gained for us so great a Redeemer!'[1]

I believe there is a way, rather than fighting our sense of fallenness, of of resting in that place and not making war on ourselves but recognizing that we are those who live in need of God's redemptive love. What I am describing is not always possible. It's hard to believe anything good can come out all things. But times of desolation can also become times of transition, times entrusted to us to listen to the Christ who promises us the Comforter, the one who will fill us with new life.

> Let us stand, then, in the interval
> of our wounding, till the silence
> turn golden and love is
> a moment eternally overflowing.
> (R. S. Thomas[2])

I think of the disciples in a locked room and I think of the Spirit that comes like tongues of fire, like a rushing wind. I believe that this Spirit will lead us.

> We have this treasure in clay jars, so that it may be made clear that this extraordinary power belongs to God and does not come from us. We are afflicted in every way, but not crushed; perplexed, but not driven to despair; persecuted, but not forsaken; struck down, but not destroyed; always carrying in the body the death of Jesus, so that the life of Jesus may also be made visible in our bodies. For while we live, we are always being given up to death for Jesus' sake, so that the life of Jesus may also be made visible in our mortal flesh. So death is at work in us, but life in you. (2 Corinthians 4.7–12)

Wonderings

I wonder if you have ever had a revelation when you have felt at the top of the world.
I wonder if you have had a revelation when you have felt at the bottom of life.
I wonder how you experience the Holy Spirit, the Comforter.
I wonder what Martin Laird means when he writes: 'The way out is the way in.'

Letter 49: The Call to Humility

July 2022

At the beginning of this month I had the huge privilege of leading the retreat for those getting ordained in the London Diocese. There were 54 women and men who gathered at the Royal Foundation of St Katherine's. There should have been 55, but Francesco, from our Nazareth Community, the Sunday before had a bad accident on his bike. I have been visiting him every day, in the critical trauma unit at St Mary's hospital. There he lies tenderly cared for by his partner Felix and his sister, and his father who has flown in from Sicily and who keeps bursting into tears. For these days it is as though he is on a precipice. It is so frightening. Francesco seems to rally when I see him. Perhaps it is all the prayers that are being offered for him. There is an outpouring of prayer, so much so that it feels palpable. Francesco being borne up by your prayers like the man whose friends carried him to Jesus. He lies looking beaten up by the accident but reaches out to hold my hand and thank me for the prayers of the Nazareth Community and for coming to see him. He keeps saying to me, almost pleading, 'I want to be ordained!' It is deeply humbling, here on the edge of our mortality, in great pain because of his head injury, to witness the calling of God within him like a light. His greatest longing is to serve God. It really is.

And thanks be to God, those prayers and all our prayers are being answered. Francesco is continuing to make a remarkable recovery. Francesco, the name that reminds us of the gentle saint of Assisi who said something like, 'Remember when you go off to the church to preach the gospel that your journey to the church is also part of your sermon.' Our journey to our destination is part of our destination. The way we get there is also the gospel. True for Francesco; also true of each one of us.

The other great Francis is this one: St Francis de Sales said, 'Have patience to walk with small steps until you have wings to fly.'[1] Witnessing the love and care Francesco is receiving, I am also made aware of the truth of St Francis de Sales' words: 'Great occasions for serving God may come seldom but little ones surround us daily.'[2] Here in this hospital room, the sacrament of service to God has already begun.

Back at the retreat, Roger, the Master of St Katherine's, welcomes me and says, 'You must be feeling very nervous taking the retreat for so many. What a huge responsibility to be preparing them for such an important moment in their lives.' Yes, I am nervous of course, but I am not nervous too because I am held in your prayers. I really know that and feel it within. Also, because I hope it is not me who will take the retreat. I must be the one who stands aside and lets them see Jesus: 'Here is the Lamb of God who takes away the sin of the world!' (John 1.29) – to be with him, to hold and be held in his presence. As John the Baptist says, 'He must increase, but I must decrease' (John 3.30). It is Jesus whom they have come to see, come to serve. To know that within me is humbling and liberating.

St Francis de Sales said, 'In everything, love simplicity.'[3] The word 'deacon' means someone called to serve at the table. It's strangely counter-cultural this idea that a true leader should really be the servant of all, especially relevant at this time when our nation's leadership has been revealed to be so lacking in truth, so self-serving. Before leading this retreat I reread a book by former Archbishop of Canterbury Michael Ramsey, published in 1972, called *The Christian Priest Today*. It's still incredibly wise and relevant not just to priests and deacons but to all those who like Peter feel this call to serve Christ the servant King.

Michael Ramsey wrote that if we want to make Christ known it is only possible by recovering this sense of true service:

It remains that there is only one kind of *person* who makes God known and realized by other people, and that is the person who is humble, because he knows God and knows God because he is humble. There is no substitute for this. It is only a humble priest who is authoritatively a man [or woman] of God, one who makes God real to [their] fellows. May it one day be said of you, not necessarily that you talked about God cleverly, but that you made God real to people … only humility can do that.[4]

Again and again in the Gospels we hear this call to humility:

After [Jesus] had washed their feet, had put on his robe, and had returned to the table, he said to them, 'Do you know what I have done to you? You call me Teacher and Lord – and you are right, for that is what I am. So if I, your Lord and Teacher, have washed your feet, you also ought to wash one another's feet. For I have set you an example, that you also should do as I have done to you. (John 13.12–15)

For we do not proclaim ourselves; we proclaim Jesus Christ as Lord, and ourselves as servants for Jesus' sake. For it is the God who said, 'Let light shine out of darkness', who has shone in our hearts to give the light of the knowledge of the glory of God in the face of Jesus Christ. (2 Corinthians 4.5–6)

But we have this treasure in clay jars, so that it may be made clear that this extraordinary power belongs to God and does not come from us. (2 Corinthians 4.7)

And all of you must clothe yourselves with humility in your dealings with one another, for
   'God opposes the proud
     but gives grace to the humble.' (1 Peter 5.5)

I wonder if you look back on your life and recognize those who really showed you the path of God and walked with you. Were they not the ones who somehow embodied this sense of humility and openness with the transparent acknowledgement that they themselves were not the know-it-alls or the saviours; rather, they pointed beyond themselves to the wonder of God who alone can lift, heal and redeem? Have we not all, stumbling under the weight of the contradictions of our lives, for a fleeting moment glimpsed the possibility of rediscovering within ourselves this place of humility, simplicity and light? Is this discovery not the discovery of Nazareth?

Our life patterns have been destabilized by a pandemic that has swept the world, and a climate crisis that is more and more impossible to ignore. We are horrified by the war in the Ukraine, shocked by duplicity in leadership, confused by the failures of nation, horrified by the self-interest of our western priorities and values. Have we not glimpsed in Christ the possibility of true freedom and authentic love? Have we not, somewhere deep within us, heard again the profound call of the gospel, the call to be bearers and messengers of hope, the call to love God and to love our neighbour as ourselves? How do we recover that? St Augustine wrote that human pride sinks us all so low that only divine humility can raise us up. But how is it we live this Nazareth call? Well, just as you learn to run by running, you learn to listen by listening, you learn to pray by praying and you learn to love by loving. At the very heart of the retreat, the words I hold on to from St Francis de Sales are 'Live Jesus'.

Michael Ramsey writes this:

We are called, near to Jesus and with Jesus and in Jesus, *to be with God with the people on our heart* ...

Your prayer then will be a rhythmic movement of all your powers, moving into the divine presence in contemplation and moving into the needs of the people in intercession. In contemplation you will reach into the peace and stillness of God's eternity, in intercession you will reach into the rough and tumble of the world of time and change ...

It means putting yourself near God, with God, in a time of quietness every day. You put yourself with him just as you are, in the feebleness of your concentration, in your lack of warmth and desire, not trying to manufacture pious thoughts or phrases. You put yourself with God, empty perhaps, but hungry and thirsty for him; and if in sincerity you cannot say that you want God you can perhaps tell him that you want to want him; and if you cannot say even that perhaps you can say that you want to want to want him! Thus you can be very near him in your naked sincerity; and *he* will do the rest, drawing out from you longings deeper than you knew were there and pouring into you a trust and a love like that of the psalmist ... I am trying to say that you will find you are 'with God' not by achieving certain devotional exercises in his presence but by daring to be your own self as you reach towards him ...

There is no by-passing the Psalmist's wisdom, 'Be still and know that I am God.'[5]

Wonderings

I wonder if you agree with Michael Ramsey that it is a person of humility who makes God known. Who is that person in your life?
I wonder how it is possible to live those words, 'Christ must increase, I must decrease.'
I wonder what you are living for.
I wonder how you can 'live Jesus'.

Letter 50: Being with Jesus – Resurrection on the Beach

9 July 2022

The story of Mary and Martha is a very identifiable one in our own lives. Martha is busy and distracted by her many tasks and annoyed with her sister Mary, who seems to have left her to do all the work while she just sits at the feet of Christ and listens to what he is saying. And much to our surprise it is Mary's side Jesus seems to take: 'Martha, Martha, you are worried and distracted by many things; there is need of only one thing. Mary has chosen the better part, which will not be taken away from her' (Luke 10.41–42). Mary certainly seems to have got the better deal. Wouldn't we all rather be sitting at the feet of Jesus than slaving away in the kitchen? Have we not all been brought up with a work ethic that makes us feel rather guilty about doing nothing? We have to do stuff, get things achieved. If we rest, it is so that we can work more efficiently. And isn't that right? Unless Martha was busy in the kitchen getting everything ready, there would be nothing to eat and no occasion for either of them to meet with Jesus.

So why does Jesus seemingly take Mary's side? This story has often been seen as advocating the path of contemplation and prayer over and against the path of action. But I think this passage is about much more than that. It is a call into relationship and physical presence with God, to meet with God and to be transformed by that meeting. But how often it is that our processes and practices begin to dominate and themselves become the end rather than the means to an end. Think of a wedding where the event planning becomes more important than the profession of love. Think of a Christmas celebration where the stress of preparation of food and gifts becomes the focus of the occasion to such an extent that the being together is like an afterthought. Think of a church where the management and meetings and the maintenance and business plans begin to dominate to such an extent that the encounter with Christ is all but pushed out and forgotten. I've just been taking a retreat for ordinands and am acutely aware of how easy it is for the externals to dominate. You can become so caught up in the busyness of being a priest that you lose the very reason you were called in the first place to come into the presence of God yourself and draw others into the presence of God too, so that you are transformed by that encounter. How many priests no longer have time to pray, to open their church or to meet people because they are too busy or overloaded?

A friend of mine, John Plummer, phoned me a couple of days ago. 'I feel so useless,' he said. 'I'm really passed my sell-by date and I can no longer do what I want to do. I am no longer fit for purpose.' I have known my friend for several years. He is a phenomenal campaigner for social justice and prison reform; he has literally given his life for it. He is the tireless writer of emails and convener of meetings, forever rallying supporters and pushing the cause of greater justice forward. But recently his health has declined and he has been in and out of hospital. I have also noticed that the busyness of all the committee meetings and campaigning has distracted us from the reason we came in the first place, which was to become prison visitors. 'I have to admit I find going to church very difficult, you see,' he says. 'I realize I am not really very interested in praying. I want to get things achieved.' I am very fond of this man. I admire him so greatly and all he does. We need people like him so much. But I remind him gently that it is not he who can save the world single-handedly, and perhaps he still needs God's help for that. The reason we come to church is that we need not only to do and achieve but to allow God, and God incarnated in the lives of others, into our lives. Make space for that, make space for relationship: it is ultimately the most important thing we have. Don't become so busy with advocacy that you lose the relationship with those you are advocating for and with. Don't become so busy that you stop being present. 'Physician heal yourself.'

You see, there is no point in being a Martha if we do not also rediscover in ourselves the importance of being Mary. Those of us who love to be busy, or love to see ourselves as busy, sometimes fear having nothing to do or nothing to control. We fear not being able to prove our worth. We would rather be in the kitchen or office, or busy on the internet, because the relationships that are most important and need time, care, conversation, listening and healing, have dried up through lack of attention.

So what does the encounter with Christ look like? What does it mean to sit with Jesus? Rather than try to explain, I will tell you the real story of such an encounter.

The Saturday before last, early in the morning, the guests of our Sunday International Group began arriving early and waiting on the steps of St Martin's. It was our annual day trip to the seaside in Worthing. We had needed some Martha-type planning to get things in place but now was the time for being with. The jackets and heavy coats and suitcases and bags that weigh down our refugees and international guests – a reminder of life on the streets – were not needed for this day and could be stowed under the stairs next door. The sky was still cloudy but blue sky was breaking through. The air-conditioned coach arrived and 50 of us climbed inside from so many different parts of the world.

It feels like liberation leaving this city behind. We are all, for this day, leaving behind the hostile environment our nation has created. We are shedding the past like a skin, and for this time together discovering the joy of the moment. We pile out of the coach on Worthing seafront, carrying Primark bags full of cheap shorts and brightly coloured beach towels. Down on the beach the young deckchair attendant, after asking who we are and finding out that many of us are homeless, decides to give us the loan of all the deckchairs for nothing. This is the day of free grace. Music is playing and along the promenade is Worthing's Gay Pride Celebration – a joyful procession with rainbow streaks on faces and children holding the hands of their grandparents waving rainbow flags.

Down on the beach our International Group have changed, shed the weight and grime of the city, and the human spirit is emerging from the chrysalis of all that weighs down and oppresses. That spirit is beautiful. 'Where has the sea gone?' asks Yubraj, mystified. He has never seen a low tide before. But then 60 boxes of fish and chips arrive with Daniel and Sarah, and with our hands we are eating fresh fish and squirting deep red tomato sauce on our chips and fingers, and everyone is sharing out cups of ice-cold water from the bottles Dan has kept in the freezer all night and which are now defrosting on the sunny beach. The fish and chips are delicious and salty and fresh and feel deserved. No one is counting calories but licking their fingers and laughing. It may be lunchtime but this is the resurrection breakfast by the Sea of Galilee, and we are sharing this resurrection breakfast because no one has had any breakfast and we are making up for lost time – alive again.

Later, we wade out into the sea, many holding hands to help each other over the sharp stones, shells and slippery seaweed until we are all in deeper water – and then swimming. Some are learning to swim for the first time and Yubraj is teaching them doggy paddle, and I am explaining how if they relax they will float. Olga from Ukraine stands in the sea in her underwear, scooping the water up in her hands. It is the happiest I have seen her since she arrived, having to leave her son behind in her war-torn homeland. Fouad, who has come from the devastation of Syria, is out deep, swimming like a dolphin, with plumes of water coming up behind him as he dives and turns and flashes through the sea.

Back on the beach where everyone is basking in the sun on beach towels, Frances has arrived with boxes of choc ices and our International Group are lavishly coating and protecting each other's backs with suntan cream that someone else is generously handing around. Everyone is helping someone else, making sure that everyone has what they need. A parable is taking place in our midst. Word is being made flesh. John, with his long beard and big heart, is struggling to get up from the beach and looking weak and breathless. And I look around and see, quick as a flash, he has helpers: Daniel and Yubraj, Angela and Michael Okoroporo are helping him, and Ebenezer is behind him, steadying him to stop him falling. They are holding him and carrying him from the beach with such care and tender respect. Wendy at my side whispers, 'It's like watching the friends carrying the paralysed man to Jesus.' They find him a seat and bring him water. If only life was always like this. It is, and it can be again. The following day I hear the elderly John has Covid and I phone Daniel, Yubraj, Angela and Michael to see if they are all right and advise them to self-test. Real kindness is sacrificial and never without its cost. Fortunately, all four remain Covid-free.

On the beach our lives opened up. The pallid winter skin, the shut-in feelings and weighed-down lives were being warmed by the sun. Resurrection came this day. And as we got off the coach everyone said it was the best day they have ever had in England. Perhaps nothing had changed but perhaps this day everything had changed. We were all human beings again, equal, unjudged and free. We discovered our humanity again. Resurrection is not a transaction or a policy or a cause, it is a gift given and received. Resurrection is being with one another. It is being in the presence of Christ. It is relationship. It is the poetry of an encounter with Christ that will stay in our hearts for ever. The one thing that is needed. We, like Mary, have chosen the better part and it will not be taken away from us. That's why we need not to be distracted by too many things, to be with one another and to be with God.

Letter 51: The Olive Tree

Ithaca, Greece, August 2022

I am writing this letter to you early in the morning, sitting down by the side of the sea in Ithaca, Greece. There is a cockerel crowing and the birds are singing, and I also hear the sound of the cicadas beginning their carefree call. Homer in *The Iliad* mentions cicadas 'that chirrup delicately from the boughs of some high tree in the wood'. It is so much the sound of this place during the heat of the day. But I am not in a wood; rather, I am surrounded by olive trees. What sacred trees. These here were planted over 100 years ago and I love their old, sinewed, twisted trunks and the bends and turns that branch out like muscled limbs into the tangle of slender shoots and the fans of their soft, arrowed leaves. The underbelly of these leaves are a pale soft green and the outer side a darker emerald glossy green. As the breeze catches them the leaves toss and turn and their different shades shimmer like pale silver in the sunlight. Their top branches stand erect and rustle like heads of tussled bleached hair. Through the dart-like leaves shine slithers of sun, dappled light and shadow, so that they magically shimmer. In these trees the small green olives are forming that will be harvested in November and December for their precious virgin oil, what Homer referred to as 'liquid gold'. They comb the olives from the branches and gather them in nets. The family here pride themselves on the taste of their own virgin olive oil, which will be enough for their extended family and guests for the year.

These trees are a symbol of abundance, wisdom, glory and most of all peace. The olive branch is of course the sign of life and hope after the great flood in Genesis: 'the dove came back to him in the evening, and there in its beak was a freshly plucked olive leaf; so Noah knew that the waters had subsided from the earth' (Genesis 8.11). Yesterday we went out for a meal and on the tables on the terrace below, along the white tablecloths, there were winding olive branches and leaves and candles floating in glass bowls to celebrate a wedding. The guests arriving, olive skinned, in soft white, pale greens and blues, seemed to be filled with the warmth of the same Mediterranean light, land and sea.

Beyond the olive trees is the Ionian sea. Its surface this morning is rippling and alive with refracting light, each ripple a mirror of the rising sun. At times a cobalt blue, at others a beautiful aquamarine sparkling in an undulating sheen of light, and above the sea the lighter cornflower blue of the sky with long trails of soft white cloud. It is a sea that constantly invites you to swim, to enter into the blue.

But I have come down to the sea this morning to pray and to write to all of you. I am alone this morning sitting here. We have been together with my brother's family, with my niece Molly and nephew Jack, who are 21 and 17. How wonderful it has been to explore this island with them and the freshness of their eyes and joy they bring. We stand at the two ends of our lives. They are beginning the race, while I for the first time am seeking to reach the finish line. Molly is in training to run the London Marathon for charity, while I sometimes feel like the marathon runner who has slowed down a little in the final stretch and, looking around for the first time, wonders if their legs will make it. My nephew and niece are so supple and fit, they run so fast, out each morning to run 9 km before breakfast. I, in contrast, have begun to feel the aches of the journey. At the same time, I have become more aware of a world alive with miracles and the wonder of this life. I want to slow down, to stop and take it all in. It's taken me all this time to appreciate all we have been given. I long to hold the moment rather than race on. This time now will not come again. With Molly and Jack I delight in the energy of their youth and their lives opening up with opportunities and future hopes, and of course, as one does for all those you love, fear for them for the unknown future we know that all must face, while trusting in their goodness. For myself I realize how much the past has made me who I am, the love, the pain, the achievements and failures. And yet how important it is to live with love now and savour the present. The stiller I become, the more attentive, the more I am astonished by the beauty of the world and the more I feel its pain.

Yesterday they left to go home. I am so aware of how holy days are a gift to be lived *now*. You have to live the wonder of the moment. For suddenly the moment is gone and days lived become a memory, an emptiness. Today my sister-in-law is on a South Western train, making the trip up to St Thomas' Hospital where she works. I told her before she left to land gently and take the light and the blue of the sea with her. She was lying on a very rickety wooden sun-lounger which was digging into her back in warm sun. In her garden in England she has an olive tree she took home from here several years ago and planted to help her through the winter. Today she texts me from the train: 'Oh, Richard, I am having to remind myself that all our fun time together wasn't just a dream. One day we will all have lots of time to enjoy ... Very clammy here and the water ban starts today. Just boarding my train and will close my eyes thinking I am swimming on an Ithacan beach. Sending lots of love from an overcrowded South Western.'

I think of London and I know that somehow each one of us is called to carry the light, the wonder of the sea and the olive branch with us and to live the future filled with a constant faith in Christ's mercy. Today it is a Thursday, so wherever we are the Nazareth Community will try to keep a time of silence and contemplative prayer together. Jamie has just sent this early morning's thought for the day for us all on WhatsApp: 'We do not seek silence to escape from the world. Rather, we seek silence to rediscover our humanity and a world infused by God. Neither do we seek silence to escape others but to find them.'[1]

The Jesus Prayer

What I am learning is that we cannot live disembodied lives. Our hearts, our heads and our bodies are one. We need to hold that life together and not let ourselves become compartmentalized, fragmented by anxiety and distraction, or let our lives become divorced from our souls. Even in the city, perhaps most of all in the city, we need to enter into that cobalt blue sea of God – all of us, all our bodies, all our memories – to be immersed in God's presence. It's not a thing we *do*. It's a relationship with all that we *are*. Jesus does not tell us *who* he is. He tells us *whose* he is. 'The Father and I are one' (John 10.30). We are not created to be in competition. We are created to rejoice, each in the beauty of the other, and to live with the beauty of the sun, the sky, the olive tree and humanity within us. How would I describe this union? This is what the Greeks call *theosis*, θέωσις – it is the place of no division – where the *mine* becomes *our*.

Lord Jesus Christ,
Son of God,
have mercy on us.

I am praying the Jesus Prayer, which comes from the ancient Orthodox tradition. It seems wholly right to be praying the Jesus Prayer here in Ithaca. 'Pray at all times,' St Paul reminds us. The Jesus Prayer is our olive branch. It is his presence within us. The noise, prattle, addiction, materialism and, most of all, fear within our modern world shatter our souls into fragments. But in this prayer Jesus draws us back into his very heart. This prayer is not concerned with abstract concepts of the mind but, through calling upon the name of Jesus, we are called into the place of encounter and the realization that nothing is outside Christ's mercy. The word for mercy in Greek is *elios* (ἔλεος) and the word that sounds very similar, which the Greek Fathers connected with the word mercy, is *elaion* (ἔλαιον) – olive oil.

I want to reflect upon how that symbol of olive oil can help us to understand the nature of mercy that is at the heart of this prayer. First, olive oil is something that we eat. In Greece the olive is one of the basic ingredients of Mediterranean cuisine. As a nutritious food and pure oil it feeds us and has been grown, eaten and used in cooking since the eighth millennium BC. Second, olive oil has long been used for cleansing. It is used in soaps and cosmetics. Not only does it cleanse but it leaves the skin moisturised and nourished. Third, since ancient times, it has been used for healing. Think of the good Samaritan who pours oil on the injured man's wounds. Olive oil is known for its healing properties, not only for the skin and for wounds but also for its ability to be a good oil, an anti-oxidant, a good cholesterol that can in fact lower the risk of heart disease. The use of olive oil as opposed to other fats can reduce blood glucose levels. Fourth, olive oil is the source of light. It is used to fill the oil lamps of the Orthodox chapels here and across the Middle East. Fifth, olive oil is sacramental; it is used for anointing as a sign of identity and belonging. You are signed with blessed olive oil at your baptism and by the bishop at confirmation. I remember watching a young boy being baptized in Kefalonia. After his emersion in the water, his whole body was covered with olive oil and he was lifted up, fragrant and shining, to be reclothed in white. It was like watching someone being reborn. When I was ordained as a priest I was anointed with oil, and the sign of the cross was made on the palms of my hands, my forehead, my lips, my heart.

The call for mercy in the Jesus Prayer is not a wallowing in our sin or guilt, it is the compassion and forgiveness that will be the food that sustains us and becomes the basis of all that we are. God's mercy will cleanse you and hydrate your body and your soul. It will be your healing outside and in, the wounds of your body and the wounds of all that is within you, touched by God. This is a healing that detoxifies and frees your heart. God's mercy will be the light of your life, a lamp that is always being refilled with oil. It will, if you receive it with gladness, keep that light within you always burning. And like olive oil, God's mercy will anoint you. It will be the seal of your belonging, your baptism, your confirmation, your sign that you are God's beloved and that nothing can separate you from that love. At the end of your life this olive oil will be the final sacrament of holy unction, the sign of the cross on your forehead, that you belong to God both in this world and beyond death for all eternity.

So in this prayer, this prayer of Jesus, we call upon the name of Jesus. His name means 'saviour'. And a name has power, for it calls the person into our presence. It names them and in so doing it makes us aware of our relationship with them and they aware of their relationship with us. It is their name, a name that is unique to them and yet, in a name, tells of the mystery of all that they are, and cannot be spoken. If you call a name, the person whose name you call will turn. In the calling of the name of Jesus we are invoking him, looking towards him to see him turn to us, calling him closer, realizing that we are not only calling him but that he is calling us by name too. The chosen one has chosen us to be our saviour and to turn to him.

In this prayer we are also repeating his name and by doing so we are entering into the uninterrupted presence of the one we name. The repetition stills the restlessness of our wandering thoughts. As it calls upon his name, it calls us back, gently, to rest in his presence. The prayer moves from lips, to mind, to heart, to silence. In this call there is both yearning and belonging. Repetition becomes rhythm, the rhythm of our breathing, the rhythm of our heart, the rhythm of God's life in us. It is what in Greek they call *hesychia* – a silence that makes room, a stillness in which we can find rest, a contemplation that finds its centre in a wisdom that is at our centre yet always beyond us, an inner and outer peace where we are freed from compulsion and where the mind, heart and body become one. In this prayer it is as if there is a to and fro – like a breathing in and a breathing out – a movement towards Jesus as we call upon his name; a moving of Christ towards us in unconditional compassion, taking away our sins. We breathe in his name, we breathe out his mercy that frees us, and with that breath, all that has held us captive.

Saying this prayer is something physical. It is a prayer that embodies all our senses and unites word, posture, breath and being. It brings our minds into our hearts as we simply go on repeating the words until the prayer prays itself and we ourselves become the prayer. Rowan Williams describes the physicality of prayer, God praying within you, in this way:

like an indistinct picture or sensation of the inside of the body, a sort of hollow, a cave, in which the breath comes and goes, with an underlying pulse ... it's a time when you are aware of your body as simply a place where life happens and where, therefore, God happens: a life lived in you ... Your own individual existence is breathed through by a life that isn't your possession.[2]

I think of my soul like the sand and shingle on the beach, which each wave of the sea sweeps over and then draws out, leaving the beach cleansed, and drawing you out with the receding wave into the depth of the sea. This in and out, this with and beyond, is the mystery of this prayer – and of course beyond the prayer it is the mystery of Christ himself, calling you to himself.

Sometimes in our western tradition we have understood mercy in legalistic terms: satisfaction, atonement for sin, Christ taking the punishment for our sin. But the mercy of which this prayer speaks is not about guilt for breaking a rule, it is the call of Christ for us to become all that God intended. Through that love of Christ there is *metanoia*, transformation of heart, the gift of freedom and renewed choice: the choice to return to God and like the returning prodigal to be clothed and raised by the one who watches and waits for all his children. This mercy is always there but is only realized when we too come to our senses and remember the one who loves us. This *theosis* becomes not judgement but deliverance and return. This mercy is homecoming. It does not negate the pain or the suffering of the cross but it reveals that God's mercy can never be defeated by the sin of the world, that this love of God is stronger even than death.

And what is required of us?
Recognition
Realizing our humility
Repeating our call to Jesus
Return
Resurrection
Again and again and again.

As I write to you the rain has begun. The clouds are now blocking out the sun. At first, I continue writing under the shelter of an olive tree, but the rain is getting harder. I drop off my things in the shelter of the house and come back to the beach to enjoy the rain. It's really pouring down now, huge droplets of rain, and rainwater is running off the hills and down gushing rivulets into the sea. The path to the beach has quickly become a stream. Morning 7.00 a.m. meditation is beginning with Angela at St Martin's. I listen to her opening prayers with rainwater running down my neck. How wonderful to be praying together with all of you across the miles. But it's too wet to sit and pray. Instead, I take off my shirt and shoes and plunge into the sea. The sea is warmer than the rain and a haze of steam is rising above the water. The water is dancing as raindrops hit the surface of the sea and bounce in millions of tiny volcanoes of silver splash through which I swim. The horizon disappears into the haze and I hear the crack of thunder. In the distance I see a yacht coming out of the blue-grey sailing towards me. What joy to swim in this rain, body warmed by the sea, face showered with pelting freshness – swimming through heaven's teardrops of new life for a thirsty land. Lord Jesus Christ, Son of God, have mercy on me. I breathe in – 'Lord Jesus Christ, Son of God'. I breathe out into the sea – 'Have mercy on me a sinner.'

Back on the land the silence is ending and Angela, live-streamed from St Martin's, is singing so beautifully our closing prayer.

Letter 52: The Busy World is Hushed

14–19 September 2022,
the Death of Queen Elizabeth II

So much has been said about the death of the late Queen Elizabeth II. On Thursday 8 September, when the news was announced, there was a storm and the rain poured down, like a biblical portent. The night was restless and disturbed with a huge sense of uncertainty and sorrow within us all. Seventy years is a very long time to be queen and most of us could not remember a time without her. Her death has awakened our own memories and histories. She has been part of all of our lives, our *common wealth*. Her life, indeed the life of her whole family and all the stories that surround them, are woven into our own stories too: the weddings, the jubilees, the tragedies and losses, the celebrations and appearances have become markers in our lives – like a national family album.

Now the clips are playing constantly – the flickering black and white shots of her as a young girl playing in the garden, wearing a uniform at the end of the Second World War, her marriage to the dashing Prince Philip, Treetops in Kenya, hearing the news of her father King George VI's death, coming down the steps of the plane upon her return wearing black on a bleak grey day, the film of her coronation in June 1953 by Archbishop Geoffrey Francis Fisher, the heavy encrusted vestments, the anointing, the heavy crown, the birth of her children, Charles, Anne, Andrew, Edward. I remember, aged ten, my Welsh primary school teacher, of whom I was terrified, saying that she was proud that her son Charles was invested as Prince of Wales. The Queen was there, dressed in yellow with a hat, like my mum used to wear, presenting Bobby Moore with the World Cup in 1966, at times of national disaster and tragedy like Aberfan, her trips all over the Commonwealth, those precious vowel sounds in her Christmas messages that sounded so posh as she wished 'mankind a very happy and blessed Christmas'. We lived alongside the marriages, the breakdowns and of course the watershed death of Princess Diana, when things seemed to change. The Christmas broadcasts softened and revealed more heart, the meetings became more real, more genuine, the human began to shine through the mask of majesty. She was there for us, at the opening of the Olympics, a nation confident to laugh at itself, and the Queen to take part with James Bond and a parachute jump, and later with Paddington Bear and marmalade sandwiches in her handbag.

I remember the Queen's visit to St Martin-in-the-Fields in 2016 for the Memorial Service for the Far East Prisoners of War. I had been so busy with the stress of organizing things that I had underestimated the impact it would have on me. As I lined up to shake her hand, I thought it would be like welcoming a very famous person or national celebrity. I had not realized her holiness. I felt it deeply within, it stilled me, her deep sense of humility. It was her faith I sensed, her prayerfulness. She knew my name and the fact that I served at St Martin's. She walked up the aisle reverently, she sat and bowed her head in prayer. I remember how proud I felt that this small woman was the head of my nation and the head of my church: a grandmother, a frail great-grandmother, with all of us under her wings.

In the week that followed her death what was so remarkable were the qualities that were being celebrated in a usually suspicious and often cynical nation, a nation whose headlines are usually dominated by failure, scandal, another damning exposure. Suddenly the same media is praising faithfulness, sacrificial service, humility, discretion, dedication, compassion, steadfast duty to others, courage in adversity, resilience and calm dignity in the face of tragedy, an ability to adapt and yet stay the same, and in all this a deep prayerfulness. How often she has spoken of the importance of her Christian faith on which all else is based. She has never answered back or paid back evil for evil. She has done unto others as she would have them do unto her. She has seen the best in people. As her family follow the gun carriage upon which her coffin is borne, I am aware how exposed they have been to all our scrutiny and how much pain she had to carry for those she loved. She has remained steadfast, holding fast to that which is good.

In these last days people have been streaming through St Martin's filling

several books of condolence with their prayers of sorrow and thankfulness. On Wednesday, while watching the 10 o'clock news, I decide to join
the queue to file past the Queen's coffin. On the news it says the queue
is only five hours long. It's my chance. 'That's very spontaneous,' says
my nephew George, who agrees to accompany me for the first couple
of hours. He feels then he must return, for it's his starting week at his
first law firm. And so we cross the footbridge at the Embankment and
my heart begins to sink as we search for the end of the queue that seems
to flow on for ever like the Thames itself. Finally we reach the end, by
Southwark Cathedral. And I start to queue. But for how long? 'That's
not a good question', advises my nephew George. 'You must treat it like
a marathon runner, just get in the zone.' I have never run a marathon
but he has and it's good advice. Be in the moment. If you constantly
think how much longer, you will never get there. He goes off to buy
me a hot chocolate while I enter 'the zone', the moment. The queue is
hushed. Indeed, London seems hushed and crystal clear, the buildings lit
up against the night sky. I love this city. We move and then stop, move
and then stop. But I am no longer rushing. I am here. George returns with
my hot chocolate and I thank him for his company and wisdom, and he
leaves.

Now the whole night has become a prayer. This is not a queue, it is a
pilgrimage. I am growing accustomed to the night and it's filling me with
its still beauty. What is more, the whole crowd that is queuing is hushed
too. They also have entered the meditation and we are quietly looking
after each other, conscious of each other's place and needs. When one of
us leaves the queue in search of toilets or a drink, the others are quietly
minding our place for us – as we flow upstream towards Westminster. I
love the diversity of our nation, here in this queue from every age, from
babies in prams to old-age pensioners, those with crutches or wheel-
chairs, and of every colour. In front of me is a young man with a brown
hooded jacket, next to me a husband, wife and two children allowed off
from school and trying to convince their mother that they don't need to
go back to school until Friday, every now and then going off in search of
food. Behind me an Indian family. These are my markers in the queue. No
one is grumbling or complaining. We have become a prayer, the prayer
of our queen, the prayer of our nation, flowing like a river, a parable of
life as we make our way towards the coffin of our queen. We are aware
of our mortality but aware too of all that lives on. Because that is why
we are here. I am travelling light, taking nothing with me. I am no longer
asking, 'How long?' I am happy for the night to last for ever.

George has lent me his earphones and I am listening to the chanting
of Benedictine monks as I slowly walk through the night past so many

places. I know the Globe, the National Theatre, the National Film Theatre, the Royal Festival Hall, behind the London Eye, towards the great St Thomas' Hospital with the statue of Mary Seacole. London is silhouetted against a clear sky. It is a beautiful night. The words of John Henry Newman's prayer fill me:

> O Lord, support us all the day long of this troublous life, until the shadows lengthen and the night comes and the busy world is hushed, the fever of life is over and our work is done; then, Lord, in thy mercy, grant us safe lodging, a holy rest and peace at the last, through Jesus Christ our Lord.

Now we are slowly walking along the Thames path in front of St Thomas', and we see the Covid memorial wall, covered with thousands and thousands of red hearts and messages to loved ones who died. The scale of the loss is overwhelming, the death of each person impacting on family, friends and the communities to which they belong – so many of them cut off when they died from those they loved. We like to think of each life as precious but when you see a wall like this it's a realization of the scale of things; this epidemic, like a battlefield in which suddenly the elderly became horrifyingly expendable, the collateral for the virus the government could not contain. I think of the Queen sitting alone at her own beloved husband's funeral.

Silence now. Slowly moving towards Lambeth Bridge. The queue stops and starts, held back, waiting, released again, getting ever closer to the Great Hall of Westminster. Then, when we seem almost there, we are filtered down into a fenced penning area, with hundreds of zigzags backwards and forwards. It's tempting to count the number of backwards and forwards tacks – it must be well over 100. Here too it's better not to count the turns but after so long on your feet this section feels like a labyrinth, so that just when you thought you had reached the centre you suddenly find yourself on the outside again, with a long way to go. Talk about the slough of despond! It's early morning and the Portaloos are in overdrive. From thinking I had arrived it's at least another two hours of ups-and-downs, and no longer the open Thames footpath, but much more like being trapped and caged in. Still there is no complaining. Perhaps it's only me feeling grumpy for the first time in the night. And then at last I am there and going through the metal detector and bag and pocket search. Huge quantities of food and drink are being discarded as they are not allowed through. But I am travelling light. The man in front has an expensive Swiss Army fruit knife which he is being told to throw in the bin. He is appealing, but to no avail. Now I am through and walking down in front of the Houses of Parliament to the entrance. All of a sudden I am inside Westminster Hall and being ushered down very wide, steep steps towards the Queen's coffin draped in a flag – it looks so small in these huge surroundings. This great hall feels like a tomb in which time has stopped still. A moment frozen in eternity. Around the coffin are the guard of honour, heads cocked forward, looking steadily at the ground, so still they could be waxworks until one moves almost imperceptibly. Attendants move forward and clear away the stalactites of molten wax that have formed from the candles. I wonder to how many of their family and friends they will tell this story.

The whole tableau is so grand, yet so movingly humble; so human, ultimately. Death, which will come to us all, is humbling. This is the destination of all our queueing: a small, still coffin. And the Queen, who has been alive all of our lives, is dead. The queue, having reached their destination, now file silently past; they sense the awe and the mystery of death but are unsure how now they should respond. All our lives I realize are part of this queue and all our lives will one day end in this same stillness and silence.

I follow the line of people down the steps. I stop, cross myself and say the Lord's Prayer to myself, wondering if someone will come and tell me to move on. There are others, who are being brought in from the other direction and have not had to wait all through the night. But while the privilege of jumping the queue may seem attractive, I do not envy or resent them because the meaning has been in the waiting. This has been a night that I will never forget. Through the beauty of the night we have waited and together been filled with a peace that is almost palpable. The first will be last and the last first. 'He has brought down the powerful from their thrones, and lifted up the lowly.'

Letter 53: My Life is with My Brother and Sister

Late September 2022

Last month I led a retreat about the fourth-century Desert Fathers and Mothers of Egypt, Palestine and Arabia, who abandoned the cities of that time to seek God in the desert. Their wisdom and teaching has been handed down to us in short sentences of wisdom, or short stories that later can be unravelled in the heart. And since Wednesday one sentence has been constantly in my mind, in this process of unravelling. It is this word from St Anthony the father of the desert, 'Our life and death is with our neighbour.'[1]

Outside my flat, as I try to write to you, there is a man on a megaphone. In fact he has been on it for the last hour shouting at passers-by. He is a so-called street evangelist. Every Saturday their pitch seems to be outside my window. Basically, they are shouting through the megaphone, over and over again, 'God loves you with an everlasting love. Jesus died for your sins.' (Repeat.) 'Jesus loves you with an everlasting love.' (Repeat.) 'Repent of your sins, or God will judge you and you will burn in an unquenchable fire.' (Repeat.) We have all heard such evangelists. I am sure they think they may be saving souls, but I wonder how many souls they drive away from God. They are certainly doing my head in. Tonight, the illogicality of what they are shouting into the megaphone seems more absurd than ever. This evangelist is not preaching good news at all; in fact, quite the opposite. His message is very threatening. How could Jesus who loves you with an everlasting love then proceed, if you fail to repent, to burn you in an unquenchable fire? We have heard some terrible stories of torture, but no torturer, however sadistic, has been able to master the art of torturing someone for ever. I wish I could turn off his megaphone for ever. Yet the gospel does contain stories of division and judgement. Think of the rich man and Lazarus, the rich man being tortured and tormented in Hades, who longs to cool his tongue from the agony of the flames because he failed to help poor Lazarus at his door.

The words I return to are these: 'Our life and death is with our neighbour.' If our life is with our neighbour then to turn your back on a brother or sister, or indeed to make war on our neighbour, is the negation of life. It is the turning away from everything God intended. We've all seen what that negation or destruction of life looks like in its extreme form. This week on our television screens we saw a steely Putin, his face rigid with hatred, threatening the western world with weapons of mass destruction. 'I am not bluffing,' he says, staring coldly into the camera. To make war on an innocent country is to sell one's soul to the devil. Make no mistake, this is hell, this all-consuming violence, this negation of life, where even innocent children are the targets of bombs and shells.

There is a different way. Like the Desert Fathers, let me tell some stories.

Our life and death is with our neighbour. His name is Lorenzo. Every day he sits on my steps. He has been diagnosed with motor neurone disease. And every day his movement becomes more difficult. I have never met a young man with such courage. After many years of homelessness, the Connection found him a place to live. But now he's finding it more and more impossible to climb the stairs. Each week he has been the most brilliant volunteer at the International Group, managing the showers that allow refugees and asylum seekers who have been sleeping on the streets to get washed and clean again. But now Lorenzo is finding it hard to hold anything in his hands, and so he comes just as a guest. He has travelled home to Europe to make his peace with his family. Now each day on my steps we chat. He knows all those who are homeless round here. They respect him. The know him to be without guile. When we had our refugee group day trip to Worthing, he gave me a roll of notes. It was £100. 'I would like to help pay for the day,' he says. 'It's money my friends gave to me.' 'Keep it for yourself,' I try to persuade him, 'it's for you to enjoy.' 'Yes,' he says, 'but this is my joy, to help all of you.' He was on my steps today, in so many ways the poorest and most unlucky; in many ways the richest young man I have ever met, facing his illness, at peace with himself, at peace with the world and with his knowledge of mortality. He has no bitterness, only goodwill. I have been a priest for 30 years but I long for his faith and his lightness of being.

Our life and death is with our neighbour. Last night I walked to Tesco. To get there I had to walk past three people lying on the street. One woman, very thin, has been lying outside Pret a Manger in the foetal position, her pale skin on raw pavement. We all walk past her, not wanting to get involved.

Last night at the supermarket I met one of the young shop assistants. He was the only one on the assisted cash till – all the other tills were self-service. I have seen this shop assistant every time I have been into Tesco. He didn't miss during lockdown. When the churches closed, and the homeless centres and night shelters were all shut because of Covid, he was there every day helping customers get their shopping so that they could eat. With his own money he often buys a bag of groceries that he gives to me because he says he knows I run a group that helps people who are homeless. He has even visited our Sunday International Group bringing contributions to our meal. No one clapped him during Covid but he went on serving in the store. Last night he told me they are going to close all the tills at Tesco and make it totally self-service to save money. 'Shame,' he said, 'because many of our customers are elderly and need a conversation or a bit of help from us.' Why are they doing that? I asked. 'Profit,' he said, 'but the people who make the decision are on large salaries in big offices. They don't know the people who come into this store. They have never been with us here on the shop floor.' What will it profit us if we gain the whole world but lose our immortal souls?

How can we say we love God? How can we say we love our neighbour as ourselves? If I love, really love, how can I tolerate the fact that so much of our world is threatened with loneliness, fear, poverty, war and climate catastrophe? Sometimes there are no answers. 'Our life and death is with our neighbour' acknowledges the struggle. And sometimes it is only when you know the bottom of things that you glimpse heaven.

Last week we saw a mini-budget that all the expert analysis says will make the gap between the rich and the poor of our nation even greater. We were told that the people who will profit from the tax concessions of this budget are those who are earning more than £150,000 a year. We were told it will help economic growth. We will be increasing the national debt to give tax concessions to the richest. The stock market itself does not agree with the logic of this and has gone into freefall.

Our lives are with our brothers and sisters. Last week our nation stopped, took stock and recognized this truth. Our newspapers proclaimed the virtues of service, of kindness, compassion and humility. We talked of a queen who dedicated her life to the service of others. And people from all walks of life, rich and poor, old and young, people of every colour and culture, came together to remember and become the diverse prayer of our nation, a prayer that celebrated unity. In the streets and in the queues to see the Queen lying in state or to see the procession, we discovered again the truth that our lives are with one another, our brothers and sisters, our neighbours. We turned Westminster into a neighbourhood.

Many of the stewards who welcomed people into our church, who had come to mourn last week, were deeply moved by what it means to be with our neighbours. 'It has been so wonderful to welcome people in this church today,' said Beverley, overflowing with joy. It is what Ruth Hutchinson, at our regular community supper known as the Archers, calls 'a hearty welcome'. If we decide that our life and death is with our neighbour, if we decide to embark on a style of life that gives life to others, we are recognizing and acting out the truth that is deepest in us. We are becoming and offering others the chance to become who they fully are.

One of the Desert Fathers, John the Dwarf, said, 'You don't build a house by starting with the roof and working down. You start with the foundation.' They said, 'What does that mean?' He said, 'The foundation is our neighbour whom we must win. The neighbour is where we start. Every commandment of Christ depends on this.[2] Our life and our death is with our neighbour.

Wonderings

If your life is with your neighbour, I wonder who your neighbours are.
I wonder how you show your love.
I wonder how you are receiving life through them.

Letter 54: Wholly, Holey, Holy

October 2022

At the top of each of the letters is a print my brother Andrew made of the leaf of a lime tree. In each of the pictures the leaf is the same but different. It is the slow weathering, disintegration, holing and dissolving of the leaves in autumn that creates the delicate, intricate patterns and colours that make each leaf unique. This ageing creates an astonishing fragile beauty.

I believe this is not just true of a leaf. It is true of each one of us. Our wholly, holey, holy bodies become the lattice work through which God's light shines and the deeper fragile patterns of our lives are revealed. Today I am sharing with you the letter that I wrote to my mother and which I read as a reflection for the wonderful disability conference entitled 'Wholly, Holey, Holy'. My mother has Lewy Body Dementia.

Dear Mum

Today, rummaging through my bedside cabinet, I find a letter you wrote to me on Wareham Station more than 17 years ago. It's you speaking to me from the past. In the letter it says that I was upset with you because I was feeling depressed and you had asked several people to pray for me. I must have wanted my depression to be a private thing, not something shared. I was afraid of my weakness being exposed. I had recently returned from a faraway place. My body at least had returned, my spirit was still far away. And now in 2022, I reread your letter to me, Mum, apologizing that you have caused me distress. And 17 years later I am so on your side. I who then was so guarded, so afraid of acknowledging my need of God's help. You write, 'All your adult life you have been such a support to me in your prayers and I have tried to support you too.' You write, 'Please try to understand that I do love you deeply and try to uphold you in the way that you should go. God bless you and keep you. Love Mum. P.S. I would be so sad if you ever felt you could not turn to me.'

Now so many years later the words open up my heart and I find myself in the middle of the night sitting on the edge of my bed reading this letter and wishing I could go back to that time and thank you. Your prayers have upheld me. Sometimes now when I visit you, you look at me with a smile and a look of puzzled recognition.

'You are Richard, aren't you?' you say.

'Yes,' I say, 'I'm your second son and you're my mother.'

'You're not going away again are you?' you say.

'No, I am not going away. I am staying with you.'

Fear is the worst thing when the person you love is suffering and you don't know what to do or how to stop it. I remember the first day we noticed your dementia, like a dark storm cloud coming in and reality getting lost. We were celebrating your eightieth birthday, staying in a hotel. You came to your party but seemed muddled and confused, began saying things that didn't make sense. 'What are you talking about, Mum?' Alarm. Fear. Later you had a fall and we spent hours in an unknown A&E. It's the unknown that is so frightening. What can we do? How can we stop this? We want answers from the hospital, but they don't give them. This is our mum. How can we protect you? This is terrifying, a wilderness which no one seems to know how to navigate. You are our mum but to them you are just another very elderly person in need. Over the weeks that follow, your confusion is becoming more and more alarming. You are agitated, restless, more and more unable to walk. You think I've got cancer. You think there are people in your bedroom who are not even there. Your mind is racing wildly. You think members of the family have died in terrible accidents when they haven't, and you need constant reassurance. And the medication is frightening too. Are the tablets the doctor giving helping or making things worse? It feels like hell.

We try to get help, write letters to the consultant doctor. But when we visit it is clear the consultant hasn't read them, isn't really listening. Each of us writes explaining Mum has *no* memory loss, she is just losing her reality. 'Yes, Mrs Carter,' says the consultant, when after months we get an appointment, 'I can see you are suffering from memory loss.' You smile at the consultant benevolently and my brother Daniel and I feel like giving up. We have waited five months to be told by a consultant something that isn't even true. And then finally we find a neurologist who does listen. He not only listens, he really understands. It's not that he can heal her or provide a solution. It's the fact that finally, finally, someone has heard us and knows the problem, and can name the symptoms and describe our fears. He tells us the truth, explains your condition. This listening and understanding offers us a way forward – a path – not a solution, but a map through the unknown. We are so thankful for his truth-telling.

Mum, we have learnt the moods of your dementia. You are still so much our mother, your essence concentrated. I see the 63 years of love for me, your flashes of anger or irritation at my selfishness, then the moments of loving kindness we call 'gentle mum', then the playing with words and poems you still remember, completing the line which I start.

'I must go down to the sea again, to the lonely sea …'

'And the sky,' you call out.

Then, suddenly, a flash of memory. As though for a short while the clouds have parted. But then the delusions too like a tangled nightmare that you are fighting to escape. You still have an ability to hold us all captive, even in the midst of your dementia. You still hold the centre.

Last month when I stayed I found you had fallen out of bed. You became really chatty in those early hours of the morning.

'You're Richard,' you said. 'Who am I?'

'You are Sally Elizabeth Carter.'

'Why don't you lie down here with me?' you said. 'You're not going away again are you?'

'No,' I said.

And so we chatted until my brother, your last-born son, Daniel, returned from walking the dog and we both lifted you gently back on to the bed and tucked you in.

I love watching the way Daniel looks after you. Caring for someone with such dignity is such a gift. I have so much to learn. But I have learnt this. Caring is not about bossing or controlling, rather honouring and giving time. It is about being alongside. It is deeply reciprocal. It's not territorial. It makes room, it creates safe, gentle space. It's like the roles of mother and child, now reversed. It's not transactional. It's relationship. It's deep patience, it's laughter, it's exasperation, but it's also a smile. It's unique to the person. And it's not easy. Coming to visit, I have consciously to stop myself wanting to interfere, telling my brother how to do it better. He knows far more than me. But I worry for him. I see him locked in. It's tiring and demanding, often answering calls and shouts through the night. It's a journey through light and darkness. I watch Daniel washing and carefully drying your feet, making sure each overlapping toe is dry. I watch him rubbing in the cream so that they will not blister or get sores. 'I have set you an example,' said Jesus, 'that you also should do as I have done to you' (John 13.15).

Later, the supper, each mouthful a gentle encouragement to open your mouth and eat – 'Open wide!'

'How do you feel about caring for her?' I ask my brother.

'I think she's so brilliant the way she allows me to do it,' he replies.

He straps the hoist sling around your waist and presses the red button of the hoist, which raises you from your seat, your arms cruciform, holding on to the straps so that you can be moved to the commode. You rise as the electric motor lifts you and stand, hands outstretched, smiling at us all. Like Christ. 'Behold your mother ... Mother, behold your son' (John 19.26).

When people ask me, 'How is your mother?' it's hard to answer.

'It must be so difficult,' they say.

'She's our mother,' I answer.

'I'm so sorry,' they say, 'it must be so hard.'

'Yes, it's hard, but she is still our mother.'

Yes, there are moments when you long for the past, and those memories like a picture in a photograph album pierce your heart with a longing for how you were before. But mostly it's you now. And we love you just as much. You still make us laugh and cry. And actually, when we live the present, I realize you are still holding us all together, creating family. You are the catalyst that makes home. It's the gift you always had that now seems magnified. Even silent in the Zoom service and Bible studies, you gather people.

'Can I say a prayer for you?' I ask.

'A pear?' you say. 'Yes, I would love a pear.'

'Not a pear, a prayer,' I say.

'A pear?' you reply.

I say the Lord's Prayer. Your lips move. On earth as it is in heaven, for ever and ever.

With love for ever and ever

Richard, your second son

Amen.

It takes a while to realize that the hole is in fact the hole the light shines through, that what you thought was burden and struggle is also grace.

'How do you feel about spending so much time caring for Mum?' I ask Daniel.

'It's the best thing I've ever done in my life,' he answers.

The miracle is that care moves outwards. It emanates, radiates from him. He may think he's just caring for my mum only, but he's caring for me too and the whole of our family, and his friends and the family of his dear friend who died. It's like abundance. True care and love multiplies, and it draws others in. I realize that Christ is bigger than us all. You may think you're wasting your time loving, but actually it's the thing that is most worth doing. And my mother with dementia, as mad as a hatter, is like the heart of this. She's a force of energy. My mother and Daniel are now hosting Ukrainians who have come to stay at their home to escape from violence. Olga and her son Svitozar, part of the family too, my brother Tim bringing food from his kitchen, Olga stuffing cabbage leaves and making Borscht, my mother's grandchildren arriving, me trying to say prayers. What is happening? We are creating Eucharist. Wholly, Holey, Holy. No, it's not us creating Eucharist, it is Jesus Christ who is creating Eucharist and we in our own small, seemingly insignificant way are learning how to magnify his love, and somehow fear, scarcity, doubt, mortality are being transformed into the heavenly banquet – a glimpse of heaven.

This is the story of my mother but maybe it is also the story of the gospel.

Christ has died, Christ is risen, Christ will come again
A memory of faithful love
A story of fear and trying to overcome it
A story of being with
Of caring and sharing
Of facing the darkness and the demons and discovering the light
    has not been put out
A gift of grace
A Eucharist
Love for someone
Disabled
And Wholly, Holey, Holy
How much we can learn about God.

I read this letter to my mother on the phone while Daniel is feeding her sausages.
'Do you like it, Mum?'
'Yes, because I know it,' she says. 'I know it all the way home.'

If I am lost, tell them I will be found by love. (John of the Cross)

Wonderings

I wonder if you have ever felt really listened to.
I wonder if really listening to someone else changed you.
I wonder when a loss became the means of grace.
I wonder when in your life you saw the shape of the gospel.

> ... Stand still. The forest knows
> Where you are. You must let it find you.[1]

Letter 55: Goodness is Stronger than Evil

11 November 2022

It is now ten years since we held a memorial service at St Martin-in-the-Fields that I will never forget. It was for Marie Colvin, the *Sunday Times* Foreign Correspondent who was killed while reporting on the war in Syria in February 2012. Her death was made particularly poignant because I had written to her asking her to take part in our Lent lecture series entitled 'Victim No Resurrection', and she had responded, 'I'd be happy to take part, bravo to you for organizing such a worthwhile event.' It was not to be.

Marie Colvin wrote:

Covering a war means going into places torn by chaos, destruction, death and pain, and trying to bear witness to that ... I care about the experience of those most directly affected by war, those asked to fight and those just trying to survive. Despite all the videos you see on television from the Pentagon or Nato briefings, what's on the ground has remained remarkably the same for the past 100 years. Craters. Burnt houses. Women weeping for sons and daughters. Suffering. One of the rules I have in covering war is: don't be afraid to be afraid.[1]

Two hours before Marie Colvin herself was killed in Homs, she had given her last interview, describing her anger and fear when faced with the shelling of civilians in the city, and her heartbreak at watching a baby hit by shrapnel die in a poorly equipped makeshift medical centre.

Marie Colvin: It's a very chaotic room. But the baby's death was just heartbreaking, possibly because he was so quiet. One of the first shocks, of course, was that the grandmother had been helping – completely co-incidentally – helping in the emergency room, and just started shouting, 'That's my grandson, where did you find him?' And then the doctor said, 'There's nothing we can do.' We just watched this little boy, his little tummy heaving and heaving as he tried to breathe. It was horrific. My heart broke ... There's been constant shelling in the city, so I have to say, it's just one of many stories ... it was just one piece of shrapnel that caught him right in the chest.

She was asked in the interview whether she thought it was right that these horrific images of the violence of the fighting should be shown and remembered, and she responded:

I feel very strongly that they should be shown ... for an audience for which the conflict, any conflict, is very far away. That's the reality [of war]. These are 28,000 civilians, men, women and children, hiding, being shelled, defenseless. That little baby was one of two children who died today, one of the children being injured every day. That baby probably will move more people to think, 'What is going on, and why is no one stopping this murder in Homs that is happening everyday?'[2]

The building from which Marie Colvin was reporting was deliberately hit two hours later by Syrian government missiles. One of the small details that I read in the *Sunday Times* was that, as she entered this house where she was staying in the Babar Amar District of Homs, she had taken off her shoes. Even in such great personal danger she had still shown this sign of respect for the culture and the humanity of those whose story she told. 'Remove the sandals from your feet, for the place on which you are standing is holy ground' (Exodus 3.5). All land, all people are sacred. Haneen, who pulled her dead body from the rubble, said, 'We cannot count the ones who die in the shelling and are buried under the rubble.' Most of those who die will not be remembered.

Yesterday I spoke with my brother Matthew, who has just returned from Ukraine. He is the CEO for Depaul International. He has been visiting the projects throughout Ukraine that his charity supports. He described to me some of the trauma faced by the victims of the war in Ukraine, the Russian tactics learnt in Syria, whole cities pounded, buildings demolished by shells, cities with no windows as winter approaches. The infrastructure of the nation is being systematically targeted and destroyed – the water, the power supplies, people's homes, and the bridges, road and rail links that bring in supplies of food. Old people are bewildered and unable to understand the violence unleashed upon them. 'We have done nothing wrong,' they say. Too frightened to leave, too frightened to stay.

Does that not seem shocking in a world in which we have learnt so much, to build skyscrapers, put astronauts on the moon, send spaceships to Mars, split the atom, travel across the world in double-decker jets, communicate with someone on the other side of the world on mobile phones, send messages and pictures and sound at the click of a computer key, create vaccines, transplant hearts? Does it not seem shocking that all around the world we are still making war, creating bombs to blow people's limbs off, bullets to tear people open, weapons to inflict the most brutal damage upon the fragile, irreplaceable flesh and bones of another? 'Father, forgive them, for they do not know what they are doing' (Luke 23.34).

Alongside the horror of violence, there is always another story that emerges, a story that without avoiding the reality of the suffering we also acknowledge and affirm. It is called resurrection. It is the story of courage and human goodness, to hold fast to all that is right. My brother Matthew also returns from Ukraine with the stories of incredible courage, kindness and solidarity – people in Ukraine who turned up on bicycles to pedal food to those across the city most in need, homeless people who became the care providers for the vulnerable; the courage and refusal of a whole nation to give up or give in to the evil of the violence; the vision and the hope that they will overcome and rebuild and be free. In the midst of suffering, such resilience, such hope. I asked Matthew how he felt when eventually he crossed the border back into Poland.

'Actually,' he said, 'I felt I wanted to stay. I had been so moved and affected by those I had visited, so welcomed, so cared for, even in the middle of a nation suffering such brutality, I felt I had witnessed the presence of Christ.'

Here, from Ukraine, living with my brother Daniel and my mother Sally, are Olga and her son Svitozar. They, like many others, have sought refuge in this country. They carry within them the pain of their nation they have left behind. It is too painful even to watch the news in their presence. 'This is Ukraine I remember,' says Olga, as she shows me the pictures on her mobile phone of the primary school children she used to teach only a year ago, so happy, so unaware when those photos were taken of the evil about to be unleashed upon her nation. And yet Olga and Svitozar still carry this pre-war goodness within them. They live with hope and goodness alive in them, even in the midst of all their fears. Here in a foreign land they have made a home with my brother and mother and brought such kindness and hope to our family too. I see Olga sitting next to my mother, helping my brother to feed her gently, looking after my mother in the same way she cared for those young children she taught in Ukraine. Goodness lives on. Svitozar is practising his English with my brother and me. They have brought joy to this house. I am practising the present continuous tense with Olga.

'What are you doing?' I ask.

'I am eating,' says Olga, and roars with laughter.

'What are you doing?'

'I am eating too,' I reply, and laugh as I take another bite of the floppy steamed cabbage roll filled with rice and ground pork called Holobtsi, which Olga has cooked for us in my brother and mother's kitchen. We are sharing Eucharist in my brother's house, in our own small way defeating all that divides our world.

Our world is still allowing Christ to be crucified. Each time we celebrate the Eucharist we are remembering the one who died for us. This is not a memory of the dead but a re-membering – a making present. We will re-member a life torn apart by violence, hatred, human prejudice, religious fanaticism and the misuse of power. But we will also remember that this broken body is also the body that gives us life and brings healing. We will say these words: 'Christ has died. Christ is risen. Christ will come again.' Or, in the words of Desmond Tutu:

Goodness is stronger than evil;
Love is stronger than hate;
Light is stronger than darkness;
Life is stronger than death;
Victory is ours through Him who loves us.[3]

Letter 56: 'Here I Am'

20 November 2022

This last week Timothy Radcliffe spoke in our lecture programme on the subject of 'What am I Living For? Life, Death and Friendship'. I was deeply moved by what he shared. One of the extraordinary things about his lecture was that while he was addressing a church of at least 250 people he also seemed to be able to address us each individually, to such an extent that when people came forward to ask questions, they seemed to speak from their very souls and he responded to them as if they were the only person in the room. And his answers modelled the friendship of which he spoke. 'I have called you friends' (John 15.15). He was ministering both to the individual and to everyone gathered. He came forward, down from the platform, to meet the questioner as he wanted to see them face to face, and in that intimate encounter somehow we were all included. This is the way Christ speaks, through the particular, the real needs of real people. He listens, speaks, meets them and in so doing meets all of us. Heart speaks to heart. God changes us face to face.

Timothy Radcliffe said that after the major surgery he went through, which lasted several hours, he lay for many weeks linked up to tubes and pipes, unable to do anything for himself. He said that as a teacher, a preacher and as a writer, clarity of mind had always seemed to be the essence of all he was valued for. But now, he said, he felt like a lump of flesh totally dependent on others. Spirituality is often embedded in corporality, the senses of the body – touch, taste, smell, sight, hearing –

but how could he pray now that these senses seemed taken away from him? He said he found it almost impossible to pray. He tried the Our Father but could not get through more than the first two sentences. The only prayer he could make at that point was the prayer of Samuel in the Temple, 'Here I am.'

Samuel in the encounter with God is at first confused. He thinks it is Eli calling, not God. I am aware how often I too do not recognize the call of God, do not realize that God speaks to us deep within our very hearts. And God often speaks most clearly not when we are full but into our emptiness. 'Here I am.' Timothy Radcliffe talked about those simple words being enough – becoming his prayer. Here I am, in the total unknown, unable to control, to understand, to act, to do anything, even to fetch the bed pan. I am mortal, I am ultimately alone. Here I am. I am totally nothing, and in this nothingness, totally yours because you are all I have. It's a prayer that strips us right down to just us and God. And it exposes us. Here I am. I can hide nothing, escape nothing, make no claim to superiority or achievement. Just me. What you see in all its hopelessness is all I've got. Flesh, bone, blood and a head full of unknowing. Me and you. And yet this 'I am' is taken up into the name of God. 'Here I AM.' Here in this nothingness, beyond pride, beyond your achievements and the need for any proof of righteousness or worthiness. 'Here I AM.' God is here, not promising miraculous intervention or even protection but affirming unconditional presence. Here I AM. Here is God and God is here and you are God's.

How often we find God's presence most fully realized in the places of abandonment:

Illness chipped away at the identity I had created and opened the door to a deeper one that was a gift to be discovered. Soon after I surfaced in the Blenheim ward of the Churchill Hospital in Oxford, a young doctor sat by my bed and asked simple questions, including: 'Where are you?' I remembered the place was connected with Blenheim but it did not look like the palace. I could not answer. I hoped that he would ask me who was the prime minister so that I could reply that I was not sure if Boris knew either! Instead he asked me who was the monarch, the only question to which I gave the correct answer ...

I lay there, connected to myriad tubes, which pumped in a sugary drip twelve hours a day and carried away waste. I was constantly injected, tested, examined. Even when the tubes began to be removed, I could do nothing, not even wipe my own bottom. I worried endlessly whether anyone would get me a bedpan in time. So my identity as an agent was also lost for a while. The nurses and doctors did their marvellous best, always asking my permission before any procedure. My fragile sense of self was nourished by their gaze and touch, their eyes and hands. We exist in the gaze others offer us.

This utter dependency was embraced by our God who became a helpless swaddled infant, incapable of anything, also needing his nose and his bottom to be wiped but held and beheld by his mother. He became the eyes and hands of God, gazing at edgy Nathaniel, at the argumentative Samaritan woman at the well, at the despised tax collector Matthew, and seeing God's friends and reaching out in touch to the sick. These nurses were ministers of the divine gaze and touch, as were my brethren who faithfully came and sat with me every day, even when I could not say anything.[1]

Timothy spoke of the way his illness had always felt like his enemy, but now slowly was becoming his teacher, his guru. 'Here I am,' the 'Here I AM' of God's eternal presence and the recognition of his own naked self, like an offering on the altar reciprocated by the total self-offering of Christ for him. Here Christ is, here and now. This is the meeting of all I am and all God is. Nothing, yet everything. And he spoke of the dawning realization of life as gift. All of life a miraculous gift. Just when we thought it was running out. Every last breath of it a gulp of the breath of God, every last sight a vision of possibility, every touch the beauty of procreation, rib of my rib, dust moulded by Jesus' own intimate hands into astonishing life. My broken flesh infused with the divine life. Perhaps we can never fully grasp that miracle unless we are in danger of losing it or have lost it. Yet in depletion we recognize the life of God poured out for us and into us, which we now must somehow pour out for others. This love is the love of the incarnation. Before perhaps we were in love with an idea, a vision, now it's made flesh, God calling us by name. Our life, our God-given life, is our reaching out too. It is learning to call others by name.

Timothy said that when we arrive in heaven we do not arrive alone. God will ask: Where are the others? Where is the love I gave you? Where is the fruit of that love? Do not stop loving because you fear no return. Rather, in your broken body let that love arise. We all have a vocation to friendship and we must never stop reaching out. This friendship, Timothy Radcliffe said, 'oxygenates us'. When you are lost you will be found by love.

A prayer

Here I am Lord
Help me to hear you when you call
Help me to know that you are always with me
Help me to know that when I call
You are already here
Here we are Lord
We have your words to live
We have your hope to share
We have your justice to bring
We have your planet to cherish and save
Lord turn our taking into sharing
Transform our fears with your love.

Now the LORD came and stood there, calling as before, 'Samuel! Samuel!' And Samuel said, 'Speak, for your servant is listening.' (1 Samuel 3.10)

Letter 57: Waiting

from Nazareth, December 2022

We know that all things work together for good for those who love God. (Romans 8.28)

I wonder how good you are at waiting. It's OK waiting when you know someone is definitely coming. It's when you are not sure that they are or, worse, if they can find you. Or if you really, really long for them to come and then they don't. The doubt sets in and, once you begin to doubt, waiting is really difficult. You keep on looking out of the window and the more restlessly you watch, the more the beloved seems not to arrive.

Last week I had an important delivery I was waiting for. I got one of those text messages to say that it would be delivered between 2 and 3 p.m., and even one of those positioning apps to show me where the delivery van had got to. But the delivery van on the app seemed to have got frozen in one place and by 3 p.m. I found myself walking up and down outside the church trying to find out where the delivery van had got to. The problem with St Martin's is there are so many different places people come to – the shop, the crypt, the church, the Connection, number 5 or number 6 – and while I was running anxiously to check the shop in the crypt, I was sure that they would arrive at number 6 or number 5, where the bell is not working. So there I was running between locations like a headless chicken. In such circumstances it is often much better to stand still and wait, wait for the delivery man to find you. I realized how hard I find it to wait, to be centred in the face of urgency.

Another moment – I set off on my bicycle to visit the hospital. I need to see Stephen, who has been taken ill, but I have to fit it into all the other things I need to do. Halfway up Charing Cross Road I can hear a bus honking its horn. He is behind me and seems to be honking at me. I steady my bicycle. What am I doing wrong? 'I'm not doing anything wrong,' I think, 'he must be honking at someone else.' The honking continues. What's wrong with him? I look round. The driver of the bus is beckoning at me. Eventually I pull in and stop and the bus stops too. The bus driver says to me, 'I saw your wallet fall out of your pocket along the road back there, that's why I have been honking you.' 'Thank you so much,' I respond in panic before I rush back along the road, 200 metres back. The street is really crowded; I'm never going to find a wallet. It will have gone by now. Nothing along the road, nothing in the gutter. And then a woman, holding up my wallet above her head.

'Are you the person the bus was honking? I picked up your wallet. Here it is!'

Suddenly all the rush is gone. I am no longer thinking of all I have to do. I am only thinking of how much more I would have had to do if the wallet had indeed been lost – total relief. But for the goodness and grace of a bus driver and a person in the street. It is as though this act of kindness and thoughtfulness is restoring my equilibrium, restoring my soul. And suddenly within I am deeply at peace, busy but at peace. We are centred by acts of grace.

Advent waiting is not a passive, lackadaisical thing. It is a finding – finding your centre. It is knowing where you stand. It is recognizing that even in the midst of struggle and uncertainty, God's grace is here and now. Our contemplative prayer is not a daydream. It's holding fast to all that is good. Prayer is attention, attention to God, attention to the other, attention to the world, attention to self. And our waiting is about not rushing thoughtlessly onwards but arriving in the present. Prayer is rediscovering your soul.

As I cycle on towards the hospital there is no longer a sense of rush within me, rather a deep thankfulness, a stillness, a recognition of the goodness of others, a warmed heart. I have been filled by the kindness of that bus driver and that woman. Inside the hospital I am no longer in a rush. I am present. I am listening. I am thankful. I am ready to share with Stephen, who is lying in a hospital bed looking so lost. I want him to realize he is found too.

The stable is in our midst. The incarnation of God's love is now. Don't miss it. You think you have no time – you are missing the star, you are overlooking the saviour in the manger of your life.

The greatest gift we have to offer is to give attention, unconstrained by time or the desire for response. Just a generous offering – a waiting upon.

Think of the very best waiter in a restaurant. It's not someone who is for-ever trying to top up your wine or persuade you to have another bottle, or continually asking you if you are enjoying the meal. It is the waiter who gives you space when you need space and is there for you when you need something. I think of a good nurse in hospital. I remember after my operation the nurse being there for me when I was in pain and afraid, but as I grew stronger, she moved on to the next patient who needed attention. At first I thought, 'Why has the nurse left me?' Then I realized that this was her job, to be with those in need, to wait on the one who needs the waiting, to recognize when the waiting is over without demand. Waiting to heal and in healing letting go.

We are told by Jesus that the greatest commandment is to love God and to love our neighbour as ourselves. But how often in our religion we do not open up that attentive space. Instead, we crowd the space with words, busyness and externalism. We cover over the spaces and gaps through which God speaks. We fill it with self-importance and our own neediness. We talk *about* people's needs; we discuss, we create commit-tees and yet we shy away from meeting the need face to face.

> Let knowledge grow from more to more,
>   But more of reverence in us dwell;
>   That mind and soul, according well,
> May make one music as before,
>
> But vaster. (Alfred Lord Tennyson[1])

Waiting – is it for a birth or death?

Over and over again, my mind returns to a time of waiting that is forever in my heart. I remember in my life waiting for the seven members of my community, the Melanesian Brothers, who had been taken hostage. For three months we held a vigil for them day and night – waiting.

'What happens', I asked our head Brother, 'if we go on praying for their safety day and night only to discover that they have already been murdered? Will that not be the failure of prayer?'

'If you visit a hospital, would you leave the person because they are dying or would you rather pray with them through death into eternity?' he replied. 'We will pray for our seven brothers whatever happens. In life and in death we will be with them.'

My time of prayer is from 2.00 to 3.00 a.m.

In my diary I describe this waiting:

At 2.00 a.m. I wake up. It is dark, and I don't want to turn on any lights as if it will disturb all that I fear. I am going over to the chapel, as I do every night. Daniel wakes. He wants to come too. Silently we slip out of the house through the hedge and across the deserted grass, past the Community graveyard, then down the footpath by the side of the square. Bare feet on wet grass and then sharp coral; I know this way even in the pitch black. I have followed this same way at least five times a day for more than ten years. And yet still, as I approach the chapel, there is an anticipation, each sense heightened, as though a meeting is about to take place that is more than anything else in my life. Fear, but it is not like the fear of darkness: holy fear, an awe of something greater and beyond anything. It cannot be seen or quantified but it is longed for. At times it seems like nothing, a yawning emptiness, and yet it is everything. It is our hope. It is everything we are waiting for. Often I will leave this chapel feeling I have just missed what I came for, or the futility of my faith is mocking me, and yet I will long to come again and be, be more deeply. It is all we have to defeat the darkness. There is a candle burning at the front; Novice Jack Alec and Novice Ishmael are there praying, solid, silent and so still, as they always are, as they have been since the beginning, for they share this hour of vigil when everyone else is sleeping.

> I feel your presence in the night
> The fragrance of God and man
> I breathe in the stillness
> And in the middle of night
> Both flesh and spirit live
> Live deeply
> Live to the brim
> Reach across time and space
> And touch eternity
> And I long for all to be drawn and held together by this invisible God
> Whose love burns in the darkness with the life of the Son
> And whose blessing touches us as softly as the rustle of the night
>   wind and rain in the trees.
> How strange that when we are most abandoned we are drawn into
>   this passion
> How miraculously you wait for us just beyond our fear.[2]

We waited upon those seven brothers and after three months of waiting we discovered that they had been killed. Now they wait for us, wait for me to live the peace, the courage and the love their life and death goes on revealing:

> In life
> In death
> In eternal life
> When we wait, really wait in love
> Death itself can also become a birth
> The poverty of a stable become the place of eternal glory
> And even a cross, the sign of resurrection and everlasting love.

Wonderings

I wonder what you are waiting for.
I wonder how you wait and if you are good at waiting.
I wonder how the meaning is in the waiting.
I wonder how you wait for God.
I wonder how God arrives.
I wonder what it means when the mind and the song make one music but vaster.

Letter 58: To Be Born

Christmas Eve 2022

The hopes and fears of all the years are met in thee.

Every birth is a miracle in so many ways – a miracle of life. I remember my father leaning out of the upstairs window to shout that my brother had just been born. I was playing in the garden with my elder brother. I came running inside, climbed the stairs, silenced, and into the bedroom where my mother was holding this little baby wrapped in a blanket against her like a small parcel of new life. Where had this new life come from? I was filled with awe.

Years later it is Christmas Eve. I am preparing to celebrate the midnight Mass in a small village on the island of Gela in the South Pacific. There are only oil lights and candles to light the stable we have built. Then in the night someone arrives asking for help. A young woman is pregnant, ready to deliver, but there are complications. In this village there are no doctors, no hospital, no maternity unit. Two members of my community rush off to her village to pray with her, for prayer is the only thing we have to offer for the life of this child and the mother crying in the night. And as the two brothers rush off, I process into a packed church to celebrate the birth of a child 2,000 years ago. Early in the morning the two members of my community return. 'What happened?' I asked. They tell me the mother's story. The girl in labour was young, only 15 years old and unmarried. No one knew who the father was. They had found her behind the village in one of the outhouses, lying on a mat. She was crying out in the night. No doctor, no nurse, the village said that her difficulty in delivery was caused by her unmarried status. Her parents were ashamed. Just one woman in the dark beside her as she cried out.

'What did you do?'

'I didn't know what to do. I have never witnessed a birth before,' he said. 'She was really screaming, so frightened, in such pain. I knelt down beside her. I took her hand and I prayed the only words that kept coming into my head.'

'What did you pray?' I asked

'I just told her this, I said, "When Jesus was born he was born just like this." I said to her, "Do not be afraid. His name is Immanuel, 'God is with us.'" Just those words again and again. God is with us. And the baby was born. It was the greatest miracle I have ever seen.'

In a world in which we have lived through this pandemic and the crisis in the NHS and in care for the elderly, we have become more aware than ever of our own vulnerability and mortality. In our world we have grown disillusioned about the misuse of power and the integrity of politicians; in Syria and now Ukraine we have seen the devastation caused by war and the horrific brutality of weapons, bombs and missiles unleashed against the innocent; it is a world in peril because of human greed and our exploitation of creation: into this world a child is born, innocent, homeless, entirely vulnerable. This child is conceived by a single mother, who has been hastily married to a carpenter who is not the real father, to avoid scandal, and will be born in an outside shed, among animals, in a divided town under occupation. The witnesses will be a group of misfits, itinerant homeless shepherds from the hills, wandering gypsies; the only other witnesses to visit will be migrants from a foreign land. In Jerusalem both the state and religious authorities are so busy defending their own positions that they see this Christ-child as a threat to their power and respond with horrific violence, in which children are massacred and our Christ-child becomes a refugee, his parents fleeing with him to save his life.

Look around our world today. The same tragedies continue to repeat themselves. And yet for those who have eyes to see, the same truth continues to unfold – God's truth, God's creative life. It begins often at the lowest point. At the point where you thought you were defeated, at the point of rejection and need. At the point of seeming death, God's life begins – and there is hope and a future and a life. As real and miraculous as a small baby gulping for air, blinking into the light, its tiny limbs, fingers, toes, eyes, nose, ears, lips, luminous skin – wondrous, a child is born unique and unrepeatable. That miracle of life belongs to each one of us. Because each one of us was once that child. And the story of the nativity says this: 'Do not be afraid. God is with us. The word was made flesh and lives among us.' His story is our story. This child changes everything, turns everything upside down. This child is the story of God's love for you – not just then but also now.

I want to pass on to you the words of Br Christian de Chergé, one of the modern martyrs of Algeria whose story is told in the film *Of Gods and Men*. They are the words he preaches on Christmas Eve, on the night their lives are threatened and they are taken hostage:

> Tonight we will celebrate the Eucharist and we will welcome the one who was born for us, absolutely helpless and already so threatened. Afterwards we will find salvation in undertaking our various tasks, in the kitchen, the garden, the home, the workplace, the church. We will all in our own lives have to resist prejudice, injustice and violence and day after day we will discover that to which Christ beckons us. It's *to be born*. Our identities as men and women go from one birth to another. From birth to birth. We must each end up bringing to the world the child of God that we are. The incarnation for us is to allow the reality, the filial reality of Jesus, to embody itself in our humanity. The mystery of the incarnation is what we are called to live. In this way what we have already lived takes root. And what we are called to live in the future is filled with possibility.[1]

Wonderings

I wonder what it means for you that Christ was born.
I wonder what it means for you to be born.

Letter 59: Learning to Empty

Castle Weary, Scotland
4 January 2023

I wake up in soft darkness. Today I have the time to do the things I do not usually do. I open the wood-burning stove in the bothy where I am staying. Inside there are still some softly glowing embers from the logs I put in last night. From the porch I take some kindling and push them into the hot ash, lifting them and blowing as I do so. They pop. I blow some more, they pop again and then there is a crackle. The orange glow intensifies, turns red, and then the first flame licks upwards. I keep blowing and add a log on top. I close the stove door leaving the air vent open as the crackle becomes a soft roar. I remember my father laying a fire meticulously in the front-room grate when I was a child. Balls of newspaper, a scaffolding of kindling and then large lumps of shining coal on top. There is something very satisfying about laying a fire that really burns bright.

Inside the cupboard there is a pack of Italian freshly ground coffee, vacuum packed. I slit it open and watch the ground coffee block crumble. I boil a kettle, listening to the sound of the bubbling water as it comes to the boil. You know the moment the electric kettle will switch off just by the sound. The morning is very still, just the sound of the bubbling water and the crackle of the firewood, then the gurgle of the water poured over the ground coffee and filling the cafetière. I press down slowly, careful that the scalding coffee does not splash back up in my face. I pour the coffee into a small saucepan and add milk and place it on top of the wood-burning stove. Each of these actions is so pleasing. There is no rush. Outside it is still pitch black. There is no sound apart from the gentle crackle of the fire.

I sit down at the table by the window to write this, and I am so focused on describing the morning that I forget all about the coffee on the stove until I hear the hiss of steam and the sound of the coffee boiling over on to the scorching surface of the stove top, and smell the burnt coffee and milk. Today I have the time to hear and smell these things, and taste. The coffee tastes delicious. I pull back the curtain that covers the door and open it. The cold winter air rushes in for a moment. I breathe in – the smell of pine, silver birch, winter and snow. Snow surrounds the bothy. It fell several days ago and in the cold it has frozen over and the edges of the furrows and the footprints are now a latticework of ice. A soft powder of snow is falling now. It is when you have time to notice that the poem begins, liminal and transcendent. The everyday that you never normally notice is astonishing. You become so attentive to the detail that each moment becomes sacramental – filled with presence and wonder.

Last night, as we drove through the fields of snow, the surface sparkled in the headlights of the car. Five-year old Lyla in the back seat cries out, 'Look, it's glitter dropped by the fairies!' True, it is a glittering field, like crossing a field of diamonds, 'icecrust and snowflake' glistening in the car's lights: 'A polished glancing. A blue frost-bright dawn.'[1] They drop me off at the bothy, the crunch of the icy snow under my boots. I walk slowly, careful not to slide, breathing in the cold air, sharp as a knife, deep into my London lungs.

I unpack slowly. I am also unpacking the stress and busyness of the last few weeks of Advent and Christmas in London – folding and putting it carefully away. Ben arrives from across the snow, carefully carrying a hot dish of steak pie with crisp, flaky pastry and small buttery boiled potatoes. I thank him again for picking me up from the station and ask him to pass on my thanks to Amy for the steak pie, and he disappears into the night. After a day on the train without eating, I eat hungrily, the crisp pastry soaking up the thick salty gravy tastes especially delicious.

I shower, a powerful gush of hot Scottish water washing away the city and a day's travel. Then a big white bath towel, stiff and rough from drying in the wind, rubbing my skin like a scouring pad so that it is red and alive. Then I climb into clean white cotton sheets and turn off the light, total blackness enveloping me like a blanket, my buzzing head and body from the city stilling. It is never dark like this in London, dark as velvet. I remember Amy's words in the car: 'When my dad comes here he says he spends the first seven days just sleeping.' This place has that effect on you. But I can't sleep.

These next hours are like a journey through the night in which I feel my body unknotting, the fibres in my lower back untwisting, the twitches and electricity of the modern city you carry with you without realizing. It's as if you are wired up to the zing of neon. But now I am not just breathing but breathing within. As though right to my marrow I have switched off the human generator of survival and opened myself to the without. I am not anxious about not sleeping. Just growing accustomed to the night.

Meditation now is not something you do but something you are, no longer seeking the stillness but inside the stillness, no longer concentrating on the breath. You are the breath and the breath is much bigger than you. It is beyond you and filling you with the stillness of the night.

They talk a lot about detox in order to sell manufactured smoothies and health supplements. But perhaps real detoxification needs us to unplug for a while from the consumables that we think power us. Our bodies can become like street bins with rubbish and packaging spilling over and decomposing within.

'Empty', this January time says to me. 'Fast. Let your fasting create the space you long for. Clear the clutter. Sweep away the debris. Slow down. Stop. Cough out the virus and breath in the fresh air of winter cleansing.' Like those with consumption who were sent to breathe the mountain air. We talk about the pollution of the planet. Well, pollution begins with our own bodies, which become the dumper trucks. So how about learning to fast again? How about realizing that replenishment does not mean consuming more but less – creating more space to touch, taste, see, smell, recognize, hear. I am convinced that after Christmas I do not need to be filled any more but emptied. I am convinced we must seek the space between things so that our lives are not just piles of stuff that overwhelm but spaces large enough to see the epiphany, see the stars. We need to create spaces of encounter that belong to no one but make space for all. We can get lost in too much stuff. We do need to bloom where we are planted but we also need to plant where the seed has space and soil to bloom.

I know that in a few days' time the city will draw me back into its frenetic heartbeat. The city is my monastery. And it will not be long before I miss the people and diversity of my home and the community of those who struggle with all the stresses and moans of the modern world and yet can still show such care and grace. People say there is no community in the city. But I have not found that to be true. What is in short supply is time – time to see, hear and be generous to those who long for community, and time to process all that takes place.

But when I return to the city, I would like to take back with me this soft blanket of the night, this smell of the winter air, this stillness, even in the midst of the rush, this silent prayer enveloping and quietening the social media of the mind – this time to love and recognize. Make this place, the place you are now, your place of meeting, the place where heaven meets the earth, the place where for a moment all our strivings cease, soft and still and fragrant and tender with the beauty of life. It is only perhaps when we let go of stuff that we find that embrace of the redeemer, but that embrace is worth giving up the whole world for.

> When I look at your heavens, the work of your fingers,
>   the moon and the stars that you have established;
> what are human beings that you are mindful of them,
>   mortals that you care for them?
> (Psalm 8.3–4)

Wonderings

I wonder what for you is both ordinary but also astonishing.
I wonder if you can describe any moment in your life that is a sacrament of the present moment.
I wonder what you need to empty.
I wonder, if you create space, what you discover.
I wonder how this year we can make the world a better place.

Letter 60: A Letter from
Emma Bresslaw – Finding Nazareth

I live in Hertfordshire and on a good day it takes me just under an hour to get to St Martin-in-the-Fields. On Wednesdays, my morning is spent with a careful eye on the clock. Household tasks and phone calls are dealt with promptly, two Labradors are given a brisk walk. I sprint the mile to the station, leap on the train, scramble through the underground tunnels at a pace, rush up the steps at Leicester Square, jostle my way through a busy pavement and then arrive at the church, slightly out of breath, hopefully before the clock strikes five. I sit down in a pew with an enormous sigh of relief. I have rushed all day for this – for nothing, for an hour of sitting in silence with a few other people. Is this nothing? No, this is everything. This is making space. This is letting go. This is 'being with'. This is prayer and God has called me here to be with God, with myself and with others who are doing the same thing, who have also been called by God to be here with me, with others and with God. It is an hour of silence. Silence within one's soul is a sacred gift that no one can take away. There may be noises of street life, and there are usually plenty in Trafalgar Square – sirens, traffic noise, music, to name but a few – but these do not distract from the inner silence that I can maintain. In fact, they remind me that my prayer life is part of the whole fabric of my twenty-first-century existence, not an adjunct to it that happens in a side room, but the very heartbeat of my existence. The distractions also remind me that prayer is not a cosy relationship between me and God, but it is about my life of discipleship in the real world and how my relationship with God, my faith, will sustain, nurture and guide me in that world.

I centre myself by emptying my consciousness of niggling, intrusive concerns and, to paraphrase the words of the poet Edwina Gateley, I say nothing and ask for nothing but just let my God look upon me and love me.[1] I have been practising contemplative prayer at home on my own for a few years, but praying silently in community with others is quite different; it is a profound and transformative experience. Surely the Holy Spirit is with us, filling this shared, intentional space to which we have each contributed and which we tenderly hold together within our safe and sacred place. The silence unites us as we unite our silences. There is a palpable presence. I have been listening, we have all been straining our ears and our hearts to hear the word of God and we may, with God's great grace, catch a priceless whisper. Our mutual, silent listening has become a new phenomenon and into this the Spirit breathes the love of God that we all inhale. I may shed the odd tear in this silent hour but, as the clock strikes six, I resurface comforted and empowered by a deep, indescribable and inexplicable sense of peace. I am becoming and have a heightened sense of belonging and of being beloved. I feel like I am coming home.

With thanksgiving
Emma

Letter 61: A Contemplative Journey Home

February 2023

Each week on a Tuesday at 11.00 a.m. I meet with a group of people at the Connection at St Martin-in-the-Fields. The Connection is our centre for those who need a place to call home, supporting people sleeping rough or homeless in the heart of London and helping them to recover and find their way off the streets. The group I lead is called Spiritual Space. It has been meeting in the art room with me (apart from during the pandemic) for more than 12 years.

We come into the room with all the struggles and pressures that each one carries – our wounds, fears and worries within.

'What is the weather you are carrying within you?' I ask.

Each person in the circle responds, telling the group how they are feeling and what mood or thoughts they are bringing into the room with them.

'My weather is changeable,' says John. 'For example, when I woke up, I was feeling dark and under the weather. But here in this room it feels that the sun is breaking through …'

'My weather feels stormy,' says J, 'too many clouds.'

After each has shared, I ask, 'What for you has been a moment of goodness and hope in the last week, a moment of blessing?'

Each person in the group shares. Simple, often ordinary but often eternal truths.

'Brockwell Park walled garden,' says Y.

'Sitting by the oak tree by York Gate,' says R. 'Yesterday was a bright sunny day and I feel happier when the sun shines.'

'The three free newspapers I can get in London,' says P.

'Washing and dressing in clean clothes at the Connection,' says M.

'My Freedom Pass and realizing I can travel free after 9.00 a.m. not 9.30 a.m. – that was a best moment for me,' says H.

'Life itself,' says D. 'And finding here someone who will listen to me, someone who will understand so I can claim back my life, find peace and connect to my creator.'

'Yesterday I spoke to a friend who phoned me. We had not spoken for twenty years, and we spoke for two hours. It was like our friendship was just continuing, like we had never parted and we were friends for ever,' says J.

'Me too,' says V. 'I was thinking I was alone yesterday but then I received a phone call and they said, "We pray for you." And I realized my prayers are answered.'

'I heard from my 11-year-old daughter yesterday,' says M, who is from Sudan. 'She told me she has been appointed the diversity representative for her class and is designing a page for the school magazine. I feel so proud of her. I need to get my hair cut so she will not be embarrassed when she sees me.'

'There is more good in the world than bad. They say the arc of history is long but it bends towards justice. I am learning to try and do good to those who have wronged me – to be more merciful. I need to forgive my father,' says J.

'Our human bodies are miracles of God and they deserve everything to take care of them.'

I listen as they share their wisdom. Then V, who was limping badly when he arrived at the group, says: 'I thank God that I am still alive. On Saturday night I was sleeping on the pavement in my small tent and about 11.30 p.m. I heard people shouting and then one of them threw a large brick on top of my tent. It fell in the place I usually put my head, but for some reason that night I had turned round so the brick only hit my legs. I thank God that he protected me.' We are all silenced and each one of us in the room feels his pain, his courage and his faith in God.

Only silence and stillness can ultimately contain all our stories. I lead them into a simple time of stillness. I play Max Richter's 'On the Nature of Daylight'. It is a piece of music that was like a theme tune for me through the lockdown. As I listened through my earphones I walked through the deserted parks and streets of London. The city that really did become my monastery.[1]

Over the music I float these words: 'Each one of you is sitting in the light of God's love for you. From the very crown of your head to the soles of your feet.'

The music has stopped. It is quiet here in this art room. The winter light floods through the window. Soft voices call from the street, a car, a bus, a distant siren from the Strand. Downstairs a door opens, a chair is moved, there is talking and laughter, someone coughs far away. But here in this room there is stillness, a deep stillness that softly breaks open the shell of our defences. A breathing in, a deep breathing in that seems to expand the soul of who we are. Gone is the need to argue, pretend, impress, grasp. We breathe in a breath larger than ourselves, larger than our humanity – a shared breath, the breath of God.

I invite the group to rise and, standing in their own space, very slowly to stretch up, hands above their heads, and to breathe in, then to bring their fingertips together and their hands slowly down, down the centre of their bodies as though gently compressing and pushing out the air from their lungs. And then from the bottom slowly raise their hands as their whole diaphragm is filled with a deep and slow intake of breath oxygenating their blood, breathing in as their hands slowly rise up, breathing out as their hands slowly descend. Our simple movement becomes like a prayer. We are breathing in and breathing out together. As I sit down, I feel a lightness within. Everyone in the room has found a centre. When the silence ends and we share our thoughts it is as though heart is speaking to heart. Though each person shares a different story, there is no division and no judgement. Rather, we all belong to a greater story, God's story of his breath of life, a greater life in us.

As I leave the group today, I am struck by how much lighter I am feeling. My soul has been stilled and filled. In a place of homelessness, we are finding our home – a home beyond borders, more expansive and miraculous than anyone of us can describe or contain, a home that cannot be possessed. Those in this group come from many parts of the world. All have made long journeys. All are alone. One would expect a room full of doom and despair. But I am struck once again that it is among those who you might think would most doubt God's providential care, that here are some who have a religious faith that is so vital and alive to them. With a faith in which something is at stake, and where their lives are in the offering, God becomes everything. They are my teachers.

I am reminded of the story I heard of two fish swimming side by side in the sea. And one fish says to the other:

'What is this thing called water?'

'It is everything that gives us life. It is that in which we live and move and have our being.'

'Well, I can't see it,' says the younger. 'How can I believe in something I cannot see?'

'If you were thrown up on the dry land, then you would see and believe, but perhaps then it would be too late.'

Perhaps we cannot see the ocean of love in which we too swim. But sometimes in a room like this, as the light floods in, as our edges soften, as a greater silence fills us, and we listen, really listen to ourselves and one another, life can be transfigured and we recognize that we are all sons and daughters, beloved of God.

Returning to St James's Park

Early in the morning I return to St James's Park and walk slowly through the London plane trees, trees that during these last years I have been with in all seasons, whose roots connect and whose seeds, trunks, branches and twigs within themselves somehow know the rhythm of the year. Now their branches are like a latticework against a pale grey-blue sky. Today among the upper twigs I notice the tight buds forming that will burst open with the spring, filling the sky with green. I follow the lake, then up, crossing The Mall, looking up towards Buckingham Palace, which in these last few years has been so much part of our national story – hope, loss, grief, betrayal, service, the longing for a greater good. Only God's love and forgiveness can heal the human heart.

There is in me a longing for goodness. Without any false piety I am convinced that life is too short to hold on to pride or bitterness, or the pride that cannot forgive my own failures. If you asked me what I would like my New Year's resolution to be, it would be to use each day of the year to see and recognize goodness in others and in the world – the goodness of God – and somehow to reflect that goodness too, simply, humbly, openly, reciprocally, a gift received, a gift given. Living goodness. Breathing in this grace. Breathing out this grace. A shared breath.

This park is a gift that belongs to all. It is a prayer, a sacrament, an encounter with God that you can return to again and again and each time feel something new. It is like the gospel itself. Each time you return, it discloses something new, reveals a deeper truth. This is the meaning of our simple Nazareth rule of life: Silence, Service, Scripture, Sacrament, Sharing, Sabbath, Staying With. It is a way to live attentively, generously, humbly. It is the way we find our way home. It is a home that is God's gift to all of us. This is what I am learning from Nazareth – how to find my way home. And he is with us, showing us the Way.

We declare to you what was from the beginning, what we have heard, what we have seen with our eyes, what we have looked at and touched with our hands, concerning the word of life – this life was revealed, and we have seen it and testify to it, and declare to you the eternal life that was with the Father and was revealed to us – we declare to you what we have seen and heard so that you also may have fellowship with us; and truly our fellowship is with the Father and with his Son Jesus Christ. We are writing these things so that our joy may be complete.

This is the message we have heard from him and proclaim to you, that God is light and in him there is no darkness at all. (1 John 1.1–5)

Wonderings

I wonder what the weather is within you.
I wonder what a moment of blessing was for you in your last day.
I wonder where you can see and share goodness today.
I wonder where your true home is and what that home is like.
I wonder what grace you need.

The Lampedusa Cross

Which has become for us the sign of our Nazareth Community
– given to each of those who join.

So many times I reach for it
Feel lost when it is lost

Yellows, blues, crimson-blood reds and flaking whites
paint of a clinker-built boat, planks and gunnel

Scraped, grazed, flaking, torn
Found on a beach in Lampedusa

Whittled, jointed, joined
above to below

drift wood to life wood
Reaching out to hold all hands

It's a cross
But how can a cross comfort or save?

This splintered boat
Puffed with water

Swept up among bright anoraks and florescent
life-jackets that didn't save

children's trainers seeping salt water
A beach in a foreign land

And a carpenter gathering the wreckage
on the shore of death and life

Skilfully he crafts the cross, threads and knots its string
And places it around my neck

Questa Croce é tratta dal legno dei barconi dei nostri
    Fratelli migranti approdati sull'isola
Portala con te come segno della resurrezione che
    nasce dal dolore

Its colours weep and bleed
Broken open by rock

This wood
Becoming splint, rift, raft, my redemption

Float me up open
Through tumble twist and tangle

To breathe with you
the breath Christ breathes in each of us

As I wear you I hold you
As you wear and hold me

You become tiller, mast, oar,
Community of the dispossessed

Possessing nothing
Possessing all

Rising beneath waves flooded with light
A cross that cannot sink

The kiss of life
The broken boat that takes me home.

Epilogue

Making Room for Us All to Belong

ROWAN WILLIAMS

Dearest Richard

'I wondered if there was a space for yet another form of religious life,' you write, reflecting on the origins of the Nazareth Community. Judging from all that this book contains, the answer is yes. But, as you go on immediately to say, the paradox is that the answer is yes because you're not thinking about what particular variety of 'new monasticism' you're trying to embody, but about the central question that the Community's life addresses: where is home? And what are we to do not only to find a home for ourselves but to make a home for each other? 'Jesus' story in Nazareth makes room for us all to belong' – there's the point where the fire of newness is kindled.

And this vision fleshes itself out with great clarity when you remind us that if finding and making a home is pretty much the central calling of human beings, then 'the world is not your battlefield'. We are not simply stuck in a space where the more of me there is, the less there must be of you – the world as a sort of lift with a sign saying, 'No more than x persons', in which we are resentfully pushed up against each other, fighting for a little extra breathing space. How much space there is will depend on us. And as you emphasize so often here, this means being willing to open doors into our own selfhood – doors that allow others to walk in, doors that allow *us* to enter more deeply into who we are, doors for God

(I loved your thoughts about Zacchaeus in Letter 34). Learning to be at home with ourselves and learning to be at home with others belong absolutely together – and they have everything to do with allowing God to be at home in us. It is our own distance from ourselves and – as often as not – our fear and denial about ourselves that feed those hasty reactions to the other out of which exclusion and violence are born.

And you have some excoriating things to say about how all this also feeds the addictive destructiveness of our approach to the world we share. 'We are trashing God's home,' you write, musing on the debris in and around the Sea of Galilee. As if, incapable of being at home with ourselves and what is around us, we subconsciously resolve that no one and nothing will be at home in the world, if we can help it. Not even its Creator.

As I'm writing this, we're all trying to make sense of proposed legislation that will once and for all guarantee that the doors of our country will stay firmly locked against people who have lost homes or left homes, in circumstances of great distress and confusion. We are encouraged to think of desperate, usually impoverished, adults and children as 'invaders', bent on taking the space that belongs to us. We are encouraged to think anything except what is the basic truth of the gospel: if we are ready to make space for God, space opens up within us for the needs of others and for the proper love of ourselves, even of those non-biodegradable elements of our stories (as you so wonderfully call them) that are our sins and failures.

When you quote the deeply moving words of the martyred Cistercian monk Christian de Chergé about Christmas being the moment when Christ is invited to embody himself in us, we can't for a moment forget the cost of this. And we can't forget that someone like Br Christian can say this with joy and conviction simply because they have found that God never fails to make space for them in all their human fullness. What comes through so plainly in these letters is that the Nazareth Community is what it is because of holding together the grateful awareness that God has always already made room for us, and the clear commitment to making room for one another and the world entrusted to us. So many of the narratives here are about your own being welcomed by strangers as much as your own exercise of making space. You've helped us see Nazareth for what it is: God accepting the hospitality of a human home, God in human flesh making divinity a home in which we may all find ourselves and each other. We make a home not by exemplary performance of our duty, not by careful policing of frontiers, not by a sophisticated system of ticketing for entry, but by discovering how recklessly we are ourselves welcomed; and for that – as our beloved Charles de Foucauld and all his followers have always said – we need the silence in which that recognition can blossom, and the sacramental sign of the Eucharist, telling us day by day that what we all, always, have in common is *being guests* in the immeasurable space of God's 'at-homeness' with God's self.

This is the mystery you lead us back to; this is the space you make for your readers. This book is another gem. Thank you so much.

With love, gratitude and blessings
+Rowan

Notes

Page ix

1 R. J. Northcott, *Dick Sheppard and St Martin's*, London: Longmans Green & Co., 1937, p. ix.

Foreword

1 Samuel Wells, *A Nazareth Manifesto: Being with God*, Oxford: Wiley-Blackwell, 2015.

Letter 1

1 Jerome Murphy-O'Connor, *The Holy Land: An Oxford Archaeological Guide*, 5th edn, Oxford: Oxford University Press, 2008, p. 425
2 Samuel Wells, *A Nazareth Manifesto: Being with God*, Oxford: Wiley Blackwell, 2015, pp. 25–6.
3 Richard Carter, *The City is My Monastery: A Contemporary Rule of Life*, London: Canterbury Press, 2019.
4 Cathy Wright LSJ, *Saint Charles de Foucauld: His Life and Spirituality*, Boston, MA: Pauline Books and Media, 2022, p. 111.

Letter 2

1 Mother Teresa, *A Simple Path*, London: Random House Books, 1995, p. 42.

Letter 3

1 R. S. Thomas, 'The Bright Field', in *Laboratories of the Spirit*, London: Macmillan, 1975, p. 60.
2 St Francis, Prayer before the Crucifix.
3 George Herbert, 'Love Bade Me Welcome'.
4 Carlo Carretto, *I Francis*, Maryknoll, NY: Orbis Books, 1982, p. 11.
5 Carretto, *I Francis*, p. 16.

Letter 5

1 Richard Carter, *In Search of the Lost: The Death and Life of Seven Members of the Melanesian Brotherhood*, London: Canterbury Press, 2006.
2 Richard Carter, in *Anglicanism: A Global Communion*, ed. Andrew Wingate and Kevin Ward, London: Mowbray, 1998, pp. 45–51.

Letter 6

1 See David Miliband, 'Accountability in the "Age of Impunity"', www.usip.org/events/accountability-age-impunity (accessed 29.04.2023).
2 David Ford, *The Shape of Living*, London: Canterbury Press, 2012; and *The Drama of Living: Being Wise in the Spirit*, London: Canterbury Press, 2014.

Letter 7

1 Carlo Carretto, *Letters from the Desert*, London: Darton, Longman & Todd, 1972.
2 Carretto, *Letters*, Introduction, pp. xv–xviii.
3 Carretto, *Letters*, chs 1—2.
4 Carretto, *Letters*, chs 5—9.
5 Carretto, *Letters*, p. 37.
6 Carretto, *Letters*, p. 55.
7 Carretto, *Letters*, p. 56.
8 Carretto, *Letters*, ch. 9.
9 Carretto, *Letters*, ch. 10.
10 Carretto, *Letters*, pp. 70–1.
11 Carretto, *Letters*, ch. 12.
12 Carretto, *Letters*, p. 93.
13 Carretto, *Letters*, pp. 121–9.

Letter 9

1 Jean Pierre Camus, *The Spirit of S. Francis de Sales*, Part I: On Religious Perfection and its Practices, Chapter II, On Mental Prayer, London: Rivingtons, 1872, p. 13.

Letter 10

1 Athanasius of Alexandria, *Life of Saint Antony*, trans. H. Ellershaw, Nicene and Post-Nicene Fathers, ed. Philip Schaff and Henry Wallace, Second Series, Volume IV, Athanasius, Select Works and Letters, Grand Rapids, MI: Eerdmans, 1892), pp. 196–7.
2 Martin Laird, *Into the Silent Land*, London: Darton, Longman & Todd, 2006, ch. 5, 'The Riddles of Distraction'. It is such a wise and insightful guide for our contemplative path through that distraction.
3 Thomas Merton, *The Wisdom of the Desert*, New York: New Directions, 1960, p. 3.

4 See Athanasius of Alexandria, *The Life of Antony*.
5 Merton, *The Wisdom of the Desert*, p. 11.
6 Merton, *The Wisdom of the Desert*, p. 6.
7 Merton, *The Wisdom of the Desert*, p. 23.
8 Rowan Williams, *Silence and Honey Cakes: The Wisdom of the Desert*, Oxford: Lion, 2003, p. 82.
9 Merton, *The Wisdom of the Desert*, p. 26.

Letter 11

1 Julian of Norwich, *Revelations of Divine Love*, tr. Clifton Wolters, Harmondsworth: Penguin Classics, 1966, p. 68.
2 St Abba Moses the Ethiopian of Scete.

Letter 13

1 Martin Laird, *An Ocean of Light*, Oxford: Oxford University Press, 2019, p. 205.
2 Laird, *An Ocean*, p. 210.
3 Laird, *An Ocean*, p. 217.

Letter 16

1 'The Cloud of Unknowing', ch. 7, in A. C. Spearing (ed.), *The Cloud of Unknowing and Other Works*, London: Penguin Books, 2001, p. 29.
2 Martin Laird, *A Sunlit Absence: Silence, Awareness and Contemplation*, Oxford: Oxford University Press, 2011, pp. 125–6.
3 Laird, *A Sunlit Absence*, p. 156.

Letter 17

1 Martin Laird, *An Ocean of Light: Contemplation, Transformation, and Liberation*, Oxford: Oxford University Press, 2019, p. 218.

Letter 18

1 Kabir (fifteenth-century Indian poet), 'You don't need to go outside your house to see flowers', in *Soul Food: Nourishing Poems for Starved Minds*, ed. Neil Astley and Pamela Robertson-Pearce, tr. Robert Bly, Newcastle-upon-Tyne: Bloodaxe Books, 2007.

Letter 20

1 Pablo Neruda, 'Keeping Quiet', *Extravagaria*, trans. Alastair Reid, New York: Noonday Press, 2001, p. 26.
2 Martin Laird, *An Ocean of Light: Contemplation, Transformation, and Liberation*, Oxford: Oxford University Press, 2019, p. 45 and chs 4—5.

3 Laird, *An Ocean*, p. 54.
4 Laird, *An Ocean*, ch. 3.
5 Laird, *An Ocean*, ch. 4.
6 Laird, *An Ocean*, p. 99.
7 Laird, *An Ocean*, p. 108.
8 Laird, *An Ocean*, ch. 4.
9 Laird, *An Ocean*, pp. 78–86.
10 Laird, *An Ocean*, p. 78.
11 Laird, *An Ocean*, p. 132.
12 Rumi, 'Out Beyond Ideas', https://nationalpoetryday.co.uk/poem/out-beyond-ideas/ (accessed 29.04.2023).

Letter 21

1 Tara Brach, *Radical Compassion*, London: Penguin, 2020.
2 Brach, *Radical*, ch. 3.
3 Brach, *Radical*, p. 42.
4 Brach, *Radical*, p. 8.
5 Brach, *Radical*, p. 42.
6 Brach, *Radical*, p. 43.
7 Brach, *Radical*, p. 43. See 'Investigate with a Gentle, Curious Attention'.
8 Brach, *Radical*, p. 45.
9 Martin Laird, *An Ocean of Light: Contemplation, Transformation, and Liberation*, Oxford: Oxford University Press, 2019, p. 205.

Letter 22

1 Rowan Williams, 'To be Fully Human is to be Recreated in the Image of Christ's Humanity', Vatican City, 11 October 2012, http://rowanwilliams.arch bishopofcanterbury.org/articles.php/2645/archbishops-address-to-the-synod-of-bishops-in-rome.html (accessed 29.04.2023).

Letter 23

1 Jon M. Sweeney and Mark S. Burrows, *Meister Eckhart's Book of the Heart: Meditations for a Restless Soul*, Newburyport, MA: Hampton Roads Publishing, 2017, pp. 184–5.

Letter 24

1 Pope Francis, *Let us Dream: The Path to a Better Future*, London: Simon & Schuster, 2020.

Letter 25

1 John Keats, 'On First Looking into Chapman's Homer'; R. S. Thomas, 'The Bright Field'; Gerard Manley Hopkins, 'That Nature is a Heraclitean Fire and the Comfort of the Resurrection'.
2 T. S. Eliot, *East Coker*, *The Four Quartets*, London: Faber & Faber, 2001.
3 V. S. Naipaul, *Literary Occasions*, London: Picador, 2004, p. 52.

Letter 26

1 Madeleine Delbrêl, *We, the Ordinary People of the Streets* (Ressourcement: Retrieval and Renewal in Catholic Thought), Grand Rapids, MI: Eerdmans, 2000, loc. 2830.
2 Delbrêl, *We, the Ordinary*, 'Part One: The Missionary 1933–1949'.
3 Delbrêl, *We, the Ordinary*.

Letter 27

1 Stephen Verney, *Water into Wine: Introduction to John's Gospel*, London: Fount, 1985, p. 190.
2 Thomas Traherne, ed. Bertram Dobell, *Centuries of Meditations*, First Century, 29, 30, London: The Editor, 1908, pp. 20–1; slightly adapted.

Letter 28

1 Rumi, 'The Source', https://pollycastor.com/2021/08/01/the-source-poem-by-rumi/ (accessed 29.04.2023).
2 Rumi, *Gold*, tr. Haleh Liza Gafori, New York: New York Review of Books, 2022, p. 31.

Letter 29

1 William Blake, 'Eternity', https://dailypoetry.me/william-blake/eternity-2/ (accessed 03.05.2023).

Letter 31

1 John Cassian, *The Institutes*, trans. Boniface Ramsey, Mahwah, NJ: Paulist Press, 2000, pp. 219–20.
2 Jean-Charles Nault OSB, *The Noonday Devil: Acedia, the Unnamed Evil of Our Times*, San Francisco, CA: Ignatius Press, 2015, pp. 27–9.

Letter 32

1 https://allpoetry.com/Absolutely-Clear (accessed 17.04.2023).
2 Attributed to Plato, quoted by Ian Maclaren, *Beside the Bonnie Brier Bush*, *1894*, Glasgow: Kennedy & Boyd, 2007.

3 Constantine Cavafy, 'Ithaka', in *Collected Poems*, Princeton, NJ: Princeton University Press, 1992, pp. 36–7.

Letter 33

1 Colum McCann, *Apeirogon*, London: Bloomsbury, 2021.
2 Alex Preston, *Guardian* review, 24 February 2020.
3 McCann, *Apeirogon*, ch. 254.

Letter 34

1 Rumi, 'The Guest House', tr. Coleman Barks, ww.scottishpoetrylibrary.org.uk/poetry/guest-house (accessed 17.04.2023).
2 https://enlightenedrumi.wordpress.com/2013/03/22/wound-is-the-place-by-rumi/ (accessed 17.04.2023).

Letter 36

1 Rowan Williams, 'Thomas Merton: Summer 1966', in *A Silent Action: Engagements with Thomas Merton*, London: SPCK, 2013.
2 Ruth Padel, 'Night Singing in a Time of Plague', used with the author's permission.

Letter 37

1 Richard Carter, *The City is My Monastery*, London: Canterbury Press, 2019, p. 241.

Letter 38

1 Hazrat Inayat Khan, a Sufi saying.
2 www.nationalgallery.org.uk/paintings/piero-della-francesca-the-baptism-of-christ (accessed 17.04.2023).
3 Henri J. M. Nouwen, *Heart Speaks to Heart: Three Prayers to Jesus*, Notre Dame, IN: Ave Maria Press, 1989, p. 22.

Letter 39

1 Liturgy of Ash Wednesday.
2 Julian of Norwich, *Revelations of Divine Love*, ch. 68. A modern translation can be found in Julian of Norwich, *Revelations of Divine Love*, tr. Elizabeth Spearing, London: Penguin Classics, 1998.
3 Richard Carter, *In Search of the Lost: The Death and Life of Seven Members of the Melanesian Brotherhood*, London: Canterbury Press, 2006, p. 233.
4 Sam Wells, St Martin-in-the-Fields.

Letter 40

1 Etty Hillesum, *An Interrupted Life: The Diaries of Etty Hillesum, 1941–1943*, New York: Pantheon Books, 1984, entry from 12 July 1942.

Letter 41

1 William Shakespeare, Sonnet 116, *The Oxford Shakespeare: The Complete Sonnets and Poems*, ed. Colin Burrow, Oxford: Oxford University Press, 2002, p. 613.
2 Jon M. Sweeney and Mark S. Burrows, *Meister Eckhart's Book of the Heart: Meditations for a Restless Soul*, Newburyport, MA: Hampton Roads Publishing, 2017, pp. 184–5.

Letter 42

1 Jerome Murphy-O'Connor, *The Holy Land: An Oxford Archaeological Guide*, 5th edn, Oxford: Oxford University Press, 2008, p. 49.
2 Cathy Wright LSJ, *Saint Charles de Foucauld: His Life and Spirituality*, Boston, MA: Pauline Books and Media, 2022, p. 97.

Letter 45

1 Little Kathleen of Jesus, *The Universal Brother: Charles de Foucauld Speaks to Us Today*, Hyde Park, NY: New City Press, 2019, ch. 4.
2 Little Kathleen of Jesus, *The Universal Brother*, ch. 4.
3 Little Kathleen of Jesus, *The Universal Brother*, ch. 4.
4 Little Kathleen of Jesus, *The Universal Brother*, ch. 4.
5 Cathy Wright LSJ, *Charles de Foucauld: Journey of the Spirit*, Boston, MA: Pauline Books and Media, 2005, p. 79.

Letter 46

1 'Dear Lord and Father of Mankind', hymn, George Greenleaf Whittier, 1872.
2 Colum McCann, *Apeirogon*, London: Bloomsbury, 2021, p. 152.
3 Carlo Carretto, *Letters from the Desert*, London: Darton, Longman & Todd, 2002.

Letter 48

1 The Exsultet, from the Roman Missal.
2 R. S. Thomas, 'Evening', in *No Truce with the Furies*, Newcastle-upon-Tyne: Bloodaxe Books, 1995, p. 19.

Letter 49

1 *Letters to Persons in Religion*, Library of St Frances de Sales, trans. H. B. Mackey, OSB, Letter XIX, 'To a Religious of the Visitation', London: Burns & Oates, 1894, p. 205.
2 St Francis de Sales, *The St Francis de Sales Collection*, London: Catholic Way Publishing, 2015, p. 295.
3 *The Spiritual Conferences of St Frances de Sales*, Conference XII, 'On Simplicity and Religious Prudence', Westminster, MD: The Newman Press, 1962.
4 Michael Ramsey, *The Christian Priest Today*, London: SPCK, 1972, p. 78; emphasis original.
5 Ramsey, *The Christian Priest Today*, pp. 15–17; emphasis original.

Letter 51

1 Richard Carter, *The City is My Monastery*, London: Canterbury Press, 2019, p. 7.
2 Rowan Williams, 'The physicality of prayer', www.archons.org/-/former-arch bishop-of-canterbury-rowan-williams-promoting-the-jesus-prayer-as-answer-to-modern-angst (accessed 19.04.2023).

Letter 53

1 From St Anthony, in Rowan Williams, *Silence and Honey Cakes: The Wisdom of the Desert*, Oxford: Lion, 2003, p. 23.
2 Williams, *Silence and Honey Cakes*, p. 25.

Letter 54

1 David Wagoner, 'Lost', in *Traveling Light: Collected and New Poems*, Chicago, IL: University of Illinois Press, 1999, p. 10.

Letter 55

1 Marie Colvin, *On the Front Line*, London: HarperPress, 2012, pp. 212–13. For details of her death, see Jon Swain's piece at the end of the book, 'The Last Assignment', pp. 529–38.
2 Marie Colvin, in an interview to Anderson Cooper for CNN. For the whole transcript, see https://edition.cnn.com/2012/02/22/world/marie-colvin-interview-transcript/index.html (accessed 19.04.23).
3 Desmond Tutu, *An African Prayer Book*, New York: Bantam Doubleday Dell, 1995, p. 80.

Letter 56

1 Timothy Radcliffe, 'Alive and No Time to Lose', *The Tablet*, 24 February 2022.

Letter 57

1 Alfred Lord Tennyson, 'In Memoriam A.H.H. OBIIT MDCCCXXXIII: [Prelude]'.
2 Richard Carter, *In Search of the Lost: The Death and Life of Seven Members of the Melanesian Brotherhood*, London: Canterbury Press, 2006, pp. 135–6.

Letter 58

1 From the French film *Des Hommes et Des Dieux* (*Of Gods and Men*), directed by Xavier Beauvois.

Letter 59

1 Ted Hughes, 'Icecrust and Snowflake', in *Collected Poems of Ted Hughes*, ed. Paul Keegan, London: Faber & Faber, 2012, p. 313.

Letter 60

1 Edwina Gateley, 'Let Your God Love You', in *There was No Path so I Trod One: Poems*, Trabuco Canyon, CA: Source Books, 1996, p. 17.

Letter 61

1 Richard Carter, *The City is My Monastery*, London: Canterbury Press, 2019.

Acknowledgements of Sources

Permission to use the following quotations under copyright is acknowledged with thanks.

A first version of a few of my earlier letters in this book first appeared in Sam Wells, ed., *Finding Abundance in Scarcity: Steps towards Church Transformation*, Canterbury Press, 2021.

Constantine Cavafy, 'Ithaca', in *Collected Poems*, Princeton University Press, 1992. Used by permission.

Pablo Naruda, 'Keeping Quiet', in *Extravagaria*, trans. Alastair Reid, Noonday Press, 2001. Permission applied for.

Brother Roger prayer, copyright © Ateliers et Presses de Taizé, 71250,Taizé, France. Used by permission.

R. S. Thomas, 'Evening', in *No Truce With the Furies*, Bloodaxe Books, 1995. Used by permission.

Desmond Tutu, *An African Prayer Book*, Bantam Doubleday Dell, 1995. Permission applied for.

Rowan Williams: *A Silent Action: Engagements with Thomas Merton*, 2013, SPCK. Used by permission.